The Handbook of Community Safety, Gender and Violence Prevention

Practical Planning Tools

Carolyn Whitzman

from Routledge

First published by Earthscan in the UK and USA in 2008

ISBN: 978-1-84407-502-7   paperback
        978-1-84407-501-0   hardback

Typeset by Safehouse Creative

Cover design by Rob Watts

For a full list of publications please contact:

Earthscan

A catalogue record for this book is available from the British Library

Library of Congress Cataloging-in-Publication Data
Whitzman, Carolyn.
The handbook of community safety, gender and violence prevention : practical
planning tools / Carolyn Whitzman.
p. cm.
ISBN 978-1-84407-501-0 (hardback) -- ISBN 978-1-84407-502-7 (pbk.) 1.
Crime prevention--Planning. 2. Violence--Prevention. 3. Community
organization. I. Title.
HV7431.W49 2008
363.32'17--dc22

                                                            2007041628

Contents

List of Figures, Tables and Boxes

Figures

Tables

Boxes

Acknowledgements

This book is the product of 20 years of learning, and I would like to thank some of my teachers and fellow students:

- my compadrés in advocacy, consulting and friendship: Ali Grant, Deborah Hierlihy, Reggie Modlich and Jennifer Ramsay;
- my fellow femocrats (and honorary femocrats) from my 10 year stint at the City of Toronto: Phyllis Berck, Wade Hillier, Sue Kaiser, Fran Perkins and Lisa Salsberg;
- the politician whom I most admire: former Toronto mayor and former head of Canada's National Crime Prevention Strategy, Barbara Hall;
- some writers who inspire me: Patsy Healey, the late Jane Jacobs, Charles Landry, Caroline Moser, Leonie Sandercock and the late Iris Marion Young.

I would like to especially thank four wonderful colleagues in Women in Cities International, who generously provided links to many resources (including their own excellent work) and also supplied feedback on the manuscript: Cecilia Andersson, Caroline Andrew, Laura Capobianco and Margaret Shaw. I would also like to thank Jan Shield, for performing the same function in Melbourne.

The University of Melbourne has offered monetary support and encouragement since I joined the institution in 2003. They also provided a publication grant that allowed me to hire Catherine Zhang, an indefatigable research assistant, to help with copyright permissions and to ready the book for publication. I would particularly like to thank Professor Ruth Fincher, former dean of the Faculty of Architecture, Building and Planning, for her ongoing encouragement of my work. Although this book was not directly supported by a grant, the ongoing financial support of the Australian Research Council and the Victorian Health Promotion Foundation for the project Gender, Local Governance and

Violence Prevention: Making the Links (LP0667605) has helped me to develop some of the ideas in this book, and to test them out in the real world of local and state politics. I would also like to thank several people working on the Gender, Local Governance and Violence Prevention (GLOVE) project for information and ideas: Melissa Afentoulis, Dee Basinski, Linda Bennett, Tracy Castelino, Deb Elkington, Trish Hayes, Georgie Hill, Shakti McLaren, Carolyn Wallace and Catherine Zhang.

Writing is an egocentric and sometimes obsessive task. I relied on an informal international online writers' support group during the writing of this book, and would especially like to thank Debra Hasler, Shelley Robinson, NancyKay Shapiro, Kathy Stoddart and Irene Svete for their support. My Melbourne friends Ruth Beilin, Andrea Cook, Stephanie Knox, Bonnie Rosen and Sharon Winocur occasionally took me out of my shell for an airing. As always, the greatest source of support and meaning in my life comes from my family: my parents, brothers, nephew and niece, and my children. I would like to lovingly thank Sheila Whitzman, Earl Whitzman, Dolly Whitzman, Stephen Whitzman, Alan Pope, Jonathan Whitzman, Megan Chadwick, Simon Hunt and Molly Hunt. And, in particular, I would like to thank my husband, friend, editor and all-round honey, David Hunt, without whom this book could not have been written.

Carolyn Whitzman
Melbourne
August 2007

List of Acronyms and Abbreviations

AIDS	acquired immune deficiency syndrome
ASBO	Anti-Social Behaviour Order
CAFSU	Comité d'Action Femmes et Sécurité Urbaine (Women's Action Committee on Urban Safety) (Canada)
CAP	Child Assault Prevention
CCTV	closed-circuit television
CEO	chief executive officer
CIA	US Central Intelligence Agency
CISCSA	Centre for Exchange and Services in the Southern Cone
CORIAC	Colectivo de Hombres por Relaciones Igualitarias (Men's Collective for Equal Relations) (Mexico)
CPTED	crime prevention through environmental design
CSIR	Centre for Scientific and Industrial Research (South Africa)
DALY	death and disability adjusted life year
EFUS	European Forum on Urban Security
FGM	female genital mutilation
FLACSO	Latin American Faculty of Social Science
GLOVE	Gender, Local Governance and Violence Prevention
GDP	gross domestic product
GNI	gross national income
GNP	gross national product
HDI	Human Development Index
HIC	high-income country
HIV	human immunodeficiency virus
ICPC	International Centre for the Prevention of Crime
IIED	International Institute of Environment and Development

ILO	International Labour Organization
iTRUMP	inner Thekwini Renewal and Urban Management Programme
LDC	least developed country
LIC	low-income country
MDG	Millennium Development Goal
METRAC	Metro Toronto Action Committee on Public Violence against Women and Children
MOU	memorandum of understanding
NGO	non-governmental organization
OECD	Organisation for Economic Co-operation and Development
PACE	Prostitution Alternatives, Counselling and Education
PNG	Papua New Guinea
PUA	participatory urban appraisal
PUKAR	Partners for Urban Knowledge, Action and Research
QALY	quality-adjusted life year
R+R	Respectful Relationships Project
SAPS	South African Police Services
SARA	scan, analyse, respond and assess
SCC	safer community council
SINAGA	Kenya Woman and Child Labour Centre
SMART	specific, measurable, attainable, realistic and timely
SWOVA	Saltspring Women Opposed to Violence and Abuse
UK	United Kingdom
UN	United Nations
UNDP	United Nations Development Programme
UNICEF	United Nations Children's Fund
UNIFEM	United Nations Fund for Women
UNODC	United Nations Office on Drugs and Crime
US	United States
VAW	Violence against Women initiative
VicHealth	Victorian Health Promotion Foundation
VIP	Violence Is Preventable project
WHO	World Health Organization

1

Introduction to the Issues

What this book is – and is not

The purpose of this book is to contribute to a less violent world by bringing together the best community safety and violence prevention information and ideas from around the world, and addressing violence in both the public and private spheres. These facts and good practice examples will be used to develop a framework for improving community safety at all scales, from neighbourhood initiatives to global coalitions.

The book is written from an interdisciplinary perspective. While my background is in spatial planning, I have worked within a health promotion framework for many years. I have also learned through reading and listening to criminologists, community development workers and political scientists. It may seem odd for someone without a degree in criminology to write about safer cities and violence prevention; but some of the most exciting work on community safety comes from governments and non-governmental organizations (NGOs) working on violence prevention from a health promotion perspective, or working on community safety as a core aspect of sustainable urban and regional development, underpinned by a commitment to democratic and participatory governance.

The Handbook of Community Safety, Gender and Violence Prevention is primarily for practitioners: people working in governments, NGOs, funding bodies and charities, the private sector, and individual activists and advisers who want to make their communities and societies safer. It is thus for people whose background may be in public health, planning and design, community development, public policy, international development, social work, education, criminology, criminal justice, or policing, but who share a common interest in the practical aspects of community safety and violence prevention. It provides a framework, guidelines, tools and case studies of innovative and effective community safety initiatives from around the world. This book is also for researchers: academics working in university settings, as well as researchers working in institutes and governments who want to develop their theoretical understanding of this issue, know more about the current state of violence prevention initiatives (most of which have not been written up in academic journals), and obtain ideas for further research in the area. Politicians and other policy-makers and advisers working at the local, national, regional and global levels will find this book useful in formulating ideas and policy. In my experience, successful community safety initiatives are like a table resting on four legs: political leadership, at all levels of governance; administrative leadership from committed senior staff people working within government structures; research leadership, providing information on good practices, evaluation and modes of dissemination; and grassroots leadership, informed by activists working in agencies and other NGOs, as volunteers or in the private sector, who make the needs of their constituents known. When the four legs are strong and equal, the table can carry a lot of weight.

Despite my professional grounding in planning and design, this book is *not* primarily about crime prevention through environmental design (or CPTED for short). I have dealt with the possibilities of planning and designing the public realms of cities to promote community safety in a previous book (Wekerle and Whitzman, 1995). While I think that physical environments within cities are important determinants of conviviality and connectedness, I have increasingly come to believe that the supreme challenge in working towards safer communities and violence prevention is how to connect the issues of violence in the public and private spheres. The greatest opportunities in making these connections lie in an interdisciplinary approach that combines traditional planning tools, such as the development and administration of place-based policy and design guidelines, with skills that are not necessarily strong within current planning practice, such as research into the incidence of violence, the development of strong programme and impact evaluation mechanisms, in place from the start of a project, and a comprehensive understanding of community development principles and practices. The 'practical planning tools' discussed throughout this book are intended to assist spatial planners – and other concerned citizens – in addressing the highly interrelated emerging priorities of the 21st century: ensuring environmental sustainability in an increasingly urbanized world, addressing growing socio-economic disparities within and between nations, and finding a way for the world's population to more peacefully and democratically 'manage our co-existence in shared spaces' (Healey, 1997, p68).

Despite the word 'gender' in the title, and the gender analysis found throughout this book, this book is *not* only for women or for feminists, and does not focus solely on violence against women. Men are a gender too. Men will benefit from a reduction in violence against women, and women will benefit in a reduction of violence against men. Men and women are, thus, equal beneficiaries of a reduction in violence, share an equal responsibility for violence prevention, and need to be involved in violence prevention on an equal basis. One of this book's central tenets is that gender, along with other grounds of difference, such as age, class, culture and abilities, needs to be 'mainstreamed', or considered as a matter of course, when looking at community safety problems, resources, actions and evaluation. If, for instance, violence against women is left out of the equation, or even dealt with as an issue that is separate, but equal, in community safety, crime prevention or violence prevention strategies, the resultant policies, programmes and products will be fatally weakened. This book is intended to be a stand-alone product that will help to develop all community safety and violence prevention strategies, not a supplemental text for people interested in 'adding violence against women in' at some later date. The consideration of gender is not an add-on, an afterthought or a separate issue. It is an essential ingredient for success. The importance of a gender mainstreaming approach in development, public health and governance issues is increasingly understood internationally, and this book is intended to further the integration of gender within the literature on community safety, sustainable cities and health promotion.

Challenging the traditional crime and punishment approach

The book is written to address two large gaps in the emerging literature on crime prevention, community safety and violence prevention. Hundreds of books, and thousands of articles and reports, have been written on crime prevention since the 1960s. Thousands of initiatives, costing billions of dollars, have been developed to prevent crime, ranging from new laws, to new prisons, to community mobilization and new social, health and recreational services. These theories and practices overwhelmingly deal with a problem that is defined as 'crime' and which focuses on a limited set of harmful acts within the public sphere. They essentially ignore violent crimes within families. To give one fairly recent example, the 1995 United Nations *Guidelines for Cooperation and Technical Assistance in the Field of Urban Crime Prevention* provide the following list of 'types of crime prevention problems to be tackled, such as theft, robbery, burglary, racial attacks, drug-related crimes, juvenile delinquency and illegal possession of firearms'(UNODC, 2003, p3). In 2002, when the UN Guidelines were revised, section 3.14 stated that 'crime prevention should pay due regard to the different needs of men and women and to different cultural identities and minorities', but continued to exclude violence within the private sphere within their understanding of 'crime and victimization' (UN Economic and Social Council, 2002, pp8, 10). Physical and sexual abuse of children, women and the elderly, mostly committed by family and taking place in the so-called private sphere of the home, has been absent from this list of international crime and victimization problems to be solved.

By focusing on a limited set of acts, it becomes easier to concentrate on a limited set of mostly male 'bad guys' as the problem, and to enact solutions based on controlling and imprisoning these people. Traditional crime prevention relies on crimes reported to the police to measure both the problem and any progress on the problem. It has also tended to focus on police and justice responses to crime as the primary aspect of crime prevention. In both high- and low-income countries, the primary mechanism to prevent crime and violence has been to lock up more offenders for greater periods of time. During 1970, there were 176 people per 100,000 in US prisons, 80 per 100,000 in English prisons, and 18 per 100,000 in Dutch prisons. By 1998, the respective proportions were 645 in the US, 125 in England and 85 in The Netherlands (Waller and Sansfacon, 2000, p1). The amount of money spent on private security responses has been growing at a rate of 8 per cent per annum in high-income countries (HICs) and 30 per cent per annum in low-income countries (LICs) (Vanderschueren, 2006, pp2–3). The 1980s saw the emergence of the 'broken windows' theory in the US, which contended that a 'zero tolerance' approach towards relatively minor crimes and incivilities in particularly unsafe areas would improve protection from all crimes (Kelling and Coles, 1996). The 'three strikes' legislation, furthermore, which was also developed in the US, enforced long sentences against people previously convicted of two serious offences, even if the third offence was minor. These punitive approaches continue to be influential throughout the rest of the world, despite the fact that they rarely work to prevent repeat crime among offenders, lower crime rates by deterring offenders or justify their enormous expense (Sherman et al, 1997; Waller and Sansfacon, 2000; Vanderschueren, 2006).

The punishment approach to crime and violence prevention is also largely irrelevant to harmful acts that take place in the private sphere of homes and families. It has long been recognized within the movement to end violence against women that the majority of acts of physical and sexual violence are unreported to the police, and may not be considered a crime by the victim, the offender, the police, the judiciary or society (Pickup, 2001; Garcia-Moreno et al, 2004). This is not only true of offences against women, but also of those against children, older people, people with disabilities, cultural and ethnic minorities, and other groups who have historically had less power within most societies. As described in Chapter 2, most acts of violence are not reported to the police as crimes; thus, there is surprisingly little information on the incidence of violence, let alone its causes, consequences and prevention. While stronger police enforcement and criminal sanctions may be a part of the solution to family violence, there have also been a plethora of other preventive responses that have been put forward, and virtually no one agrees that 'lock 'em all up' is an appropriate sole solution. Furthermore, if everyone who had committed a violent crime against a family member, including physical assault against a child, was arrested and charged for their offence, prevalence statistics suggest that the majority of adults, male and female, in almost every society, would be incarcerated.

The 1970s and 1980s saw the emergence of a strong movement condemning violence against women, which developed services for female victims of violence and advocated changes to laws, as well as developing a gender analysis that explained both the causes and relative invisibility of violence in the private sphere. Directly or indirectly informed by this feminist analysis, the 1990s and the present decade have seen a growing literature and practice that have slowly been transforming traditional crime prevention. Governments around the world have begun to shift from a sole focus on police-reported crime to looking at the broader issues of crime and violence against both women and men. They have begun to consider violence that occurs in both the public and private spheres – acts which may or may not be against the law, but which are increasingly recognized as causing harm to individuals, families and communities. While developing appropriate police and justice responses has been one of the emphases of this work, so too have public awareness and community mobilization to change societal attitudes and behaviours, and social and economic development projects that would increase the life choices of victims and offenders. The work has mostly occurred at the local level, but has been disseminated and promoted by global organizations such as the World Health Organization (Krug et al, 2002; Garcia-Moreno et al, 2004), the World Bank (Moser and McIlwaine, 2006; World Bank, 2006), UN-Habitat (Smaoun, 2000; Vanderschueren, 2006), Oxfam (Pickup, 2001), the Commonwealth Secretariat (2003) and the International Centre for the Prevention of Crime (Shaw, 2001a, 2006). Increasingly, the terms 'community safety' and 'safer cities' have been utilized to describe efforts to prevent all forms of crime, violence and insecurity, with an emphasis on mobilizing and coordinating a broad range of partners.

Aside from this first gap – the tendency to limit consideration of crime and violence to a specific number of acts that take place in the public sphere – there is a second gap, which is to focus solely on ideas and examples from high-income countries, variously referred to as developed countries, the North or the West. Living, as I do, in Australia, a country with a high average household income that is usually found in the south-east of world maps, I find the latter two terms inaccurate and the first term highly condescending. I therefore use the terms high-income countries and low-income countries, which refer to average household incomes within nations (see Box 1.1). Many of the best ideas and practices on preventing crime and improving community safety have come from places that have the greatest problems and the fewest resources to tackle these problems. This book develops an international and cross-cultural approach to community safety, while recognizing that every society, like every individual, has unique characteristics.

Box 1.1 *What are high-income and low-income countries?*

In this book, I will be using high-income countries (HICs) and low-income countries (LICs) as an admittedly simplistic division between nations. There are many shorthand ways to describe the huge differences between nations' resources. Following on the lead of several international organizations, including the World Health Organization (WHO), I use the World Bank's classification of national economies. This uses per capita gross national income (GNI) – a concept similar, but not identical, to gross national product (GNP) as a way of categorizing countries. The World Bank's classification was developed in the mid 1970s to determine lending categories, and is not meant to reflect every aspect of welfare or human development (a better measure for this would be the Human Development Index, or HDI; see below). Furthermore, the measure takes no account of disparities within nations. There are huge disparities in income, as well as health, between aboriginal Canadians or Australians and the rest of the population, and wealth disparities in countries such as Saudi Arabia or the US are also considerable. However, the classification is a useful shorthand for the amount of resources a nation has to fight problems and improve human development outcomes, including the prevention of violence (World Bank, 2007a).

High-income countries

HICs have a GNI per capita of at least US$10,726 (measured in 2007 US dollars). There are 56 national economies classified as high income, many of them supporting very small populations (e.g. the Channel Islands and Andorra). About one sixth of the world's population lives in HICs. They are located mostly in Western Europe; North America and the Caribbean (including the US and Canada, as well as several smaller Caribbean islands such as Bermuda); West Asia (including Israel and Saudi Arabia); East Asia (including Japan, South Korea, Singapore, Brunei, and Macao and Hong Kong, if considered as separate economies from the rest of China); and the Pacific (Australia, New Zealand and a few smaller islands such as Guam). There are no HICs in South America or Africa. Most of the larger HICs are members of the Organisation for Economic Co-operation and Development (OECD).

Medium- and low-income countries

Medium-income countries have per capita GNIs of between US$875 and US$10,725, and are often broken further into low medium and high medium, while LICs are those with per capita GNIs of less than US$875. While the average per capita GNI for the world is approximately US$6500, most of the

HICs have a per capita GNI of US$20,000 or more. Thus, there is far more difference between HICs and middle-income countries than there is between the latter and LICs, and the two are grouped as LICs for the purpose of this book. Medium- and low-income countries are often called developing countries. Low-income countries are sometimes called least developed countries, or LDCs.

Developing countries

Developing countries have standards of living that are considerably below HICs. Many have economies in transition, and deep and enduring poverty.

Economies in transition

These are countries that have recently either established or re-established market economies, including former Communist countries, such as Russia and China.

Human Development Index

This index measures the average national achievement in three areas:

1   life expectancy at birth;
2   adult literacy and school enrolment; and
3   standard of living as measured by gross national product (GNP) per capita.

The HDI is probably a better measure than GNI in measuring nations' social and economic capacity; but sufficient data is not updated on an annual basis, so classification becomes more problematic.

Developing a new framework for community safety and violence prevention

The international shift of focus, away from a traditional emphasis on crime in the public sphere and punishment as the primary response, towards a more holistic and nuanced understanding of how to prevent violence in both the public and private spheres, is just in its starting phase. Even within the emerging research and practice on violence prevention and community safety that has emerged during the last 10 to 20 years, there are still several 'silos' that separate subcategories within the discourse on violence prevention. As Canadian researcher Holly Johnson (2007, p79) has recently stated:

Crime prevention discourse and practice has tended not to incorporate a gender perspective. Efforts to prevent violence against women have evolved separately and remain outside traditional crime prevention work.

The majority of work on violence prevention focuses on 'youth violence' in the public sphere, with an emphasis on guns, gangs and illegal drugs as problems, and a set of prevention techniques that derives from police practices. Co-existent, but largely separate, is a substantial body of well-established work on preventing violence against women, with a genesis in grassroots service provision to victims and advocacy on their behalf (Johnson, 2007). Then there are other silos of work on abuse of children, the elderly and people with disabilities, and hate crimes against cultural, religious and sexual minorities, although at least half of these demographic groups are women, and everyone was once a child. Violence is still largely treated as a number of separate and largely disconnected issues, not only in the realm of research and writing, but also in the actions of governments and the private and non-profit sectors. However, as Chapters 2 and 3 of this book examine, there is a web of connections between harmful acts committed in public and in private, and acts committed against oneself, strangers, acquaintances and peers, and family members.

There are three emerging approaches that go beyond an emphasis on policing and justice responses to crime, and which are beginning to include a gender analysis that allows both public and private violence to be addressed. One is the health promotion approach. This approach analyses violence and insecurity as a health and well-being problem, and uses techniques that have stopped people from taking up smoking and prevented infectious diseases from spreading to be adapted to community safety and injury prevention (Mohan, 2000; Krug et al, 2002). The second is an urban planning and management approach, which sees violence and insecurity as human rights issues that stunt the development of individuals, communities and societies. This approach uses partnership and participatory governance techniques that have worked to highlight environmental sustainability concerns to be adapted to community safety (Smaoun, 2000; UN-Habitat, 2005a). The third is a poverty reduction approach, also known as a sustainable livelihoods or international development approach, which focuses on the economic costs of violence to individuals and societies, and often develops strategies based on livelihood concerns (Moser, 2004; Moser and McIlwaine, 2006). Health promotion, urban development and poverty reduction approaches draw on practices in both HICs and LICs, and seek to promote cross-cultural learning. All three approaches are capable of a gendered analysis that recognizes violence against women and men in its many forms. They all prefer the terms community safety and violence prevention to crime prevention, although the poverty reduction approach takes a broad view of violence prevention that includes property crimes as economic violence. However, these approaches still largely operate in isolation from one another, although the planning and management and poverty reduction approaches are beginning to merge in addressing the Millennium Development Goals (MDGs) (UN, 2007). Within all three approaches, the gender analysis is still in its nascent stage, with a tendency to insert violence against women into a list of issues to be addressed, rather than mainstreaming gender into a discussion of all violence, as several writers, including myself, have recommended (Smaoun, 2000; Shaw, 2002; Shaw and Capobianco, 2004; Whitzman, 2004; Shaw and Andrew, 2005).

This book thus brings together three streams of literature: violence prevention, particularly from a public health perspective; planning partnership and poverty reduction approaches to sustainable development; and an emerging gender analysis that is beginning to affect these two sets of literature (see Figure 1.1). The literature I draw upon is largely contained in recent local, national and international government and charitable organization reports because academic theoretical literature has not yet caught up with practice – the work of Caroline Moser and her colleagues being one of the few exceptions to this generalization.

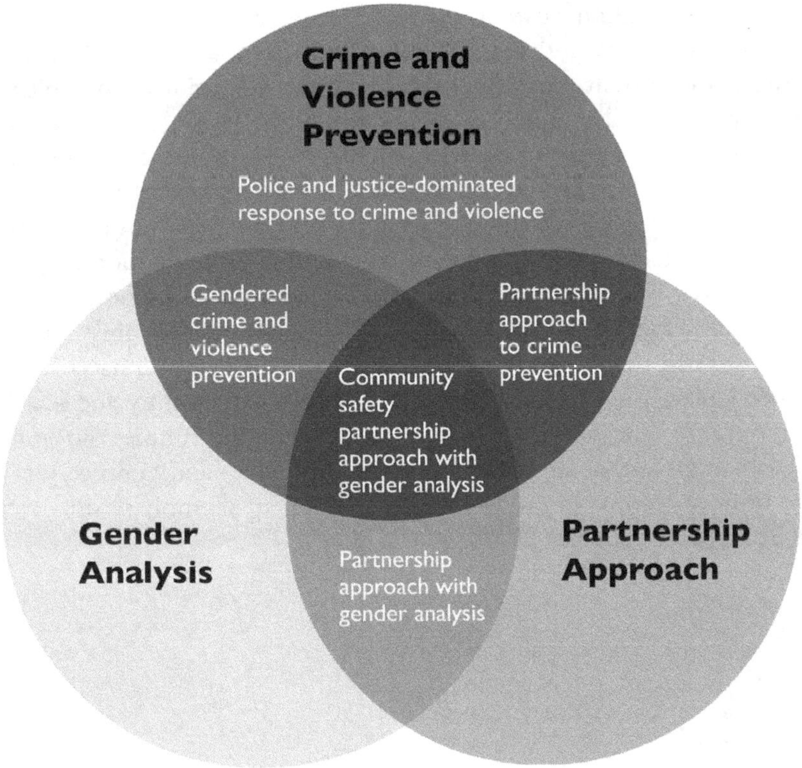

Crime and Violence Prevention

Police and justice-dominated response to crime and violence

Gendered crime and violence prevention

Partnership approach to crime prevention

Community safety partnership approach with gender analysis

Gender Analysis

Partnership approach with gender analysis

Partnership Approach

Figure 1.1 *Conceptual diagram of the book's focus*

Brief outline of the rest of the book

Throughout this handbook, I emphasize interdisciplinary research and theory on the incidence and consequences of violence, partnership-based approaches that seek collective responses to deal with the root causes of violence, and rigorous evaluation that allows us to identify 'what works, what doesn't and what is promising' in violence prevention (Sherman et al, 1997). The book proceeds along four stages that are commonly used in any health promotion campaign, including one on community safety and violence prevention (Krug et al, 2002). I begin by describing the current state of knowledge about the incidence of violence and insecurity in a global context. Second, I move on analysis: the risk and resilience factors that cause or prevent violence, the relationships between different forms of violence, and the theories and evidence behind successful violence prevention. I then describe successful partnership-based interventions at five different scales of governance: neighbourhoods, cities and localities, nations, regions and the globe. The longest chapter looks at the process of community safety: how initiatives develop, learn, grow, resolve conflicts, and monitor and evaluate their work. The book then turns to potential components of a multifaceted community safety plan: working at the individual, family, community and social scales of intervention. It ends with a summary of current opportunities and constraints in developing a global approach to community safety and violence prevention that can integrate both a gender analysis and an equal emphasis on violence in public and private spheres.

2

Defining the Problem: The Prevalence of Violence and Insecurity

Defining community safety and violence

There are now hundreds of 'safe community' and 'community safety' initiatives at the local level across the world, but there is no consensus on what these terms actually connote. In the UK, for instance, community safety is defined as a positive outcome of crime prevention, 'an aspect of quality of life in which people, individually and collectively, are protected as far as possible from hazards or threats that result from the criminal or anti-social behaviour of others, and are equipped or helped to cope with those they do experience' (Community Safety Advisory Service, 2007). All local authorities in England and Wales were mandated as of 1998 to develop Community Safety Partnerships, although the name of these initiatives in England was latterly changed to Crime and Disorder Reduction Partnerships. The International Centre for the Prevention of Crime also defines community safety as a more positive way of conceptualizing crime prevention, noting an international policy shift from 'the relatively narrow focus on crime prevention to the broader issue of *community safety and security* as a public good' (Shaw, 2001a, piii, italics in original). These definitions focus on intentional injury, assuming that a threat to people's safety comes from a conscious or voluntary act by a victimizer. In contrast, the World Health Organization (WHO) Collaborating Centre for Community Safety, based in the Karolinska Institute in Sweden for over 20 years, defines community safety as all injury prevention, including intentional injuries such as violence, crime and suicide, as well as unintentional injuries, such as traffic and other accidents, fires and natural disasters, 'where the leading role is played by the community itself' (WHO Collaborating Centre on Community Safety Promotion, 2007). Over 50 local governments throughout the world are accredited as 'safe communities' according to this classification. These contrasting understandings of community safety, whether it is equivalent to the prevention of crime and insecurity, or whether it encompasses all injury prevention, have a very small area of overlap: violent crime. Property crimes, traffic accidents, suicide and self-harming behaviour, and protection from natural disaster, are excluded from one definition or the other.

The term 'community' used in these initiatives is usually defined as a group of people who share a geographic territory, and who may also share a culture and institutions. This geographic sense of community might be found in a particular housing estate or a neighbourhood, or may stretch to a rural region or a metropolitan area. Occasionally, the term community is used to describe people who have a set of shared experiences or common culture, experiences or background, although they do not necessarily live in the same geographic area. These communities of interest are infinite in number and can include young people who feel excluded, urban indigenous populations, lesbians, new immigrants or people with disabilities (Shaw, 2006, p3). Both uses of the term 'community' have been glorified and vilified since the early 1990s. On the one hand, community has been rediscovered as a locus for successful intervention under the terms 'place management', 'whole-of-government' approach, 'networked government' or 'joined up governance' (Waller and Sansfacon, 2000; Lee and Herborn, 2003; Homel, 2005). On the other hand, the term community has been critiqued as too vague to be meaningful (Crawford, 1999) or inherently dependent upon a false sense of shared interests, and thus exclusionary of minority voices (Young, 1990; Pain and Townshend, 2002; Mitchell, 2003). 'Community safety' has been critiqued as too formless and all encompassing to evaluate (Sherman et al, 1997), and as shifting the burden of solving communal problems away from governments to individuals and non-governmental organizations (NGOs) (Lee and Herborn, 2003). It has been suggested by more than one researcher that the community safety approach is not necessarily the best way of preventing crime and violence (Tilley and Laycock, 2000; Homel, 2004). Despite these criticisms, the term 'community safety' has been widely embraced by local, national and global governance bodies (Mohan, 2000; Shaw, 2006; Vanderschueren, 2006).

This book emphasizes the intentional injury, or violence and insecurity prevention, aspect of community safety, although aspects of unintentional injury prevention (particularly road safety) and crimes other than violence (particularly interpersonal property crime) are considered as related topics. The book focuses on violence for three reasons. First, it is remarkably endemic, directly affecting close to half of the world's population and indirectly affecting everyone. Violence is among the leading causes of death for men and women aged 15 to 44 (Krug et al, 2002, p3), and a recent Australian study found intimate partner violence to be the leading cause of premature death and disability for women in that age group (VicHealth, 2004). Even if we were to exclude violent deaths from wars and suicide, interpersonal violence alone would account for half a million deaths per year, 'the equivalent of three long-haul commercial aircraft crashing every single day, week in and week out, year after year'; and death is only 'the tip of the iceberg' when it comes to the injuries and suffering caused by interpersonal violence (Butchart et al, 2004, p2; this metaphor occurs often in the literature).

Second, despite or perhaps because of its omnipresence, the harm caused by violence is still hidden, denied or treated as normal in most societies. As is discussed throughout this book, the vast majority of societal resources spent on 'crime', 'violence' and 'community safety' addresses a very small part of a much larger problem, using costly interventions that are known not to work. Some of the most prevalent forms of violence, such as child abuse and rape within marriage, are legal and socially sanctioned throughout much of the world. An increasingly important issue such as elder abuse was the subject of the first formal study – using the term 'granny battering' – in 1975, and is still largely uncounted in terms of prevalence and costs to society (Krug et al, 2002, p125). The individual and societal costs of violence are often under-reported or taken for granted, such as the fact that millions of girl children in India and China are 'missing' due to infanticide and childhood neglect (Pickup, 2001, pp88–89; Sen, 2005, p224), or that private security responses, including for-profit prisons and gated communities, are rapidly growing expenditures in all societies, despite the fact that the work done by these profitable companies may result in increasing, rather than decreasing, violence and insecurity (Vanderschueren, 2006, p3).

Third, violence is eminently preventable, perhaps the least expensively preventable of leading causes of mortality and disease. It is seldom recognized that a public health approach has worked over the past century to virtually eliminate previously fatal diseases such as polio and diphtheria, and that even before 'wonder drugs' were invented, the conditions that allow these diseases to spread were being prevented effectively (Mohan, 2000, p4). A growing body of evidence suggests that a public health approach to preventing the underlying causes of violence works as well (Butchart et al, 2004). While tackling the underlying causes of violence would involve a great deal of economic, social and cultural transformation, it is as difficult (or more so) to address the underlying factors behind the growth in cardiovascular disease, diabetes and many cancers, or human-induced climate change. Preventing death and disability from violence does not require expensive medicines and unethical research on animal or human subjects; nor does it cost more than a small proportion of the hundreds of billions of dollars currently spent worldwide on policing, courts, private security and the incarceration of criminals. It is simply a matter of individual and collective will, and effective and democratic governance.

Despite disputes over the definition of community safety, I use this term to highlight that any form of health promotion, including prevention of violence and unintentional injuries, works best when coordinated at the local community level. The terms 'community safety' and 'safer communities' also present a positive goal, rather than merely preventing a negative event. Talking about 'community' highlights an aspect central to the growing understanding of both violence and fear of violence: that these intentional injuries harm not only individuals, but communities, and that positive change must begin with a change in communities' understanding of the realities of violence. Finally, the emphasis on community fits well with the growing literature on crime and violence prevention in relation to citizenship: the right of both men and women to participate fully in community life, both formally, in the sense of politics, and informally, in the right to use and influence change in public space (Young, 1990; Pitts, 1998; Mitchell, 2003; Whitzman, 2004; Fenster, 2005).

Although most of the literature on the injury prevention aspect of community safety focuses on unintentional injuries, such as vehicular and pedestrian accidents, poisons, falls and fires, it still provides a set of public health and human rights principles that are highly useful in discussing violence prevention. For instance, successive declarations adopted at World Conferences on Injury Prevention and Control recognize safety as a fundamental human right and a basic precondition for individual and community health and well-being, economic and social development, peace and justice, and realization of higher aspirations (Mohan, 2000, p3; Fifth World Conference on Injury Prevention and Control, 2000; Sixth World Conference on Injury Prevention and Control, 2002). This understanding of safety is based on Abraham Maslow's (1987) hierarchy of needs, where freedom from assault or murder and the threat of such violent acts, along with food, shelter and water, are seen as basic preconditions for any further human development.

In the injury prevention literature, 'safety' is defined as 'a state in which hazards and conditions leading to physical, psychological or material harm are controlled in order to preserve the health and well-being of individuals and the community' (Mohan, 2000, p3). Both the crime prevention and injury prevention definitions of community safety accept that there are two dimensions to the issue: an objective behavioural and environmental aspect, and a subjective 'feeling of safety'. The two affect one another, and it is essential to consider both (Mohan, 2000, p3).

Since making it a policy priority in 1996, the World Health Organization has greatly increased its research and advocacy on the violence prevention aspect of injury prevention. According to the magisterial *World Report on Violence and Health*, the WHO defines violence as:

> ... *the intentional use of physical force or power, threatened or actual, against oneself, another person, or against a population or community, that either results in or has a high likelihood of resulting in injury, death, psychological harm, mal-development or deprivation.* (Krug et al, 2002, p5)

The World Health Organization's 'mapping' of violence prevention appears as Figure 2.1, while definitions of particular terms are found in Box 2.1. As can be seen, the violence typology includes divisions based on victim (child abuse), offender (intimate partner violence), setting (community violence) and motive (political violence).

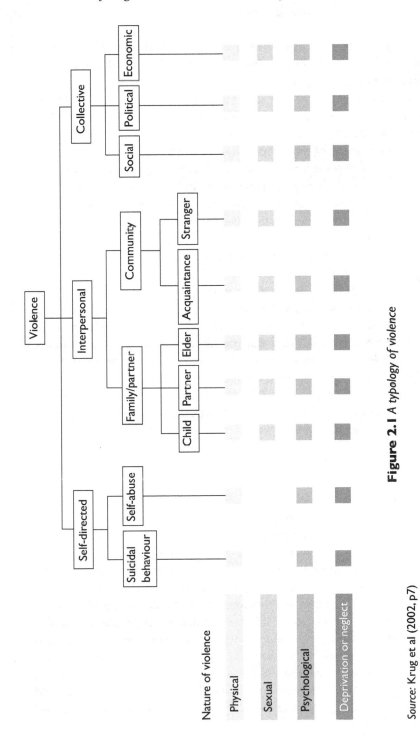

Figure 2.1 *A typology of violence*

Source: Krug et al (2002, p7)

Box 2.1 *Violence: A lexicon*

Most of the following definitions are drawn from the World Health Organization's *World Report on Violence and Health* (Krug et al, 2002, p6; see also Butchart et al, 2004, p1).

Self-directed violence: violence a person inflicts against himself or herself, including suicide, attempted suicide, self-mutilation and suicidal thoughts. Self-directed violence may or may not be considered a crime, depending upon the situation and the laws of the country where the violence takes place.

Interpersonal violence: violence that is inflicted by an individual or small group of individuals against another individual or group of individuals. Interpersonal violence is usually divided into *family violence*, where there is an ongoing relationship between the offender(s) and victim(s), and *community violence*, where the violence is between unrelated people.

Family violence includes *intimate partner violence*, which is usually violence by husbands against wives (*wife assault*), as well as violence by unmarried long-term male heterosexual partners (who usually, but not necessarily, co-habit), male and female same-sex partners, and violence by female partners against male partners. Family violence also includes violence against children where the offender is a relative (most, but not all, *child abuse* and maltreatment, including violence by siblings, as well as parents and other older family members), and violence against older members of the family (most, but not all, *elder abuse*). While usually the violence is committed by the family member with more physical, social and economic power, it also includes less common abuse, such as that of children against parents where the parent is not elderly. Family violence is sometimes called *domestic violence* because incidents usually, although not exclusively, take place in the home. Family violence may or may not be considered a crime, depending upon the particular laws of the country where it takes place. It is certainly grossly under-reported to the police and other authorities in almost every country.

Community violence is violence between people who are unrelated and who may or may not know one another. If the victim(s) and offender(s) know one another, this violence is sometimes called *acquaintance violence*, and if they do not, it is called *stranger violence*. Community violence includes much of what is sometimes called *youth violence*, where the violence involves young offenders and/or victims (youth usually being defined as people between 15 and 29 years old). It includes random acts of violence, as well as physical and sexual assaults by strangers and acquaintances (including *date rape* or sexual assault within casual relationships). Since these offences often, although not exclusively, take place outside the home, collective violence is sometimes called *public violence*, although the violence can occur in workplaces, institutional settings, schools and other places that may not be owned by the public or open to public view. Because an increase in community violence is sometimes associated with urbanization, it is occasionally called *urban violence*. Home invasions, carjacking, robbery and extortion are included under the definition of *community violence* since the primary purpose – acquisition of money or property – is accomplished by force or threat of force. *Sexual trafficking of women and children*, within countries or across borders, which has an economic motive, would also be included under the definition of community violence. While most of these acts of violence are defined as crimes in most countries, community violence is also grossly under-reported to the police and other authorities.

Collective violence is defined by the WHO as 'the instrumental use of violence by people who identify themselves as members of a group – whether this group is transitory or has a more permanent identity – against another group or set of individuals in order to achieve political, economic or social objectives' (Krug et al, 2002, p215). *Social violence* to advance a particular social agenda includes organized *hate crimes* that 'manifest prejudice based on race, religion, sexual orientation, disability or ethnicity', particularly those that involve mob violence (Shaw and Barchelat, 2001, p2). *Political violence* includes wars and related violent internal and international conflicts, *state violence* committed by governments, and other acts carried out by large groups, including rape as an instrument of war. *Economic violence* can include denying access to essential services, as well as attacks carried out for the purpose of disrupting economic activities. There is a great deal of disagreement about to what extent violence committed by sovereign states, particularly in the administration of justice, should be included within collective violence. Is executing a woman for adultery, or executing a man for murder, state violence? Is cutting off a man's hand for theft, or imprisoning a 16-year-old boy for a drug offence, also state violence?

A number of researchers, including Caroline Moser, would use the tripartite division of social, economic and political motives to define *all* violence: interpersonal, community and collective (Moser and McIlwaine, 2006, pp93–94). In this alternative classification, *social violence* would include sexual assault, abuse of women, children and older people within relationships, and violence between individuals and societies for the purpose of social control. *Economic violence* would include street crime, robberies, and killing and rapes committed during the commission of economically motivated crimes for the purpose of economic advancement of individuals or gangs. *Political violence* would include terrorism, armed conflict between parties and political assassinations motivated by a desire to attain or retain political power. A subset of political violence would be the *institutional violence* committed by armies and police forces, doctors and teachers, and lynching by communities of suspected criminals.

> *Gender-based violence, woman abuse and violence against women*, like the terms elder abuse and child abuse, defines itself by using the identity of the victim. It includes a wide range of violence against women and girls, including interpersonal physical and sexual violence by family members, acquaintances and strangers, trafficking of women and children, and collective violence such as rape as an instrument of war. The overwhelming majority of these violent acts are committed by male perpetrators. It is common for the term gender-based violence to be used as a synonym for violence against women (Pickup, 2001; Commonwealth Secretariat, 2003). It is uncommon for gender-based violence to include violence committed by men against other men, even if the violence is based on conflicts over gender roles or sexuality.
>
> Cross-cutting all of these categories are four modes of violence: *physical, sexual* and *psychological* attacks, and *deprivation* or *neglect*. Physical and sexual violence are easier to detect; but the impacts of psychological violence and neglect can also be severe on individuals, families and communities.

The prevalence of violence: An overview

During recent years, both health promotion and international development organizations have come to a growing understanding of the individual and collective costs of violence, insecurity and unintentional injury. Perhaps the most startling information comes from an international analysis of the changing causes of death and disability. While the mortality rate of living is 100 per cent, one of the universal collective quests of humankind has been to prevent premature death and disability through economic and social measures, such as medical research, laws and regulations, and indirect environmental mechanisms, such as improving sewerage and water supplies. Most individuals would prefer to attain the highest possible level of both health and well-being for themselves and their families. We want ourselves and the people we love to be as healthy and happy as possible. It is increasingly understood that low levels of health and well-being affect not only individuals and families, but also communities and societies. It is impossible to develop socially, culturally and economically when dealing with the consequences of injury and disease. Conversely, health problems thrive where social, economic and environmental inequalities are stark and increasing. This is true whether the health problem in question is HIV in Africa or Asia, or alcohol-related diseases in the former Soviet Union and Eastern Europe.

According to projections made for the World Health Organization and the World Bank (Murray and Lopez, 1996), the disease burden (death and disability adjusted life years, or DALYs) of many communicable diseases, such as lower respiratory, pre-natal and diarrhoeal diseases, is decreasing (see Figure 2.2). This

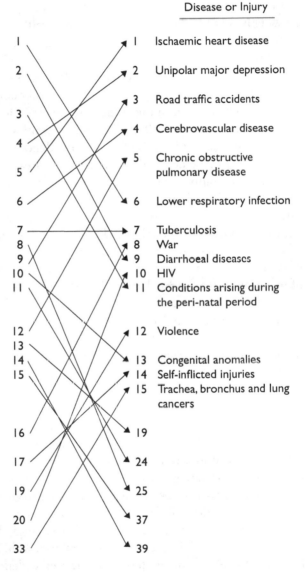

1990			2020

Disease or Injury

Disease or Injury

Lower respiratory infection	1	1	Ischaemic heart disease
Diarrhoeal diseases	2	2	Unipolar major depression
Conditions arising during the peri-natal period	3	3	Road traffic accidents
		4	Cerebrovascular disease
Unipolar major depression	4		
Ischaemic heart disease	5	5	Chronic obstructive pulmonary disease
Cerebrovascular disease	6	6	Lower respiratory infection
Tuberculosis	7	7	Tuberculosis
Measles	8	8	War
Road traffic accidents	9	9	Diarrhoeal diseases
Congenital anomalies	10	10	HIV
Malaria	11	11	Conditions arising during the peri-natal period
Chronic obstructive pulmonary disease	12	12	Violence
Falls	13		
Iron-deficiency anaemia	14	13	Congenital anomalies
Protein-energy malnutrition	15	14	Self-inflicted injuries
		15	Trachea, bronchus and lung cancers
	16	19	
	17	24	
	19	25	
	20	37	
	33	39	

Figure 2.2 *Change in rank order of disease burden for 15 leading causes worldwide, 1990–2020 (as measured by DALYs)*

Source: Murray and Lopez (1996)

is good news because these diseases carry off a high proportion of children and young people in many low-income countries (LICs). Chronic diseases, which are closely related to lifestyle factors such as diet and exercise, are increasing. While heart- and stroke-related diseases kill a higher proportion of older people, a growing body of evidence suggests that the health futures of many young people in high-income countries (HICs) may be grimmer than their parents due to obesity-promoting diets laden with fast food and obesity-promoting lives filled with physical inactivity (Leeder et al, 2006). In LICs, a perfect storm is brewing: while there are growing rates of obesity and obesity-related diseases, such as diabetes, there are continuing and, in some cases, increasing levels of malnutrition-related diseases, as well as older public health problems associated with lack of clean water (Leeder et al, 2006). The incidence of uni-polar major depression (as opposed to bipolar 'manic depression') is already the fourth leading cause of death and disability internationally, and is set to become the second by 2020. Depression affects both young and old, in high- and low-income countries. Furthermore, violence, war and self-inflected injuries are rapidly becoming leading causes of death and disability (Murray and Lopez, 1996). Since the majority of victims and perpetrators of interpersonal violence are young adults, high rates of violence can cancel out many of the health gains achieved through the control of infectious diseases (Butchart et al, 2004, p2).

One of the common problems in counting the health, social and economic costs of any health problem is its occasional hidden nature. A health problem is not a health problem until it is named as such. This is as true for the previously hidden issue of depression as it is for a relatively new disease such as AIDS. Violence would fall in the category of a health issue that is still largely overlooked as a destroyer of lives and economies.

As the most extensive current summary of research on the prevalence of violence, the World Health Organization's *World Report on Violence and Health*, points out, mortality figures on violence are underestimated, particularly with regard to deaths as a result of child abuse and woman abuse, and injuries as a result of violence are grossly underestimated (Krug et al, 2002, pp59–61, 93). The *World Report* is not without its flaws. Its categorization of violence leads to unnecessary duplication. For instance, information on child sexual and physical assault is in four chapters on youth violence, child abuse, violence by intimate partners and sexual violence. A life course approach, such as is commonly used in other discussions of the health impacts of violence (Commonwealth Secretariat, 2003), would be more integrated. There are significant omissions in the report, including very limited discussion of racist or homophobic hate crimes, violence against people with mental and physical disabilities, psychological abuse and neglect, and the subjective element of fear and insecurity. However, it is undoubtedly the best current meta-source, or summary, of previous studies on the incidence of violence and will be used as a basic text in this chapter.

A follow-up *Multi-country Study on Women's Health and Domestic Violence against Women* (Garcia-Moreno et al, 2004), a survey of women in nine LICs and Japan, is another extremely useful recent international statistical resource on the prevalence of violence, as is Francine Pickup's (2001) *Ending Violence against Women*.

In 2000, 1.6 million people are estimated to have died worldwide as a result of self-inflicted, interpersonal or collective violence (Krug et al, 2002, p9). Rates of violence vary widely by region, age, gender and other grounds of difference. For instance, the global average rate of violent deaths is 28.8 per 100,000 population; but LICs have an average of 32.1 death per 100,000, while HICs have an average of less than half this figure, or 14.4 deaths (Krug et al, 2002, p10). The balance between suicide and homicide also varies by region. In Africa and the Americas, homicide rates are more than double suicide rates, while in Europe, suicide rates are 2.5 times homicide rates, and in the Western Pacific region (China, Japan, Australia, New Zealand and the Pacific Islands), suicide rates are fully six times the homicide rates (Krug et al, 2002, pp9–10). Generally, there is an inverse relationship between homicide and suicide: regions and countries with high suicide rates have low homicide rates, and vice versa. Colombia, for instance, has one of the highest homicide rates in the world – 146.5/100,000 within the male population; but the suicide rate is a very low: 4.5/100,000. In Europe, the homicide rates are relatively low – an average of 8.4/100,000; but suicide rates are relatively high, particularly in Eastern Europe: an average of 19.1/100,000, rising to rates of over 36/100,000 in Hungary and Latvia (Krug et al, 2002, pp185–186).

One factor that increases violent death rates in Africa and Latin America, the two most violent regions in the world, is collective violence: violent conflict between and within states, as well as state-perpetrated genocide. Population surveys suggest that over 132,000 died in Guatemala's civil war between 1960 and 1996, fully 100,000 more than official estimates, while tens of thousands of East Timorese were killed by Indonesian troops during the late 1990s, although the true number may never be known. Between 500,000 and 1 million people died in less than four months in Rwanda in 1994, and as many as 2.5 million people have died in the Congo during the 1990s (Krug et al, 2002, p157). While genocide is hardly a new phenomenon – it is estimated that at least 6 million people died in the slave trade over the past four centuries and at least 10 million indigenous people died during the European conquest of the Americas alone – the number of people killed in collective violence, whether in an official war or not, has increased rapidly. During the 19th century, it is estimated that 19.4 million people died as a result of civil or international conflict. In the 20th century, the figure increased to 109.7 million, or three times the rate of population increase in that century (Krug et al, 2002, p218). Collective violence is usually committed by young men; but the victims usually include adults and children of both genders. It would certainly appear that the global fear of collective violence, in the form of terrorism, has never been higher.

Although rates of violence vary between HICs and LICs and between regions, they vary far more within regions: Colombia's male homicide rate is almost a dozen times greater than Cuba. They also vary widely within countries: the US's homicide rate for young people aged 15 to 24 is over 12 times greater for African-Americans (38.6/100,000) than for European-origin, non-Hispanic Americans (3.1/100,000) (Krug et al, 2002, pp9–10). Homicides are heavily concentrated in the 15 to 29 age group (Krug et al, 2002, pp8–9). The majority of recognized homicide victims, 77 per cent, are men (Krug et al, 2002, p9), and although the *World Report on Violence and Health* is weak on the subject of the gender of perpetrators, the majority of perpetrators are acknowledged to be young men as well (Krug et al, 2002, p25).

Contrary to the popular belief that suicide is concentrated in youth, the majority of deaths from suicide occur among older people, particularly older men, with rates rising throughout the life cycle and peaking after age 60. In most countries, more men are successful in suicide attempts, with 60 per cent of recognized suicide victims being male, although women are two to three times more likely to engage in non-fatal suicidal behaviour (Krug et al, 2002, p191). The exception to this international trend is the world's most populous country, China, where slightly more women than men kill themselves (Krug et al, 2002, p186). Indigenous people in Canada and Australia have much higher rates of suicide and self-harming behaviour. The suicide rate in Queensland, Australia, is 14.5/100,000 overall, but 23.6 among Aboriginals and Torres Strait Islanders, while the suicide rate among Inuit in Arctic Canada ranges from 59.5 to 74.3, between four and five times the Canadian average of 15/100,000 (Krug et al, 2002, p190). Suicide rates are also higher among sexual minorities, such as lesbians and gay men, although there is an absence of comparable national data (Krug et al, 2002, p195). In the case of these at-risk groups, it is young people, both men and women, who are the primary victims of self-directed violence, not older people.

We enter far more uncertain territory when examining non-fatal violence. Non-fatal violence encompasses a large continuum, from hitting another person or hurting one's self once, to repeated acts of severe violence that can result in long-term disabilities. A United Nations-associated project, the *International Crime Victim Survey*, has been developing a standardized survey since 1987 that has now been used in 47 countries; but the results are slow in coming out (as of 2007, there was still no report summarizing international data from the 2000 survey, broken down by gender and age), and the survey has several limitations, including a lack of distinction between community and familial assaults (UNICJRI, 2007). However, the survey helps complement the *World Report on Violence and Health* (Krug et al, 2002) by providing regional data on violent crimes such as robbery, which is not covered in the latter report. In Latin America, 6.3 per cent of respondents reported having been robbed in the previous year, compared to 4.1 per cent in sub-Saharan Africa, 2 per cent in Europe, and 1.4 per cent in Oceania and North America (UNODC, 2005, p60).

Most of the surveys employ as a minimum level of violence an act that would require some form of medical treatment; but many victims do not have the wherewithal to seek or find medical treatment. Many forms of violence are not illegal (see Box 2.2), and even when there are laws against violence, only a small proportion are disclosed to police or to social and health professionals. There is a great deal of discretion and variation used by police and justice officials in deciding which complaints to record, which offences to investigate, and which charges are to be laid and who will face charges. Most information on non-fatal violence across the life course thus comes from victimization surveys of different population groups and, sometimes, from self-reporting studies of violent activities (Krug et al, 2002, p11). It is also important to remember that emotional and psychological abuse and neglect are also considered forms of violence; but there is little research on their incidence (Pickup, 2001; Krug et al, 2002; Commonwealth Secretariat, 2003).

Using victimization surveys to compare prevalence of violence can be problematic for a number of reasons. One reason is wide variance in the questions asked. For instance, asking someone whether they have ever been raped will invariably lead to a lower response rate than asking someone whether they have ever had sexual contact against their will. There are often concerns about *reliability* (the extent to which surveys are consistent in different countries or over time) and *validity* (the extent to which the questions asked were the right ones) (Walklate, 1995, pp2–3). Another problem with victimization surveys is that they are rare because they are costly, time consuming (it takes many more questions to probe actual experiences of physical assault, rather than asking flat out 'has anyone ever hit you') and challenge the 'private' and hidden nature of much of the violence (Garcia-Moreno et al, 2004). Stanko (2000) raises a more theoretical concern about victimization surveys, especially as they have been used in her home country: England. To her, surveys divide the world neatly into victims and perpetrators, without recognizing that people can be both at the same time, and the situations they find themselves in are more complex than evil/good. While it is undoubtedly true that quantitative surveys are far less nuanced than qualitative studies, and that at this point in history we *do not* know much more than we *do* know, the next sections will focus on recent quantitative surveys in order to provide an international overview of current knowledge on the prevalence of violence across the life course. Somewhat arbitrary divisions have been used to separate different phases of the life course: 'childhood' for the first 15 years of life, 'youth' for the next 15 years, 'adulthood' for the subsequent 30 years, and 'old age' for life after 60.

Box 2.2 *Violence versus crime*

Most countries talk about 'crime prevention', rather than 'violence prevention', and measure violence using police-recorded crime statistics. However, crime and violence are very different phenomena. In most countries, most recorded crimes are not violent, and most violence is not reported to the police and thus not counted as crimes in the countries' statistics. To give one example, according to international police data, the police-reported rate for assaults is 409/100,000 for Southern, West and Central Africa, and 55/100,000 in North America, while the most recent *International Crime Victimization Survey* provides self-reported rates for assault as 3100/100,000 in sub-Saharan Africa (7.5 times the official rate) and 2300/100,000 in North America (42 times the official rate) (UNODC, 2005, p57).

Crime is any offence that is against the laws of a government. In most countries, using 'reasonable force' violence in disciplining children is not against the law. In many countries, there is no law against sexual assault within a married relationship. In some countries, adultery is a crime punishable by death. In some jurisdictions, chewing gum or asking for money in a public place are both considered crimes. There are, in short, huge cultural differences in the labelling of crimes and the meting out of punishments. For these reasons, we prefer the more cross-cultural term 'violence prevention', and only use the term 'crime prevention' when referring to a particular initiative that labels itself as such.

Violent crimes or *crimes against the person* are those serious offences against the laws of a country that involve force or attempted force against a person. Depending upon the categorization used by the particular country, implicit threat of force may not matter in terms of violent crimes, leaving out violence such as harassment based on sexism, racism or homophobia, or *stalking* (continued harassment by an ex-intimate partner). Violent crimes usually include murder, attempted murder, assault, sexual assault (which may be narrowly defined as *rape*, sexual assault involving forced penetration of the vulva or anus, or may have a broader definition, encompassing unwanted sexual harm of any nature) and, in many but not most countries, robbery and extortion (theft of money and property that involves the use of violence or threat of violence, including *home invasions* and *carjacking*), as well as kidnapping. Most deaths and injuries involving motorized vehicles are not included as violent crimes, even if the driver of the car was responsible (driving while under the influence of alcohol or drugs), although some countries have a charge of *vehicular homicide*. Sexual assault sometimes includes the crime of *statutory rape* or sexual relations below the age of consent (or, in the case of people with severe intellectual disabilities, where consent may not be properly understood). The age of consent to sexual acts varies across jurisdictions, and sometimes there are different ages depending upon gender or the nature of the act. For instance, anal sexual intercourse, which would be considered a violent crime in some jurisdictions even if both partners are willing, often has a higher age of consent than 'heterosexual' penis–vagina sexual intercourse in countries where it is legal. While possession of a weapon is not considered a violent crime, possession of a weapon with intent to use it in a crime is sometimes included in the category of violent crimes.

Terrorism is considered to be criminal acts, usually involving violence, against civilians by groups or individuals for political goals. There are broad disagreements about the extent and nature of terrorism – for instance, whether it includes acts of terror or torture by sovereign states as well as non-governmental organizations. An opponent's terrorist is a supporter's freedom fighter. For that reason, we usually use the term *collective violence* instead of terrorism.

Property crimes are those serious offences that do not involve direct violence against a person, and which usually are motivated by desire for money or property. They include thefts from homes, workplaces or public spaces; vehicle theft; the growing crime of identity theft; fraud, or obtaining money under false pretences; many *white collar* or *corporate crimes* (crimes committed by individuals or companies within business transactions); and large-scale damage to property (e.g. through arson). It should be noted that some corporate crimes lead to widespread death – in cases such as Union Carbide's criminal negligence, resulting in death by chemical poisoning of thousands of people in Bhopal, India, in 1984. In some cases, corporate crime, because of its transnational and long-term nature, should probably be classified as organized crime (see below); but the two are generally kept separate. It should also be noted that most property crimes can have impacts upon people's heath and well-being, and upon their use of scarce resources, particularly in low-income communities. While property crimes will be discussed at various points throughout this book, the emphasis is on violent crimes as they are generally more destructive to both individuals and communities. Property offences are usually considered less serious than violent crimes in most societies. However, it is not unusual in many countries for convicted property criminals, particularly repeat offenders, to receive heavier sentences than violent criminals.

There is a large category of crimes that do not involve direct violence towards persons or damage to property, but are, nonetheless, commonly agreed to be criminal activities and sources of harm. These include trafficking in illicit drugs (and, in some cases, trafficking in alcohol and prescription drugs), and trafficking in pornography or sexual images (particularly child pornography). These offences, along with sexual trafficking in persons and prostitution, are usually categorized under the term *vice*. Sometimes, self-harming behaviour, such as illicit drug use, under-age drinking or suicide attempts, are considered crimes and are punished as such, sometimes very harshly, as in the case of repeat drug offenders (including those in possession of insufficient drugs to be trafficking) going to prison for life.

Organized crime refers to a group of people engaged over a relatively long-term basis in criminal activity, which may include violent crimes (kidnapping, extortion, trafficking of women and children, or drugs), weapons sales and property crimes (particularly those involving cars or computers). Organized crime rings are often transnational in nature, moving goods or people long distances in the commission of a crime. Because both corporate and non-corporate organized crime is transnational, international organizations are becoming increasingly involved in the issue of organized crime, including the United Nations Office on Drugs and Crime (UNODC, 2005).

Incivilities, disorder and *anti-social behaviours* are acts that may not be considered offences, or are considered minor offences, by the state, but are still seen as a threat to public order. Some incivilities are not against the law, and criminal judgements usually tend towards fines or community service orders rather than imprisonment. Examples include littering, graffiti and other relatively minor acts of property damage and shoplifting. What is considered a non-criminal incivility in one place might attract regular criminal enforcement in another jurisdiction, including spitting, harassing language, or public urination or defecation. While some commentators (Kelling and Coles, 1996) feel that enforcing criminal sanctions against incivilities are a powerful way of deterring more serious crimes, and have a direct positive impact upon fear in public space, other commentators (Mitchell, 2003) argue that focusing on incivilities destroys the civil liberties of particular groups (e.g. visible minority young men and homeless people) and has a long-term negative impact upon insecurity and public life.

Violence across the life course

Infancy and childhood (ages 0 to 14)

Any discussion of violence across the life course should begin pre-natally, with violence against pregnant women, mostly committed by their male partners (Commonwealth Secretariat, 2003, p3). In 48 recent local, national or regional surveys, between 10 and 69 per cent of women report having been physically assaulted by their male intimate partner – their husband or boyfriend – at some point in their lives (Krug et al, 2002, p89), with a high proportion of those who are physically abused reporting sexual assault by their partners as well (Krug et al, 2002, p151). Estimates of this violence range from 3 per cent of women who are in a relationship having suffered at least one incident over the past 12 months in the US, Australia and Canada, to 38 per cent of married women in Korea and 52 per cent of married Palestinian women in the West Bank and the Gaza Strip having recently experienced violence by their husbands (Krug et al, 2002, p89). Pregnancy is often a trigger to sexual and physical violence by intimate partners: the most recent Australian survey, in 2005, found that 36 per cent of women who had experienced violence by a male former partner reported that the violence occurred while pregnant, and 17 per cent experienced violence for the first time in their relationship while pregnant (Australian Bureau of Statistics, 2006). Impacts of physical violence, which will be discussed more thoroughly in the section on adults, include pre-natal injuries and loss of the mother's reproductive rights. Impacts of rape include forced childbirth or forced abortion. Research in Leon, Nicaragua, found that after controlling for other factors, the children of women who were physically and sexually abused by partners were six times more likely to die before the age of five than children of women who had not been abused. Another study in two Indian states found that women who had been beaten were significantly more likely than non-abused women to have experienced an infant death or pregnancy loss (Krug et al, 2002, p103).

Indian economist Amartya Sen talks about 'natality inequality', or selective abortion and infanticide, and 'survival inequality', including inadequate and inequitable peri-natal and post-natal care for mothers and girl infants as two reasons for approximately 100 million 'missing women' in India and China, the two most populous countries of the world. In contrast to the average of 95 girls per 100 boys born in Europe and North America, only 86 girls are born to every 100 boys in China, and in some states in India, there are only 79 girls born to every 100 boys (Sen, 2005, pp224–225; see also Pickup, 2001, pp88–89; Commonwealth Secretariat, 2003, p72; and UNICEF, 2006, p4). Most abortions and infanticides are performed by the mother, her family or traditional midwives, and point to a devaluation of women in these societies that may continue through the life course. Damage from maternal pre-natal drinking and drug-taking may also have a significant impact on a child's life chances, and it is also possible that genetic damage may eventuate from paternal abuse of alcohol and drugs. It is certain that HIV infection is a large and growing health issue for women, and these might all be considered indirect forms of pre-natal violence.

According to the *World Report on Violence and Health* (Krug et al, 2002), injuries against infants take many forms. Head trauma as a result of abuse is the most common cause of violent death in young children, with children in the first two years of life being most vulnerable. Most perpetrators of severe 'shaken child syndrome' are male, and the majority of victims are less than nine months old, with the evidence suggesting that about one third of severely shaken children die as a result and the majority of survivors suffer long-term consequences, such as mental retardation, cerebral palsy or blindness (Krug et al, 2002, p61). There are no absolute numbers or rates on this form of violence since death and injuries due to infant maltreatment are not adequately screened in most countries. Overall, recorded rates for infant and child homicide are higher for males than females and decrease after infancy (Krug et al, 2002, p61).

A 1995 study in the US found that a little less than 5 per cent of parents reported hitting children with an object, other than on the buttocks, kicking the child, beating him or her, or threatening with a knife or a gun. A similar proportion of children in Romania self-reported severe abuse, ranging from being hit by objects to being burned; nearly half the parents surveyed in that country admitted to beating their children 'regularly'. In Korea, two-thirds of parents say they whip their children, and 45 per cent confirmed that they had hit, kicked or beaten them on at least one occasion. In Egypt, 37 per cent of children say they have been beaten or tied up by their parents, and 26 per cent reported injuries such as fractures, loss of consciousness or permanent disability (Krug et al, 2002, pp62–63). The gender of perpetrators of physical abuse is not analysed in these studies.

While rates of severe violence may vary by country, the absence of legal protection for children is a constant in most countries. Despite the United Nations Convention on the Rights of Children requiring states to protect children from 'all forms of physical and mental violence' while they are in the care of parents or other caregivers, the majority of states do not have a law banning 'corporal punishment' of children. Sweden became the first country in the world to ban corporal punishment of children in 1979, and as of 2002, its lead had been followed by at least ten more countries (Krug et al, 2002, p64).

Female genital mutilation (FGM) is the removal of the clitoris and sometimes the labia of girl children, often accompanied by stitching up the vagina to leave only a small hole for the flow of urine and blood. It is carried out at any age from three days old to puberty, and is practised in 26 African countries and by some migrant communities in other countries. It is estimated to affect between 120 million and 135 million women, including almost all women in Djibouti, Mali, Somalia and large parts of Ethiopia and Sudan, and about 50 per cent of women in Kenya. Although associated by some with Islam, most Muslims do not practice FGM, and many FGM victims are not Muslim. Health impacts are severe and include infections, severe pain and haemorrhaging that can cause toxic shock and death when performed, as well as ongoing infections, infertility, prolonged pain and extremely painful sexual intercourse and childbirth (Pickup, 2001, pp89–90). Generally, the perpetrators are other women, usually family members or respected elders in the community.

According to the United Nations Children's Fund, 1.8 million children, mostly girls, are engaged in commercial sex work (UNICEF, 2006, p4), and a total of 8.4 million children are engaged in child slavery (slavery, trafficking, debt bondage, forced army recruitment and other forms of unpaid labour). A further 200 million children and young people aged between 5 and 17 are engaged in paid labour (Anti-Slavery International, 2007). Child labour, like physical abuse, is contrary to the United Nations Convention on the Rights of the Child; but it is common and legal in many countries, and is associated with higher rates of both physical and sexual abuse. This is particularly true in relation to young girls' domestic work, which is unregulated and takes place in the 'privacy' of the home (UNICEF, 2006, p48).

Children are being increasingly recruited into armies as combatants, especially in African countries. At least 300,000 children, mostly boys under 18, are taking part as combatants in various civil and transnational conflicts around the world. This transformation has partly been facilitated by light and easy-to-use small arms, as well as the decimation of adult male populations in war-torn nations. Girls who are child soldiers or refugees in war-torn nations suffer from rape, forced prostitution and other forms of violence, and boys are frequently forced to kill their families or neighbours, or to rape girls, as a form of 'army training' (Pickup, 2001, pp94–95).

There is some evidence that physical violence against girls and boys occurs at roughly equal levels, but that girls are more at risk for sexual violence. For instance, in the 2005 Australian *Personal Safety Survey*, one of the few comprehensive national surveys to ask the same questions of women and men, approximately 10 per cent of men and the same proportion of women said that they had experienced at least one incident of physical abuse before the age of 15. However, 12 per cent of women, as opposed to 4.5 per cent of men, said that they had experienced at least one incident of childhood sexual abuse (Australian Bureau of Statistics, 2006). International studies suggest an average rate of 20 per cent for childhood sexual abuse among girls, and 5 to 10 per cent among boys, with no information given by the *World Report on Violence and Health* as to the gender of the perpetrator (Krug et al, 2002, p64). The *Multi-country Study on Women's Health and Domestic Violence against Women* found rates of between 1 and 21 per cent for sexual abuse of girls before the age of 15, with male family members other than the father or stepfather being the most common perpetrator (Garcia-Moreno et al, 2004, pp49–51). Other than family members, acquaintances in position of authority – teachers, religious leaders and family friends – are common perpetrators. In South Africa, a survey of girls' experiences of rape before the age of 15 found that school teachers were named as those responsible for almost one third of rapes, and this kind of institutional abuse by male school teachers has also been indicated in other African studies (Krug et al, 2002, p155). Another South African survey, of school pupils aged 10 to 19 in grades 6 to 11, found 11 per cent of males and 4 per cent of females claimed to have forced someone else to have sex, and 66 per cent of these males and 71 per cent of these females had themselves been forced to have sex (UNODC, 2005, p58). What limited information exists on sexual assault against boys and young men suggests that the perpetrators are predominantly men and, as in the case of female victims, are family members or acquaintances in positions of authority. Settings can range from the home, to schools, to institutional settings such as police stations, prisons and armies, to refugee camps. Young men who show sexual interest in other men may be punished by rape (Krug et al, 2002, p154).

Forty per cent of girls' first sexual experiences in Peru were described by them as 'forced', as were 11 per cent of boys. In a study of nine Caribbean countries, 47.6 per cent of women and 31.9 per cent of men said that their first sexual experiences were 'forced' or 'somewhat forced'. In the US, a little over 9 per cent of women said that their first sexual experience was forced (the same question was not asked of men), and in Dunedin, New Zealand, 7 per cent of women and 0.2 per cent of men said their first sexual experience was forced (Krug et al, 2002, p154). The *Multi-country Study* ties these large variations of forced first sexual contact into customs of early marriage in many South American, African and South Asian countries (Garcia-Moreno et al, 2004, p51). In Nepal, 7 per cent of girls are married before age 10 and 40 per cent are married by the age of 15. In Rajasthan, a state of India, the equivalent percentages are 17 and 56 per cent, respectively. In Ethiopia and parts of West Africa, girls married by the age of seven or eight are not uncommon (Krug et al, 2002, p156). The minimum age for marriage in Chile, Ecuador, Panama, Paraguay, Sri Lanka and Venezuela is 12 (Pickup, 2001, p90). There is some evidence that the AIDS epidemic has created a demand for much younger female sex partners and wives because men believe young girls are less likely to be infected, and that some HIV-positive men actively seek out virgins in the erroneous belief that sex with virgins can cure them (Commonwealth Secretariat, 2003, p6). There are other culturally specific forms of sexual violence against young girls, such as forced inspections for virginity in parts of West Asia (Krug et al, 2002, p156). The health impacts of child rape, whether under the rubric of early marriage or not, are severe. Pregnancy-related death is the leading cause of mortality for girls aged 15 to 19 worldwide, and giving birth before pelvic bones are fully formed can result in infertility and other injuries, such as fistulas that cause chronic leaking of urine and faeces and resultant social ostracism (Pickup, 2001, p98).

Less severe violence, such as bullying, harassment and fighting, is very common among school-aged children in many parts of the world and is often associated with pressure to live up to particular notions of masculinity. An international average of one in three students report having ever been involved in school fights, with males two to three times more likely to fight than females (Krug et al, 2002, p29). Twenty-two per cent of adolescent males in Sweden, 44 per cent in the US, and 76 per cent in Jerusalem, Israel, say that they have been involved in schoolyard fights over the past year (Krug et al, 2002, p11). A study of school-aged children in 27 countries found that the majority of 13 year olds in most countries had engaged in bullying at least some of the time (Krug et al, 2002, p29). A Canadian study found that 23 per cent of girls in secondary schools had been sexually harassed by male peers (Krug et al, 2002, p155).

Yet another form of violence affecting children is witnessing intimate partner violence, particularly violence by a father or stepfather against the child's mother. Children are often present during incidents of adult violence: in one study in Ireland, 64 per cent of abused women said that their children regularly witnessed the violence, as did 50 per cent of abused women in Monterrey, Mexico. Studies from North America indicate that children who witness violence between their parents frequently exhibit many of the same behavioural and psychological disturbances as children who are themselves abused, including anxiety and depression, poor school performance and disobedience, nightmares and physical health problems (Krug et al, 2002, p103).

Psychological threats and humiliation, and neglect or abandonment, are highly contested grounds when it comes to child abuse. What might be considered normal by one family or one culture is considered grossly unacceptable by another. Almost half of parents surveyed in the Philippines have threatened their children with being ejected from the household or being abandoned, and 12 per cent have actually locked their children out of the house. However, rates of severe physical violence are lower in the Philippines than they are in rural India or Egypt, and rates of cursing at the child are near zero (as opposed to 24 per cent in the US and 51 per cent in Egypt). In rural India, 58 per cent of parents say that they slap children on their head, as compared to the US (4 per cent); but fewer parents in India (70 per cent) 'yell or scream' at their children than in the US (85 per cent). In Kenya, physical neglect and abandonment are common forms of abuse brought up by parents and children, and in the case of Canada's child welfare services, neglect and lack of adequate supervision (including in relation to school attendance) are common causes of child abuse cases brought to authorities' attention (Krug et al, 2002, p65).

Youth and young adulthood (ages 15 to 29)

The fact that the majority of victims and perpetrators of crimes reported to the police are young men is often brought up in a manner disassociated from high rates of child abuse, the under-reporting of many crimes throughout the life course, and the social construction of masculinities and femininities in early childhood and adolescence. Children are suddenly seen as having individual and sole responsibility for perpetrating crimes at ages as young as ten, and any discussion of mitigating factors or early childhood intervention to prevent criminality becomes seen as 'soft'. For instance, the so-called Project Respect in the UK records thousands of Anti-Social Behaviour Orders against adolescents, mostly male, forbidding behaviour that is mostly sub-criminal (ranging from spitting to under-age alcohol use), but becomes a criminal act when breached. Yet, the project says little about upstream approaches that might prevent violent childhoods and that respect the integrity of children and adolescents (Crime Reduction UK, 2007). The *World Report on Violence and Health* begins its chapters on specific forms of violence with 'youth violence' and only later turns to child abuse as a separate topic. However, it does recognize the importance of physical and sexual abuse in childhood as shaping later violence, and the importance of identifying and responding to childhood aggression before children continue on a pathway to adult criminality (Krug et al, 2002, p30). Other reports (Pickup, 2001; Commonwealth Secretariat, 2003) discuss the importance of providing education to children on non-violent ways of being masculine and feminine as a way of preventing youth violence.

In any case, the first 30 years of life are the most dangerous in terms of risk of death from interpersonal and collective violence. An average of 565 children, adolescents and young adults aged between 10 and 29 die every day as the result of interpersonal violence alone. Homicide rates among young people vary even more widely than overall rates, from less than 1/100,000 youth in Europe, parts of Asia and the Pacific, to 17.6 in Africa and 36.4 in Latin America. For every fatality, there are between 20 and 40 young people requiring hospital treatment. As is the case with overall homicide rates, youth homicide rates are almost everywhere lower for females than males. This is especially true in countries with high rates of fatal violence, such as Venezuela and the Philippines, each of which have male-to-female homicide ratios of over 16:1. In contrast, in countries where homicide rates are relatively low, such as The Netherlands and Korea, male-to-female ratios are 1.6:1. Across cultures, female homicide rates vary much less than do male homicide rates (Krug et al, 2002, pp25–27).

Female homicides are also different in nature than male homicides. Studies from five countries indicate that 40 to 70 per cent of female murder victims were killed by their husbands or boyfriends, frequently in the context of an ongoing relationship, while the obverse, men being killed by their wives, ex-wives or girlfriends, is relatively rare, between 4 and 8.6 per cent (Krug et al, 2002, p93). Male homicides are far more likely to be committed by acquaintances or strangers. In other words, fatal violence between men is much more variable across cultures than fatal male violence against women, which remains a constant in most cultures.

It should be cautioned that female homicides are far less likely to be recorded as such. Dowry-related murders in India, Pakistan and Bangladesh are often disguised as accidents or suicide. For instance, in Greater Mumbai, fully one in five deaths of women between the ages of 15 to 44 is ascribed to 'accidental burns' in kitchen fires, most of which result from dousing a woman with kerosene (Krug et al, 2002, p93). Human rights organizations estimate that over 6000 deaths a year are the result of dowry killings, with the number on the rise, despite dowries being illegal since 1961 in India (Pickup, 2001, p91–92). 'Honour killings' of women who have been raped are also commonly under-recorded as homicides. One study in Alexandria, Egypt, found that 47 per cent of women who had been raped were subsequently killed by a family member (Krug et al, 2002, p93). A survey in Yemen found 400 honour killings in 1997 alone, and in Pakistan, over 1000 women were victims in 1999 (Pickup, 2001, p91).

Apart from the US, with death rates at 11/100,000, most of the countries with youth homicide rates above 10/100,000 are LICs experiencing rapid social or economic change. Young male homicide rates have increased in recent years, particularly in developing countries in Africa and Latin America, and in countries in economic transition, such as those in the former Soviet Union. Increases in youth homicides have been associated with increases in the use of guns in attacks (Krug et al, 2002, pp25–27).

Hate crime data is rarely collected systematically, or even legally recognized, in most countries. Hate crimes are generally motivated by societal stigmatization on grounds of ethnicity, 'race', religion, sexual orientation or another aspect of exclusion from the majority society. The US, Canada and some countries in Western Europe, such as Germany, France, England and Wales, have begun standardized data collection (most of them excluding at least one of the grounds described above); but most of the evidence on hate crimes, including violent crimes as well as property destruction, is qualitative and anecdotal at present. One Canadian survey has found that 14 per cent of elementary school children suffered intimidation on the basis of their perceived race (Shaw and Barchelat, 2001, p12). An Australian study of adult lesbians, gay men, bisexuals, trans-gendered and inter-sex people found that 17.3 per cent of males and 7.2 per cent of females had faced a physical attack on the basis of their sexual or gender orientation, and 19.3 per cent of males and 13.3 per cent of females said that fear of prejudice or discrimination caused them to modify their daily routines (Pitts et al, 2007, pp48–50). While this is by no means an issue confined to young people, harassment and violence based on grounds of identity have been posited as one reason for high suicide rates among lesbian and gay teenagers.

Guns and other weapons can escalate the injuries caused by fights and harassment at school and in other public spaces. In Cape Town, South Africa, almost 10 per cent of males and over 1 per cent of females say that they bring knives to secondary school. In Scotland, 34 per cent of males and almost 9 per cent of females aged 11 to 16 said that they have carried a weapon at least once during their lifetime, while in the US, a national survey of children aged 14–18 found that 17.3 per cent had carried a weapon during the previous 30 days, and almost 7 per cent had carried a weapon onto school premises (Krug et al, 2002, pp29–30).

Youth violence, particularly among males, is rarely isolated from other crimes and risky behaviours, ranging from truancy to substance abuse, to reckless driving, to unsafe sex (Krug et al, 2002, p25). Alcohol, in particular, is a precipitator of violence. In one Swedish study, about three-quarters of violent young offenders and about half of the victims of violence were intoxicated at the time of the incident (Krug et al, 2002, p31). In Australia, 34 per cent of men reporting their most recent physical assault stated that it occurred in licensed premises (Australian Bureau of Statistics, 2006). There is evidence that the majority of young people who commit serious violence during adolescence do not go on to be violent in later life (Krug et al, 2002, p31). However, the importance of adolescent experiences of violence in shaping masculinities and femininities during the later life course may be, once again, underestimated in much literature on the issue.

For instance, discussion of 'youth violence' associated with male-on-male violence is often separated from discussion of physical and sexual assault of young women and men. This silo phenomenon certainly occurs in the *World Report on Violence and Health* (Krug et al, 2002), and is also a constant in most local, national and international policy documents. However, young women are also highly subject to men's violence, albeit in different settings and through different circumstances. The *Multi-country Study* found that incidence of both sexual and physical assault by intimate partners is most prevalent in women aged 15 to 29 (Garcia-Moreno et al, 2004, p32). Non-intimate partner violence against women also appears to be concentrated in younger age groups. Between 11 and 38 per cent of women reported non-partner physical and/or sexual violence since the age of 15, a lower rate than intimate partner violence rates of between 30 and 60 per cent, but still highly significant. The most common category of non-partner perpetrator of physical violence was a family member (fathers, stepfathers, male family members and female family members were the most common in this category), an acquaintance (teacher, male friend of family, female friend of family, boyfriend, person at work, or religious leader were most common in this category), or a stranger (police/soldier was common in this category). The most common category of non-partner perpetrator of sexual violence was acquaintances and strangers. Although the results are not broken down by age, the preponderance of family members and teachers as perpetrators suggests that the victims were aged between 15 and 29 (Garcia-Moreno et al, 2004, p46). According to the 2000 *International Crime Victimization Survey*, 2.8 per cent of respondents in sub-Saharan Africa, 2.2 per cent in Latin America, 1.5 per cent in Europe, 0.9 per cent in Oceania and North America and 0.7 per cent in Asia reported having been sexual assaulted during the previous year. This data was not broken down by gender or age (UNODC, 2005, p59). Young women aged 15 to 29 are infected by HIV in sub-Saharan Africa at rates between three and five times greater than men, with women's infection rates approaching 15 per cent in Botswana, Lesotho and Namibia. While many of these infections were due to consensual sex rather than rape, these differential rates are associated with young women's early marriage, forced sexual experiences and lack of power over sexual health (UNICEF, 2006, p11). International data thus suggests that 'youth violence' occurs at very high rates among women as well as men.

Aside from this 'everyday' gender-based violence, every year, thousands of young women and girls around the world are bought and sold into prostitution or sexual slavery. Research in Kyrgyzstan, a Central Asian republic that was formerly part of the Soviet Union, has estimated that approximately 4000 people were trafficked from that country in 1999, with the principal destinations being China, Germany, Kazakhstan, the Russian Federation, Turkey and the United Arab Emirates. Of those trafficked, 62 per cent said that they were forced to work without pay, and over 50 per cent said that they were physically abused or tortured by their employers. Over 200,000 Bangladeshi women have been trafficked between 1990 and 1997, and 5000 to 7000 Nepali women are illegally brought into India every year. According to the CIA, an estimated 45,000 to 50,000 foreign women and children are trafficked annually to the US. A study of about 2000 trafficked prostitutes in Italy found that most of these women were under 25 years of age, and many were between 16 and 18 years old: the principal countries of origin being in Central and Eastern Europe. Trafficking also takes place internally within some countries, mostly from rural areas to cities (Krug et al, 2002, p155).

Whether trafficked or not, sex workers are at particularly high risk of violence. One study of sex workers in the UK found that 30 per cent had been punched, slapped or kicked by a client, 13 per cent had been beaten, 11 per cent had been raped, and 22 per cent had experienced attempted rape. A study of Bangladeshi prostitutes found that in the previous year, 49 per cent had been raped and 59 per cent beaten by the police. In Ethiopia, a study of sex workers found violence particularly high against child sex workers (Krug et al, 2002, p155). Although there are female and male sex workers (as well as a higher proportion of trans-sexual, trans-gendered and inter-sex people than in the general population), young women still comprise the majority of sex workers.

Another increasing aspect of international migration, particularly for women, is the market for foreign domestic workers. Domestic work, like sex work, has been associated with increased risks of physical and sexual abuse, and low levels of recourse to local laws (Yeoh and Huang, 1998; Pickup, 2001, p163). As in the case of internationally arranged marriages, women may correctly fear that their right to remain in the new country will be threatened if they report or attempt to escape violence (Pickup, 2001, p130).

Adulthood (ages 30 to 59)

The age at which women and men are considered fully mature and responsible adults varies across cultures. However, some time between the latter half of the teen years and their late 20s, most people in most countries leave school (if they have not left school already), move away from their parents or other childhood caregivers to form their own households, including forming intimate partner relationships, commence the search for paid employment, or begin child-rearing. The emphasis on young people as perpetrators and victims of violence deflects attention from experiences of violence as adults. And it is true that the risks of certain forms of violence decrease over the life course, particularly male-on-male stranger and acquaintance violence in public space.

To give one example, the 2005 Australian *Personal Safety Survey* found that a little under 40 per cent of women, and a little over 50 per cent of men, report having been the victim of at least one incident of physical assault since the age of 15. Thirty-seven per cent of men who reported being physically assaulted over the past 12 months were between 18 and 24 years of age, while only 26 per cent of women were in that age group. Of men who were physically assaulted over their lifetimes, 71 per cent were assaulted by a male stranger. Of women who were physically assaulted over their lifetimes, 44 per cent were assaulted by a previous male partner. Sixty-four per cent of assaults by men against women occurred in the home of the victim and/or offender, while 69 per cent of assaults by men against men took place either outdoors or in licensed premises (Australian Bureau of Statistics, 2006). This particular national survey suggests that as men move on to lesser risks of violence in adulthood, particularly violence in public spaces, women retain the risk of being victims of violence in the supposedly safe space of their home.

The idea that women and men suffer equally from intimate partner violence, a currently controversial topic in the US based on research on high school and college-age relationships, is simply not borne out by the vast majority of international research (Garcia-Moreno et al, 2004, pp37–38). In Canada, for instance, females are three times as likely as males to suffer injury, five times as likely to be admitted for medical attention, and five times as likely to fear for their lives within violent relationships (Krug et al, 2002, pp93–94). Dozens of surveys suggest that there is no country where intimate partner violence does not victimize a significant proportion of women in relationships with men, with incidence ranging from 10 and 69 per cent (Krug et al 2002, p89). A ten country standardized survey on male intimate partner physical and sexual violence against women conducted recently by the World Health Organization found lifetime rates of between 19 and 76 per cent of physical and/or sexual violence against adult women, with most sites recording levels of violence between 26 and 60 per cent, and with intimate partner violence in most sites representing about 80 per cent of the violence (Garcia-Moreno et al, 2004, p46). While it is true that men have often not been asked the same questions, in the countries that have asked similar questions of both men and women, men report much lower rates of intimate partner violence (e.g. Australian Bureau of Statistics, 2006).

The health, social and economic impacts of overwhelmingly male-on-female intimate partner violence on individuals and on families is profound. As the *World Report on Violence and Health* states:

> *The fact that women are often emotionally involved with and economically dependent on those who victimize them has major implications for both the dynamics of abuse and the approaches to dealing with it.* (Krug et al, 2002, p89)

For one thing, the violence tends to be recurrent. In a US study, women who were being assaulted by their male partners reported an average of three violent incidents per year; in another study in London, England, the average was seven times a year. Violent behaviours such as slapping, hitting and kicking are often combined with forced intercourse (rape), denial of the right to contraception or sexual protection, constant belittling and humiliation, isolating the woman from friends and family, and monitoring and limiting movement outside the home (Krug et al, 2002, pp89, 149–150). This has huge implications for a woman's ability to be economically and emotionally independent, to talk with friends and family about the abuse, or to take any legal steps to remove herself and her children from her violent partner. Women are often conscious that trying to extricate themselves from a violent relationship can be harmful or fatal. Evidence from Canada, the US and Australia (where some of the most detailed studies have taken place), suggests that a significant proportion of femicides – women being killed – occur when the woman is trying to leave an abusive partner (Krug et al, 2002, p96). Aside from death, either through homicide or suicide, health impacts upon women range from temporary or permanent physical disabilities; abdominal injuries (connected to pregnancy often being a trigger for violence); loss of reproductive rights through miscarriage or forced pregnancy; sexually transmitted diseases; substance abuse and smoking; depression and anxiety; sleep and eating disorders; and post-traumatic stress disorders. Economic impacts include lower incomes and homelessness. These health and economic impacts have been recorded in LICs such as Nicaragua and Pakistan, as well as HICs such as the US and Australia. Health impacts upon the children of women who have been abused have already been discussed; but there are further health impacts upon any other dependent relatives, such as parents or disabled adult family members. Societal impacts include lost productivity, more unemployment, expenditures for mental and physical health, and greater likelihood of ending up on government income supplementation in countries that have social safety nets (Krug et al, 2002, pp101–102; Garcia-Moreno et al, 2004, pp55–71).

Like child abuse, 'discipline' of adult women by their husbands and partners is seen as legitimate across many countries and cultures, with some delineation between 'acceptable' violence and 'going too far'. Studies of both LICs and HICs show a similar list of events that are said to explain and at least partially justify acts of physical or sexual violence: not obeying the man; not having food ready on time; arguing back; not caring adequately for the children; questioning the man about money or girlfriends; refusing the man sex; going somewhere without the man's permission; or suspicion of infidelity. In Cambodia, women are given the following advice by the national government to prevent assault by their husbands: 'Be a good wife; take care of your house; serve your husband. Don't say bad things when he comes home from work. It's your karma; you must be patient. Cook food better. Don't burn the food. The man is very strong; don't refuse him; give him what he wants' (Pickup, 2001, p29). Eighty per cent of rural Egyptian women say that men have the right to discipline their wives in certain circumstances, including refusing to have sex with them, and the notion of 'just cause' comes up often in qualitative studies from around the globe (Krug et al, 2002, p95; Garcia-Moreno et al, 2004, pp39–41). The move to criminalize abuse by intimate partners has moved more rapidly than is the case with child abuse, with 24 countries in Latin America and the Caribbean alone passing domestic violence legislation between 1992 and 2002 (Krug et al, 2002, p104).

Men are more likely to kill and die in the collective violence of war and internal political conflict. Aside from the direct physical impacts of death and injury upon both men and women victims, and the psychological impact upon men who are trained to kill, collective violence has particular, often hidden, impacts upon girls and women. Organized mass rape as a war strategy was practised by the Japanese against women in their occupied territories, particularly Korea, during World War II, by India against Kashmir in that longstanding conflict, and by Indonesia against East Timor (Krug et al, 2002, p155). Rape as an aspect of state torture in internal conflict has been documented in South Africa, Guatemala, Rwanda, the former Yugoslavia and other countries (Pickup, 2001, pp95, 99). Armed conflict can also lead to economic and social disruption, forcing women into prostitution or leaving them as heads of households in refugee camps, where they are at high risk of rape. A study of 'boat people' fleeing Vietnam during the 1970s found that 39 per cent of women reported being abducted or raped by pirates (Krug et al, 2002, p155). The consequences of torture and rape on individuals can be felt for decades after the experience and carry over into new countries of settlement. These include depression, aggression, inability to show physical affection to one's husband or children, and other forms of long-term trauma (Pickup, 2001, pp99–101).

Disability is both a risk factor and a possible consequence of all forms of injury, from unintentional injury to suicide and collective violence. Up to one quarter of disabilities, in some countries, result from injuries and violence (UN,

2006). The United Nations estimates that around 10 per cent of the world's population lives with a disability, and this figure is rapidly increasing through population growth, medical advances and the ageing process. In countries with life expectancies of over 70 years, individuals spend on average about eight years living with disabilities. Disabilities can be physical: mobility, sight and hearing impairments, as well as chronic physical diseases; mental: living with depression, schizophrenia or another short-term or chronic mental disease; or intellectual. Women and girls with disabilities are particularly vulnerable to abuse. A survey in Orissa, India, found that virtually all the women and girls with disabilities were beaten at home, 25 per cent of women with intellectual disabilities had been raped and 6 per cent of disabled women had been forcibly sterilized (UN, 2006). As is the case with hate crimes, there are simply not enough national studies on violence against people with disabilities to provide useful cross-cultural statistical information.

Old age (age 60 onwards)

Like the abuse of children and women, elder abuse is still often hidden and denied in many societies. One issue in cross-cultural comparisons is that studies of elder abuse are exceedingly rare. Information on the extent of elder abuse in the *World Report on Violence and Health* (Krug et al, 2002) relies on five surveys from HICs in the past ten years since there are no reliable studies from the developing world. Another issue is that defining 'old age' is even more culturally contingent than defining 'youth'. In HICs, old age is commonly associated with retirement between the ages of 60 and 70. In LICs, where life expectancies are lower, the age at which a person is considered old may also be lower. Whenever people lose their productive or reproductive functions, when they 'because of physical decline can no longer carry out their work or family roles' (Krug et al, 2002, p125), when they become economically dependent instead of independent, they are considered old and potentially less valuable to their societies. The fact that in almost every country, suicide rates are highest in people over 60 (Krug et al, 2002, p125), yet the majority of attention focuses on youth suicide, points to a social, as well as an individual, devaluation of life in the third age.

As life expectancies increase and birth rates fall in most countries, the proportion of older people grows ever larger. A doubling of the worldwide population of people aged 60 or more is expected between 1995 and 2025. Throughout the world, the population of those aged over 60 grows by 1 million every month, 80 per cent of whom live in the developing world. In most nations, there are more old women than old men, although nations ravaged by AIDS are the exception to the rule that women live longer. Only 30 per cent of older people are covered by pension schemes. In both HICs and LICs, structural inequalities against women (lower wages, lower participation in the paid workforce, lack of educational opportunities, lower-quality health services, unjust divorce or inheritance laws) lead to older women being poorer and more vulnerable to abuse (Krug et al, 2002, pp125–126). There are also culturally specific forms of violence against older women. In Tanzania, an estimated 500 older women a year are still murdered as 'witches' (Krug et al, 2002, p128), and widespread cases of 'witch-killing' have also been reported in the state of Bihar, India (Pickup, 2001, p93).

Elder abuse can be physical, psychological/emotional, financial, sexual or can consist of abandonment and neglect. By financial abuse, the *World Report* includes extortion and control of pension money, theft of property (e.g. the expulsion of a parent from the family home by their children) and exploitation of older people by forcing them to care for grandchildren. Sexual abuse includes incest and rape, but also culturally specific practices such as the forced marriage of a widow to her husband's younger brother, which can occur in Africa and India. Neglect and abandonment are also culturally determined. For instance, in China, failing to care for an older relative in one's home would be considered elder abuse (Krug et al, 2002, p127). If all of these aspects of elder abuse are included, rates in the five HICs that have conducted surveys on the issue (Canada, the US, The Netherlands, Finland and the UK) vary between 4 and 6 per cent over the past year (the first three studies) or 'since retirement' or 'the past few years' (the latter two studies). Only one of the studies, from Finland, found a significant difference in prevalence among female and male victims: 7 and 2.5 per cent, respectively. The Canadian study found that men were more likely to report financial abuse than women (Krug et al, 2002, p129).

In many high- and low-income countries, institutional care is beginning to overtake family care as the norm. About 4 to 7 per cent of the elderly population of HICs currently live in nursing homes, while in Latin America the rate is between 1 and 4 per cent. While there is no national data on abuse within these settings, there have been well-publicized cases in all countries of physical, financial, sexual and emotional abuse in nursing homes (Krug et al, 2002, p129).

The relationship between violence and insecurity

Despite the World Health Organization's community safety principles, which declare that perceptions are as important as observable realities, there is virtually no mention of fear of violence or insecurity within the *World Report on Violence and Health* (Krug et al, 2002). International comparative studies on the issue are also rare. One problem, even more acute than is the case with non-fatal violence, is coming up with reliable and comparable statistics. It is now widely presumed that asking questions about fear of crime increases anxiety among correspondents (Pain, 2000; Lemanski, 2004); that there is a complex relationship between fear, risk and behaviour that can only be understood through qualitative surveys

(National Community Crime Prevention Programme Australia, 1998; Lupton, 2000; Pain, 2000); that specific groups, such as men, may underestimate their fear because of concerns that it is weak to admit fear (Pain, 2000; Lemanski, 2004; Brownlow, 2005); and, perhaps most importantly, that the usual questions asked in fear of crime surveys firmly anchor the problems of crime and violence in the public sphere (Lupton, 2000; Pain, 2000, 2001; Whitzman, 2007).

However, 20 years of research, mostly within HICs, but increasingly within LICs, suggest that fear of violence has extensive costs at the individual and family levels, including loss of educational, employment and leisure opportunities; negative self-image, anxiety and depression; and loss of trust in neighbours and fellow citizens (Gordon and Riger, 1989; National Community Crime Prevention Programme Australia, 1999; Pain, 2000; National Crime Prevention Council US, 2001). At the community and societal levels, fear of violence has been posited as the motor behind an increase in private-security gated communities and other aspects of the 'architecture of fear', restrictive and discriminatory by-laws and vigilantism against the homeless and other vulnerable groups, and an increasing disregard of civil liberties by individuals and private and public security providers, especially with regard to visible minorities, during the past 20 years (Mitchell, 2003; Vanderschueren, 2006). Concerns about 'stranger danger', as well as traffic safety, have been given as the main reason behind a huge decrease in the number of children allowed to walk independently to school, neighbourhood parks, shops and their friends' houses in many HICs over the past 20 years (Hillman et al, 1990; National Crime Prevention Council US, 2001). Fear of violence is related to the question of citizenship, which is central to much of the literature on community safety – namely, the right to participate not only in formal politics, but also in the informal politics of community life. This can also be constituted as the 'right to the city': the right not only to feel comfortable and welcome in public space, but to influence its physical form and the social relations that take place in public space (Lefebvre, 1996; Fenster, 2005). Tovi Fenster argues that 'the lack of freedom to move in space by imprisonment at home' is as brutal a violation of human rights as actual physical violence (Fenster, 1999, p3).

We use the term 'fear of violence' rather than 'fear of crime' because numerous HIC studies have shown that the crime that has the greatest impact upon fear in women is sexual assault, while the crime that has the greatest impact upon fear in men is assault (Gordon and Riger, 1989; Pain, 1997; National Community Crime Prevention Programme Australia, 1998). Fear of violence is usually constituted as a public space phenomenon: the most common question asked in surveys is some variant of 'How safe do you feel walking alone in your neighbourhood after dark?' (Grabosky, 1995). Most fear of crime surveys find that gender is the most important variable explaining differences in rates of fear, with adult women reporting fear at rates three times greater than men (Grabosky, 1995;

National Community Crime Prevention Programme Australia, 1998; National Crime Prevention Council US, 2001). A study in Edinburgh found that 83.8 per cent of women avoided certain streets or areas, 70.1 per cent of women avoided certain types of transport, and 35 per cent sometimes or always avoided going out alone because of fear of sexual attack. The same study found that fear of sexual attack affected the work lives of 41.6 per cent of the women surveyed, while 53.6 per cent said that it affected their leisure activities and 76.9 per cent said it affected their social lives (Pain, 1997).

While the gender gap in fear of violence statistics appears to be cross-cultural, recent surveys in the UK and South Africa suggest that living in low-income areas may be a greater determinant of insecurity (National Crime Prevention Council US, 2001; Crime Reduction UK, 2004; Lemanski, 2004), and that self-identified 'race' and income may be a better predictor of whether fear affects use of public space than gender. It should be noted that the at-risk households identified by the *British Crime Survey* – led by single parents and/or people with disabilities, often in public housing estates – are often women led, as are the plurality of low-income urban households in most countries, including the US and South Africa. The US survey, for example, found that an average of 17 per cent of respondents said that they somewhat or significantly reduced their activities because of fear. The difference between men and women was twofold: 22 per cent of women and 11 per cent of men said that they reduced activities, as was the difference between those earning under US$20,000 a year (16 per cent) and those earning between US$20,000 and $39,000 a year (30 per cent). The difference between African-Americans (42 per cent) and whites (12 per cent) was more than threefold. Identities are never simple and unchanging, and age, class, 'race'/culture, gender and sexuality often intersect in ways that cannot be captured by binary divisions such as man/woman or black/white. A number of UK studies show how women from South Asian backgrounds fear both racist and sexual attack when using public space (Burgess, 1998; Scraton and Watson, 1998). Age (young children and older people are more likely to report fear of violence and limitations on activities because of fear), physical abilities and sexual orientation have also been shown to have significant impacts on the incidence and impacts of fear (Pain, 2000, 2001).

Numerous commentators have noted the so-called irony that women (or older people) fear crime in public space more than men (or young people); yet young men are more likely to be victims of crime in public space, particularly with regard to those crimes reported to police. These commentators do not appear to recognize the gendered and age-specific social context within which people develop a sense of risk and choices around public space. Fear of violence among older people appears related to a sense of greater frailty in defending oneself against potential attackers and a greater risk of serious impacts if attacked, which are both quite legitimate fears (Pain, 2001). Fear of violence among older people might also be affected by previous experiences of violence in their lives. As for gender, qualitative studies in Canada and Australia suggest that experiences in both the home and workplace have an impact upon the constitution of fear of violence in public space. Johnson and Sacco (1995), discussing the first national violence against women survey conducted in Canada in 1993, record the common daily 'sub-violent' experiences of 'unpredictable situations that could *potentially* turn violent', including flashing, obscene phone calls, being followed, repeatedly being asked for a date despite saying 'no' and threats of losing your job if you do not submit to sexual relations (Johnson and Sacco, 1995, pp297–299). In Australia, Lupton's female interview subjects described disquieting incidents, such as being followed, stared at, approached or shouted at by men on the street or in public transport (Lupton, 1999, p10), while some of her interview subjects also described experiences of childhood and adult sexual violence in the home as having an impact upon their sense of fear in public space (Lupton, 1999, pp11–12). In the UK, Pain's female interview subjects reported more worry about being sexually assaulted 'outside' by strangers than in their homes by someone they knew, which was also the case in the Australian and Canadian studies. However, 29.3 per cent reported that they had been the victim of a physical and/or sexual assault, almost all involving men they knew (Pain, 1997). Their first-hand experiences of what being a victim of violence felt like almost certainly affected their perceptions of safety in public space. The *Multi-country Study* (Garcia-Moreno et al, 2004) found that between 10 and 62 per cent of women surveyed in ten countries had experienced physical violence, and 1 to 12 per cent had experienced sexual violence by people who were *not* their intimate partners. Many of these assaults took place outside the home: in schools, workplaces and in public space. The *World Report on Violence and Health* acknowledges studies that show that many women who are physically assaulted by their intimate partners fear for their lives at some point in the relationship (Krug et al 2002, p93); however, these fears are almost never captured within 'fear of crime' surveys. How men develop their sense of risk and choices has only recently been addressed by researchers (Brownlow, 2005).

So why is fear of violence constituted in public discourse as fear in public space? Lupton and Pain both point to a powerful cultural mythology, at least in Anglo-American HICs, that posits home as a safe and controllable space, and women needing a man to protect them in potentially unsafe spaces outside the home. Children, particularly girl children, are instructed from childhood to be fearful of 'strange men', while adolescent boys are encouraged to deny vulnerability and not to display fear (Lupton, 1999, p10; see also Pain, 2000, and Brownlow, 2005). Lupton also speaks of the importance of 'mythologized spaces', such as the town centre, or some public housing estates as hotbeds of crime within the media and 'localized circuits of gossip and knowledge', whether or not reported crime statistics, let alone victimization surveys, back up these myths (Lupton,

1999, p8). Pain contends that fear in public space is less about the space itself than it is about fear of men, and it is far more culturally acceptable to say that you fear strange men than to say you fear the men you know (Pain, 2000, p372). Fear of crime statistics is also misused for political ends, with figures either misrepresented or overstated to back certain programmes or policies; these misleading 'fear discourses' are often blamed on the media, but are as likely to be generated by political leaders (Pain, 2000, p367). The fear discourses then become self-reinforcing: politicians, saying that they are responding to public fears, proceed to fund efforts to 'design out crime' with measures such as closed-circuit television (CCTV), increased lighting, increased 'zero tolerance' policing in certain areas, and removal of benches and other elements that might attract 'undesirables'. These measures reinforce the emphasis on unsafe public space versus the safety of homes, and may increase fear and avoidance of the former spaces, as well as increase social exclusion of certain groups constituted as threats (Pain, 1997, p233; see also Pain, 2001; Mitchell, 2003; Speak, 2004). Finally, the impact of the questions themselves cannot be underestimated: most national surveys, focusing as they do on fear in the public sphere, further reinforce the dichotomy of good/safe/private versus bad/unsafe/public spheres (with home constituted as a safe space because it is harder for strangers to gain entry), which denies the existence of violence in rural areas, gated communities, rich suburbs and homes in general (Pain, 2000, 2001).

Although the emphasis in this book is on direct forms of violence, the impact of offences against property, particularly when backed up by intimidation by the offenders, should not be underemphasized. This can be a particular issue in low-income communities, whether they are in HICs or LICs. Moser (2004, pp3–5), drawing upon her work in Latin America, includes interpersonal property offences in her 'roadmap of violence and insecurity'. In one qualitative study of a small town in Ecuador, one in five women's houses was broken into and robbed by young men known within the community. Because these young men were known and retribution was feared if officials took action, the women's responses were individual and restrictive of their freedom and choices. Women dropped out of night school and reduced their evening social activities. Scarce resources went into grilles on the windows of their homes and reinforced doors. In short, the wave of thefts 'eroded assets of the poor and affected their livelihoods and well-being' (Moser, 2004, p3).

A study of fear of crime in immediate post-apartheid Cape Town, South Africa, found that while fear was rapidly increasing in wealthy white neighbourhoods between 1994 and 1997, the impact in poor black areas was far more devastating, mostly because the richer communities had the means to insulate themselves from those whom they considered threatening (Lemanski, 2004). While virtually all whites (95 per cent) felt 'very' or 'fairly' safe in their daytime residential areas, only just over half of blacks (52 per cent) and coloureds

(56 per cent) felt that way. At night, the differences were even starker: very few blacks (11.9 per cent) and coloureds (9 per cent) felt safe in their residential areas, as opposed to half of whites (55 per cent). These figures are confirmed by levels of victimization: while most (79.2 per cent) of white victimization, both personal and property offences, occurs away from their residential areas, most black (51 per cent) and coloured (55 per cent) victimization occurs within their residential areas (Lemanski, 2004, p105). The impacts of this fear in rich areas include fortifying entire neighbourhoods with high walls, electrified fences, closed street access, sophisticated alarm systems utilizing CCTV, and armed-response private security. The smaller number of blacks and coloureds who could afford some measure of protection mostly relied on dogs, window grilles and high fences (Lemanski, 2004). The impacts upon social exclusion, urban segregation and the authority of local governments (many, if not most, of the street closures were constructed in contravention to local planning laws), as those with money retreat to fortified communities, has been detailed in both South Africa and the US (Blakely and Snyder, 1997).

Recent safety audits in Delhi and Mumbai, India, suggest that while women are using public spaces to a greater extent during recent years, they still labour under a 'tyranny of purpose' – that is, they still feel more comfortable when doing a specific task or moving from point A to point B than they do in lingering in public spaces (Phadke, 2005). Female students at the University of Delhi follow a 'rape schedule', where they limit their use of the campus after dark and avoid situations where they are alone (Baxi, 2003). These findings in India echo studies 20 years ago in the UK which suggest that fear of violence results in a *de facto* 'curfew on women' (Walklate, 1995, p61). The problem, as Danish urban designer Jan Gehl has pointed out, is that it is precisely those optional social activities, accomplished outside regular work hours, that are essential to creating genuinely 'social spaces' (Gehl, 1987, p13). These spaces allow mixture and casual learning of different cultures through undemanding conversation with strangers and acquaintances, and are also the source of pleasure and interest for children and adults. Lingering people, particularly if they are mixed in gender, can provide a sense of safety through informal surveillance (Gehl, 1987, p17; see also Jacobs, 1961, and Whyte, 1980). The 'excessive thinning out of people and events', the destruction of what Gehl calls 'life between buildings', is inimical to good social space (Gehl, 1987, p48). Where this kind of denudation of urban life has occurred, whether through urban design measures, including 'designing out crime', or through people abandoning public space for a variety of reasons, including fear of violence, the concept of social space becomes lost and the sense of collective responsibility for safe communities may also disappear.

Because fear of crime surveys almost never discuss their findings in the context of the realities of violence in both private and public space, the traditional government reaction to findings that adult women and older people fear violence

Box 2.3 *A short note on 'race' and violence*

The term 'race' will be put in single quotation marks throughout the book because there is no evidence that there are biologically determined 'races', let alone characteristics that can be ascribed to race. Despite that fact that analysis by 'race' is common, terms vary widely between countries. For instance, the term 'black' refers to many different groups, depending upon the country where it is used. In the US, black means African-Americans, usually descendents of slaves, although there are a growing number of recent black migrants from the Caribbean and Africa. In Canada, black means people of African origin as well, usually first- or second-generation migrants from the Caribbean, although there is a smaller, more established, community descended from refugees from slavery in the US. In the UK, black usually means people of South Asian descent, who may be new migrants or who may be second- or third-generation citizens. In Australia, black means the indigenous people or Aboriginal Australians, who are descendents of inhabitants who predated European settlement by over 40,000 years. In South Africa, black means the indigenous people as well, although settlement by particular black groups may predate European settlement by only 100 years or so, and in that country blacks comprise the majority. Despite race being an imprecise and essentially meaningless term, certain individual groups are *racialized* by being assigned characteristics based on what is sometimes one element of their heritage or identity. For instance, some Americans or Australians might be considered black even if only one grandparent was of African or Aboriginal origin, respectively. This may or may not correspond with their self-identity. A larger problem is *racism*, the belief of a more powerful group that less powerful groups act in certain ways perceived as negative because of innate or cultural deficiencies. There is a large difference between saying that certain groups, such as African-Americans or Australian indigenous people, have higher rates of violence and so therefore need the resources to identify and solve these problems, and locating 'the problem of violence' within these communities, usually accompanied by a demand that they 'act more like us'. It is unjust to stigmatize a particular community for having more violence, particularly without looking at the underlying economic, social, spiritual and cultural causes of this violence. It is also likely to be ineffective to say that simply by acting more like 'mainstream' society, a high violence community will be able to solve their problems. One thing is certain, much higher imprisonment rates for 'blacks' in many high-income countries and in South Africa has not led to lower rates of violence, either within these communities or in countries as a whole.

in public space more than young men is to assume that the former groups are 'irrational' and to dismiss their concerns and ideas for action (Walklate, 1995, pp57–58). Unfortunately, as Carina Listerborn points out, even some feminists working on violence prevention issues repeat the notion that focusing on reducing fear of violence in public space is somehow a misuse of community resources, or that *any* attempt to utilize a planning or urban management approach to limiting public violence is necessarily restrictive of others' rights, as well as ineffective (Listerborn, 2002a). The opposite reaction, taking knee-jerk repressive approaches, particularly against low-income and visible minority young men under the rationale of reducing fear of crime, is equally destructive to people's rights and to public space (Mitchell, 2003). While fear cannot be completely designed or legislated out, it is both ethical and sensible to engage with and listen to people who express fear of violence in public space since these perceptions have real impacts upon people's lives and livelihoods, and the alternative is for people with any choice in the matter to abandon public spaces and public life altogether.

Conclusion: A largely private issue or a public concern?

As the information in this chapter indicates and as Box 2.4 summarizes, violence and insecurity are endemic across most societies and iterative throughout the life course. It is not simply a problem of war-torn or poverty-stricken countries, although the issues of violence there are more severe and, in some ways, different from people living in HICs. It is not simply a problem concentrated within a particular demographic: 'at-risk' young men as perpetrators and/or victims. The incidence of violence crosses class, ethnicity, religious and other lines. This is particularly true when discussing violence within families and in homes, as opposed to community or public violence. It is only in recent years that the incidence of so-called 'private' or 'domestic' violence in household and institutional settings began to be publicly discussed as an international social, economic and health problem. Reliable, comparable international information on the nature and extent of violence, particularly against children, women, older people, people with disabilities, and ethnic, religious and sexual minorities, is still lacking. However, it is increasingly acknowledged that 'everyday violence', a term coined by the Council of Europe (2004) to distinguish interpersonal violence from extraordinary circumstances such as terrorism or war, affects us all.

What we know about the prevalence of violence suggests that male infants under five years of age are at slightly more risk of fatal injury than girl infants in most societies, but that some societies have higher rates of selective abortion and infanticide for girls. Both male and female children between the ages of 5 and 14 are at roughly equal and high risk of both fatal and non-fatal (but serious and

Box 2.4 *Violence in a global city: A thought experiment*

Table 2.1 summarizes available information on global violence. In order to make sense of these numbers, imagine that we live in a city with a population of 400,000, with equal numbers of men and women. The birth rate is fairly low in this city and public health is generally good, so the usual 'age pyramid' does not apply. There are equal numbers of children under 15, young people aged 15 to 29, adults aged 30 to 59, and older people over 60 years of age. The city is neither rich nor poor. It is not a hotbed of sexual trafficking, and harmful traditional cultural practices such as female genital mutilation, witch hunting and honour killings are uncommon. It is not in the middle of a civil or international war, and has not been the target of terrorist attacks. We, its citizens, like to think of ourselves as decent law-abiding people, living in a relatively safe city.

In our city, three unrelated children under the age of five have recently been murdered by their parents. Between 5000 and 67,000 children are regularly hit, kicked, whipped or locked out of the house by their parents, and somewhere between 10,000 and 20,000 children under the age of 15, both girls and boys, are being sexually abused, mostly by family members. No one is quite sure of the numbers because there is no particular public outcry and no systemic research into the issue. After all, what happens in homes and within families is a private affair, isn't it?

Twenty-three young people, 19 of them men, have been murdered, mostly by other young men. This seems to be a problem concentrated in the poorer parts of the city, so it isn't a big concern to the rest of us. We'll just avoid those areas. Another 28 young people have killed themselves. A lot of these deaths could have been prevented; but it is their own responsibility, isn't it?

Then there are the thousands of young men, anywhere between 20,000 and 37,500 of them, who have got into fights in schools, on streets and in licensed and unlicensed drinking premises. About 12,500 young women, and an unknown number of young men, have been sexually assaulted by boyfriends, teachers, older family members and strangers. But isn't that a normal part of growing up? Tens of thousands of people, particularly women, don't like using public transport to get to work or to go out, in general, by themselves, particularly after dark. Well, it is their right to take precautions, although they seem a little irrational in their concerns. Perhaps they should not go out by themselves or at least attire themselves decently should they venture out alone. They might want to buy themselves tens of thousands of cars, or at least all buy themselves mobile phones, whether they can afford to or not. Again, it is people's individual responsibility to take reasonable precautions, isn't it?

Table 2.1 *Prevalence of violence over a life course:*
Rates per 100,000 population

Age 0 to 14	Men/100,000	Women/100,000
Homicides	6 (0–4)	5 (0–4)
	2 (5–14)	2 (5–14)
Suicides	2 (5–14)	2 (5–14)
Non-fatal physical violence[1]	5000–67,000[2]	5000–67,000[2]
Non-fatal sexual violence	5000–10,000[3]	20,0000[3]
Age 15 to 29		
Homicides	19	4
Suicides	16	12
Non-fatal physical violence[1]	40,000–77,000[4]	10,000–69,000[5]
Non-fatal sexual violence	Unknown[6]	33,000[7]
Age 30 to 59		
Homicides	19 (30–44)	4 (30–44)
	15 (45–59)	4 (45–59)
Suicides	22 (30–44)	12 (30–44)
	28 (45–59)	13 (45–59)
Non-fatal physical violence[1]	Unknown	10,000–69,000[5]
Non-fatal sexual violence	Unknown[6]	25,000[8]
Age 60 plus		
Homicides	13	5
Suicides	45	22
Non-fatal physical violence[1]	4000–7000[9]	4000–7000[9]
Non-fatal sexual violence	Unknown[9]	Unknown[9]

Notes:
1 Does not include self-directed violence.
2 Most national surveys on physical violence against children are not broken down
  by gender; limited evidence (e.g. Australian Bureau of Statistics, 2006) suggests
  similar rates for boys and girls (Krug et al, 2002, pp62–63).
3 Estimates are from Krug et al (2002, p64).
4 Based on limited national and local surveys of school fighting among adolescent
  boys (Krug et al, 2002, p11); the Australian *Personal Safety Survey* estimates

lifetime prevalence rates for physical violence among men of 50 per cent, mostly concentrated in the 15 to 29 age group, and mostly acquaintance or stranger assault (Australian Bureau of Statistics, 2006).

5 Based on a large number of recent national surveys of physical assault within intimate partner relationships (Krug et al, 2002, p89).

6 The Australian *Personal Safety Survey* found that 2 per cent of men said that they had been sexually assaulted as adults.

7 Based on several national surveys of forced first sexual experience (Krug et al, 2002, p149).

8 Based on a large number of recent national surveys of sexual assault in adult women (Krug et al 2002, p149).

9 Based on limited national surveys of elder abuse, most of which are not broken down by gender (Krug et al, 2002, p129); most national surveys do not include experiences of physical or sexual assault, by intimate partners or not, after the age of 60; but these experiences certainly exist.

About eight women in our Global City have been killed by their boyfriends or partners over the past few years, several of them as they tried to extricate themselves from their relationships. I guess they made some bad choices, didn't they? There are also somewhere between 10,000 and 69,000 women aged 15 to 59 who are being sexually and physically assaulted by their intimate partners, many with young children witnessing the abuse. They should probably all just move away from the guy, get a job and another place to live, and deal with their problems. Then there is the growing number of people, about 45 men and 22 women, who have been killing themselves as they get older. But I'm sure they all had their good reasons to be depressed, and there isn't much we as a society can do about it. There's a rumour that some older people, maybe 4000, maybe 7000, are being abused by their adult children; but those old folks can be a real pain sometimes.

More and more people are moving into guarded apartment buildings and gated communities, and fewer people than ever are using the streets, public squares and parks around town. When people go out in the evenings, they tend to take their cars instead of public transport, and some parts of the city appear to be 'no-go' areas, where the local economy is suffering and residents feel stigmatized. Most kids seem to be spending their time in front of the television or computer, rather than playing on the street or roaming around by themselves, like their parents used to when they were kids. Maybe they should be driven by their parents to extra-curricular sports lessons or they will get fat.

Of course, we are concerned about crime. We have a large police force, and a nice new courthouse and jail. The last city hall meeting came up with some good solutions to the crime problem in our city. Young people who spray graffiti on the city's walls need to be fined and probably caned by their parents, as well. Those homeless guys downtown have been making a real nuisance of themselves, so we've passed a by-law saying they can't ask for money from us. If young hooligans keep on stealing to feed their drug habits, how about locking them away for life? After all, we want to be a safer community, don't we?

recurrent) violence, most commonly committed in homes and within families. The gender breakdown of perpetrators of child physical abuse is not yet clear, although the majority of perpetrators of sexual abuse are known to be men. Adult men, particularly young adults, are most at risk of fatal violence, committed by other men who are strangers or acquaintances, usually in public space. Girls and women are most at risk of serious, recurrent and sometimes fatal violence in the private sphere, most commonly committed by men who are intimate partners or family members, but who sometimes are strangers and acquaintances. Older people, particularly men, are most at risk of suicide, and there is growing understanding on the nature and risks of elder abuse within families and in institutional settings. Throughout the life course, people stigmatized on the grounds of 'race', religion, ethnicity, disabilities and sexual orientation suffer higher risks of violence, including self-inflicted violence, than their age-equivalent peers.

Relaying available statistics on the perpetrators of violence does not imply that men are 'naturally' more violent, or that women are 'naturally' more inclined to be victims than perpetrators of violence. First, reliable and comparable information of the gender of perpetrators of child and elder physical abuse is still lacking. Second, even with high rates of violence in many societies, somewhere between a substantial minority and a clear majority of women and men have little direct experience with violence, either as a victim or a perpetrator. Having said that, there is clearly a question of how social and cultural norms of masculinities and femininities are constructed within and across cultures, and how various forms of violence against people with less power are tolerated within most societies.

Risk of dying from collective violence has increased over time, and fatal community violence among young men has increased in LICs during recent years. Other than these two phenomena, there is not enough information to decide whether fatal and non-fatal violence has increased over time, or whether societies are only now beginning to recognize the magnitude of violence. Over 20 years ago, Elizabeth Wilson warned against the romanticization of earlier generations, which is common in HICs, reminding readers that public floggings and hangings were common less than a century ago, and violence in both families and institutional settings were taken for granted and thus not 'counted' as violence until relatively recently (Wilson, 1983, p29).

The unfolding realities of violence are not yet reflected in popular perceptions of violence. Particularly in HICs, violence is still treated as a rare occurrence, predominantly located in particular 'dysfunctional' cultures (e.g. adolescent male children of single-mother households and certain ethnic, religious or 'racial' minorities) or localities (e.g. public or low-income housing in HICs and slums in LICs). Hume (2004) discussing violence in El Salvador, examines how international funders and national and local governments give a high profile to the young gang problem, which is seen as an issue of 'citizen security', while the high prevalence of domestic violence is invisible and, thus, tacitly acceptable. In both HICs and LICs, the public face of violence is that of youth gangs, guns, drugs and graffiti, and the vast majority of governmental and NGO resources on crime and violence prevention are channelled into this stream (Smaoun, 2000; Shaw, 2002).

Tackling the full and interrelated magnitude of this severe and costly problem is still not a priority for most governments, non-governmental organizations, community activists or researchers. When violence, particularly in domestic settings, is discussed, it is sidelined as an issue within police and justice, crime prevention and injury prevention responses. 'Family violence' is simplified as intimate partner physical violence and put in a silo as a 'women's issue'. Elder abuse, child abuse, school bullying, sexual assault, suicide, self-harming behaviour and fear of crime are placed within other silos. Much hidden violence is seen as disconnected from the community safety or crime problem, and also as disconnected from one another. Some forms of violence and crime are seen as police and justice issues; others are seen as health issues or as urban development issues. However, as Chapter 3 describes, whether in private or public space, committed by family members or strangers, violence is similar in motivations and impacts. Prevention can best be accomplished by taking a comprehensive community safety approach that acknowledges the full range of violence throughout the life course.

3

Analysing the Problem: Causes, Consequences and Prevention of Violence

The previous chapter focused on the prevalence of violence and argued for a reframing of the problems of community safety, violence and crime, using a gendered approach that encompasses violence in both the public and private spheres. In this chapter, we turn our attention to redefining the root causes of these problems and the resources that exist to address these causes. The emphasis is on links between forms of violence; the health, social and economic impacts of violence; the risk factors of becoming a victim and/or a perpetrator of violence; and the resilience factors that help to prevent initial victimization (primary prevention) and re-victimization (secondary and tertiary prevention).

Root causes of violence and risk/resilience factors

Given that the manifestations of violence are so diverse, it is hardly surprising that the *World Report on Violence and Health* concludes that no single factor can explain why some individuals are more violent than others, why some violent relationships last longer than others, or why violence is more prevalent in some communities (Krug et al, 2002, p16). Rather, there are different causes of violence, operating across different scales. Figure 3.1 portrays the *World Report's* conceptualization of an ecological model, with four different scales, that can be used to discuss the incidence of violence, the risk factors for violence, the costs of violence and the interventions that might decrease violence. There is also a fifth scale, the global; but it is not explicitly addressed in the *World Report's* discussion of the ecological model.

At the scale of the individual victim or offender, biological and personal history risk factors discussed by the *World Report* include inability to control

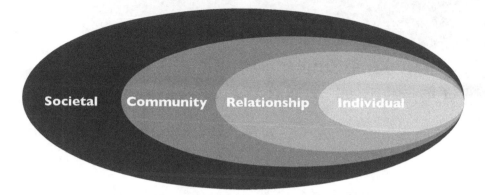

Figure 3.1 *World Health Organization ecological model of violence*

Source: Krug et al (2002, p12)

angry impulses, substance abuse, and prior history of violence and abuse, either as a victim or a perpetrator (Krug et al, 2002, pp12–13). Inability to control anger may be a hereditary or genetic issue; but more often it is based on people modelling behaviours that they see around them, which is why it is frequently related to childhood maltreatment. Substance abuse not only affects the impulse control of offenders, but is a common coping mechanism for victims, one that can lead to further inability to escape violent situations.

The relationship scale includes interactions with family, peers and intimate partners. Risk factors, such as sharing a domicile or a familial or legal relationship, increase the risk of repeat abuse of women, children and older people. Low educational attainment of any or all members of a household is linked to low socio-economic status, which, in turn, means fewer choices for legal employment for both potential offenders and people seeking the economic resources to escape economically dependent relationships with abusive family members. Family members who are being victimized are often in economically and emotionally dependent situations with their abusers. It may be both socially unacceptable and financially difficult to take steps to become independent. Peer support has a large impact upon people's toleration of violent acts, or lack thereof. Again, it is a matter of going along with the behaviour that you see all around you.

At the community scale, the *World Report* discusses interactions in various settings, such as schools, workplaces and neighbourhoods. High scales of unemployment and poverty can influence peer and individual relations dominated by hopelessness and despair, and can also lead to limited social networks in which to seek help. Physical deterioration of communities, and lack of institutional supports such as social services and appropriate policing, also play a role in developing excluded communities that are more likely to encourage violent individuals. Ready availability of weapons and drug trafficking create reasons to commit economic violence (obtaining money to purchase these items), and weapons increase the harm that can be done through violence. The *World Report* also identifies high scales of residential mobility, heterogeneity and high densities as characteristics of high violence communities, although low densities and homogeneous neighbourhoods may lead to problems as well (Krug et al, 2002, p13).

At the societal scale, cultural norms that support violence as an acceptable way of resolving conflicts, regard suicide as a matter of individual choice rather than a societal issue, give priority to parental rights over children's welfare, entrench male dominance over women and children, and support excessive force by police and other arms of the state against citizens have all been identified as factors that create an acceptable climate for violence, reduce inhibitions against violence, and create and sustain inequalities that allow violence to reign unchecked (Krug et al, 2002, p13). More indirect societal risk factors include health, educational, economic and social policies that encourage or maintain disparities between individuals, groups and communities, and rapid societal change, such as the erosion of the social welfare net that has accompanied former communist countries moving towards a market system. Finally, when societies are in wars and civil conflicts, this not only leads to direct collective violence, but indirect impacts, such as the destruction of economies and family breakdown. Even after conflicts have ended, there may be a generation that has known nothing but war and violence.

Figure 3.2 shows shared risk factors for all interpersonal violence (physical and sexual violence between individuals), using the World Health Organization's (WHO's) ecological model.

While the *World Report* does not explicitly discuss the global scale, other commentators have noted that supporting violence as an acceptable way of resolving political, economic and social conflict within and between nations is another part of the 'web of causal connections' that links individuals to global structures, processes and behaviours, and that economic, health and social disparities between nations also have the potential to generate violence (Kurtz and Turpin, 1997, p208). Economic globalization has also been blamed for increasing polarization of the rich and poor in many nations, as well as the proliferation of an international criminal economy trafficking in drugs, women and guns (Moser and McIlwaine, 2006, p90). The increasing mobility of individuals and families means that the impacts of torture and repression may accompany refugees into their new countries (VicHealth, 2003). However, the positive impacts of globalization should not be underestimated, including increased international attention, funding and dissemination of information and research on violence prevention, and allowing relatively safe havens in high-income countries (HICs) for refugees from violent countries.

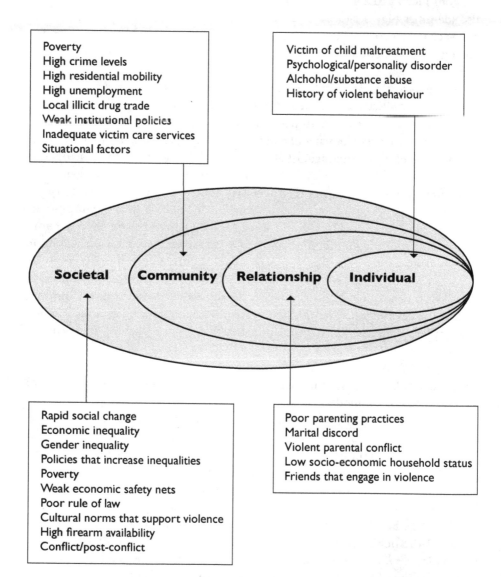

Figure 3.2 *World Health Organization ecological model showing shared risk factors for interpersonal violence*

Source: Butchart et al (2004, p4)

In most cases, the protective or resilience factors that would tend to prevent violence from occurring the first time, or enable escape from violent relationships and situations, are the opposite from these risk factors. Potential social individual-resilience factors include childhoods with supportive and non-violent adult figures, high education levels and specific education on resolving interpersonal conflicts non-violently. A sense of rights, self-worth and responsibilities towards oneself and others is a strong resilience factor: knowing that violence is wrong and that there are alternatives. Individual wealth, or at least access to economic resources, is also a resilience factor. To state the obvious, the more economic assets that individuals can directly access, the more choices they have in terms of combating violence and insecurity, whether this involves leaving a violent partner, hiring private security guards or moving to a less violent community or country. Individual social capital, such as increased knowledge of people and resources, is supported by education, but is also assisted by employment in the formal economy and being able to make health-supportive choices.

Family-scale resilience factors include economic and social supports to parents of young children, as well as financial and social autonomy for married women and older people. Community-scale resilience factors include the provision of adequate and appropriate services, such as healthcare centres, employment training and safe schools; police and justice systems that are trusted by the people whom they serve; strong and supported leadership to make positive changes in communities; and public spaces that bring diverse people together. Societal-scale resilience factors would include addressing gender inequalities, rationalizations for violence against less powerful (and more powerful) people, and improving equitable access to education, employment, housing, transportation, and other goods, services and opportunities (Krug et al, 2002, pp15–16; Moser and McIlwaine, 2006, pp98–99).

These risk/resilience factors vary substantially from more traditional popular and scholarly explanations of the causes of violence, which tend to see violence as a result of individual biological abnormalities, 'natural' aggression and innate evil at both individual and societal scales, to the decline of social networks solely as the result of urbanization (Turpin and Kurtz, 1997, pp3–7). Violence against women is often explained away as the result of alcohol, the victim's behaviour or the natural expression of men's violent nature or sexual urges (Pickup, 2001, p18). One issue with these explanations is that they assume that very little can be done to prevent violence other than locking up people who are the most egregious and socially unacceptable offenders. These explanations depend upon an understanding that violence is a relatively rare occurrence, and that offenders are unusually aggressive or evil individuals who can be clearly identified as outside the norms of society. But if violence is endemic across the life course and violence is woven within the very fabric of most societies, a 'lock 'em up and throw away the key' response will be unfeasible as well as unproductive.

Simplistic explanations of violence tend to arise when different forms of violence are put into silos. For instance, the family-based explanations for youth violence in the Sherman report and the subsequent book on evidence-based crime prevention include 'poor child-rearing, poor supervision, and inconsistent or harsh discipline' (Farrington and Welsh, 2002, p22), thus emphasizing neglect by single mothers and refusing to consider the absence of fathers or actual abuse by parents as a strong causative factor for youth violence. The primary explanation for violence against women in a recent book published by the international charity Oxfam, *Ending Violence against Women* (Pickup, 2001, pp19–22), is patriarchy, or unequal power relations between women and men. Men who do not commit violence are resisting 'hegemonic masculinity' and women who commit violence are 'bargaining with patriarchy'. This explanation comes dangerously close to biological explanations for violence: some 'natural' difference between men and women that makes the former aggressors and the latter nurturers. While unequal power relations between men and women undoubtedly play a huge role in child abuse, hate crimes and genocide, as well as more traditionally defined gender-based violence, there is enough variation in violence against women across cultures that are strongly patriarchal (e.g. Japan versus Colombia) to reject patriarchy as a single explanation for all forms of gender-based violence, let alone violence as a whole.

In contrast, the Commonwealth Secretariat (2003, pp6–8) takes a more holistic approach to describing the causes of gender-based violence: moving from the economic and other decision-making authority of men within some families as a prime cause of domestic violence to political instability and economic hardship at the community and societal levels, particularly as they are compounded by unequal rights to education, employment, credit and property for women in many, if not most, cultures, and the particular stresses of societies in civil conflict and immediate post-conflict situations. Like the causes identified by the *World Report on Violence and Health*, there is an emphasis on connections between scales, such as inequalities at the societal and community scales having an impact at the individual and family scales, and vice versa. They provide associations between the characteristics of victims and offenders of violence, and suggest that individuals can be both at the same time. Furthermore, they suggest key areas of intervention, such as development of institutional supports such as better and more equal educational and employment opportunities at the community scale that can help to reduce risk factors and improve resilience factors.

A number of other causal models reinforce these linkages. Caroline Moser and a number of her colleagues have developed a 'roadmap of categories and manifestations of violence' that complements and, in some cases, challenges, the *World Report*'s discussion of violence (Moser, 2004, p5, Figure 7; see also Moser and McIlwaine, 2006, p96). As discussed in Chapter 2, their typology of violence is categorized by distinctions between economic, political, social and institutional violence, rather than the categorizations used by the World Health

Table 3.1 *A road map of violence and insecurity*

Category of violence	Types of violence by perpetrators and/or victims	Manifestations
Political	• State and non-state violence	• Guerrilla conflict • Paramilitary conflict • Political assassinations • Armed conflict between political parties
Institutional	• Violence of state and other 'informal' institutions • Includes the private sector	• Extra-judicial killings by police • Physical or psychological abuse by health and education workers • State or community vigilante-directed social cleansing of gangs and street children • Lynching of suspected criminals by community members
Economic	• Organized crime • Business interests • Delinquents • Thieves	• Intimidation and violence as a means of resolving economic disputes • Street theft, robbery and crime • Kidnapping • Armed robbery • Drug trafficking • Car theft and other contraband activities • Small-arms dealing • Assaults, including killing and rape in the course of economic crimes • Trafficking in prostitutes • Conflict over scarce resources
Economic/ social	• Gangs • Street children (boys and girls) • Ethnic violence	• Territorial or identity-based 'turf' violence; robbery and theft • Petty theft • Communal riots
Social	• Intimate partner violence inside the home • Sexual violence (including rape) in the public arena • Child abuse (boys and girls) • Intergenerational conflict between parents and children • Gratuitous/routine daily violence	• Physical or psychological male–female abuse • Physical and sexual abuse, particularly prevalent in the case of stepfathers, but also uncles • Physical and psychological abuse • Incivility in areas such as traffic, road rage, bar fights and street confrontations • Arguments that get out of control

Source: Moser (2004, p5)

Organization. It is based on comprehensive local, regional and national surveys of violence in Latin America, which is considered the most violent region in the world. Moser's definition of violence is broader than the categories described by the *World Report*, encompassing institutional violence by police, education, health workers and state-tolerated vigilante groups; economic violence in the form of endemic robberies and thefts from homes and on the street; and incivilities, such as road rage and aggressive driving. She also explicitly includes violence by 'victims', including lynching of suspected criminals by community members, theft and robberies by street children abandoned by their parents, and riots by those wanting a greater share of society's scarce resources. Moser, who worked for many years for the World Bank, as well as individuals associated with the United Nations (Smaoun, 2000; Vanderscheuren, 2006) draw a much stronger link between lack of democracy in low-income countries (LICs) and resultant individual and institutional violence than does the World Health Organization.

When turning to the causes of violence, Moser makes a useful distinction between structural causes of violence and 'trigger risk factors' (2004, pp7–8). Structural causes are issues related to unequal power relations (between men and women, rich and poor, adults and children), while trigger risk factors include drug and alcohol abuse, and ready availability of weapons. While acknowledging the usefulness of the ecological explanatory model used by the WHO, Moser and colleagues have developed another causative model based on three linked inter-related concepts that help to explain violence: structure, identity and agency. The question of structure is related to the notion of *power*: those who have more power in a given situation and how they use that power. Power is infinitely complex, related to the concept of democracy at the community and societal scales, yet also encompassing power inequalities at the individual and household or family scales. For instance, nations have the power of life and death over individuals because they have the power to make war and to enact and prosecute (or ignore) laws that protect citizens, and many nations still have capital punishment. On the other hand, there are individuals and corporations who are able to ignore national laws with relative impunity because victims are afraid of retribution if they report a crime or because what the offenders are doing (beating a child or setting up a polluting industry) is not perceived as a crime. Doctors have power over patients, teachers have power over pupils, and security forces armed with weapons often have both power and impunity in relation to abuses of their authority. One person may have power over another person (a man over his pregnant girlfriend, a woman over her child), but might not have any other power over their lives – for instance, their ability to find employment or decent housing. Power is also linked to the control of resources, particularly property and land. In many LICs, married women still have limited rights to own property, and the land tenure system is still heavily inequitable, with a few rich families owning the majority of land. In Moser's model, the state, large landowners and family members such as stepfathers are all powerful actors at their different scales, who can commit violence with relative impunity, particularly in undemocratic societies.

Francine Pickup provides a useful corollary to this notion of power, providing examples of four very different types of power. *Power over* is generally the form of power associated with repressive societal structures and is the power to control other individual's actions, thoughts and beliefs. However, power over may be useful in terms of changing laws and norms. *Power to* refers to individuals' liberty to make decisions, to express themselves or to earn a living. *Power within* refers to the power to transform a situation and could refer to community as well as individual power. Finally, *power with* connotes the power attained by individuals and communities who work together to accomplish common goals (Pickup, 2001, pp33–37).

Structures are often linked to notions of *identity*, a complex and contingent (it may change over time and across settings) mix of gender, age, ethnicity, sexuality, abilities and class. Class, in turn, is a combined result of educational attainment, occupational status and income/property or financial capital, which is often intergenerational in nature. Identities may be adopted by individuals; but often they are assigned to individuals against their will. People are put in identity boxes, with values ascribed to those boxes. According to Moser, some groups – women, children and ethnic minorities – are at risk because they are identified as a relatively powerless group and because their relative powerlessness allows others more power. This is related to, although broader than, the concept of patriarchy discussed by Pickup (2001, pp19–22). Other groups – such as low-income or visible minority young men – are at risk because they are identified as criminals, whatever their actual behaviour. It can be argued that the identification of a single group, such as young men, as being the sole locus of violence and criminality relieves other groups from responsibility for the multiple forms of violence in any society.

Finally, human *agency* is related to the notion of choice: the concept that individuals are actors who face alternative ways of dealing with situations, depending upon their resources and their understanding of their choices. Street children and prostitutes are two examples of groups where individuals have relatively few choices over where they live, how they make money and from whom they can seek help. If a woman's only choice in reaching a safe haven country is to prostitute herself (Pickup, 2001, p24), then she has limited agency, resulting in a violation of her human rights. One goal of violence prevention is therefore to improve choices and promote *autonomy*, the self-reliance and resilience abilities of individuals. Agency is related to the aspects of 'power within', 'power to' and 'power with' discussed by Pickup (2001).

Along with her colleague Cathy McIlwaine, Moser has been using a consultation technique called participatory urban appraisals, or PUAs (see Chapter 5), to improve understanding of people's perceptions of the causes of crime. A causal flow diagram drawn by a mixed-sex group of nine adults in Agauazul, Colombia, helps to illustrate the interrelations of these three concepts of structure, identity and agency (see Figure 3.3).

Violence in the home is connected to trigger factors such as alcohol and individual personality factors, such as lack of ethical values ('lack of love of God'), but also structural factors, such as lack of education, money and understanding of the consequences of violence. Violence in the home is also related to violence between neighbours, partially because of similar trigger factors such as alcohol, but also because of weak and divisive social relations ('gossip'), and the fact that in this village, households are related. Envy, which is related to tensions over scarce resources, leads to lack of collective action. Finally, violence over land is associated with both these forms of violence since people do not trust their neighbours or people in positions of authority.

Violence prevention therefore must operate at both the structural level by, for instance, creating a culture where the human rights of individuals are legally and socially protected, while also addressing immediate trigger factors, such as easy availability of weapons and substance abuse. An example of a place where rates of violence have increased dramatically in recent years, Russia, illustrates this point. When post-communist economic reforms eliminated social safety nets, such as welfare and full employment, absolute poverty increased, as did economic disparities. These structural factors, combined with continuing social and economic inequalities between men and women, with the added trigger factor of increased individual drug and alcohol abuse as a coping strategy, helped lead to a situation where 20 per cent of adult female deaths are caused by domestic violence and 75 per cent of rapes occur while the offenders are under the influence of alcohol (Waters et al, 2004, p36).

One of the most famous explanations of the manifestations of violence is 'the wheel of power and control' developed by the Domestic Abuse Intervention Project based in Duluth, US, during the 1980s (see Figure 3.4 and Chapter 4). The model focuses on individual and family-based characteristics of the abuser, particularly the use of economic, physical and emotional controlling behaviours. It is intended for use as an educational tool with abused women and abusive men. It is not explicit in clarifying why some men abuse their intimate partners, although it does explain how they do and why some women stay in abusive relationships. Similar wheels have been developed on equal, as opposed to abusive, intimate relationships and on child abuse. The power and control wheel touches on several aspects already discussed in Chapter 2, such as economic dependence, the use of threats to get women to back down from taking action and isolating the victim.

More recently, a project associated with the Duluth Domestic Violence Intervention Project called Mending the Sacred Hoop has used indigenous American philosophy, combined with the wheel image, to develop a vision of a mutually

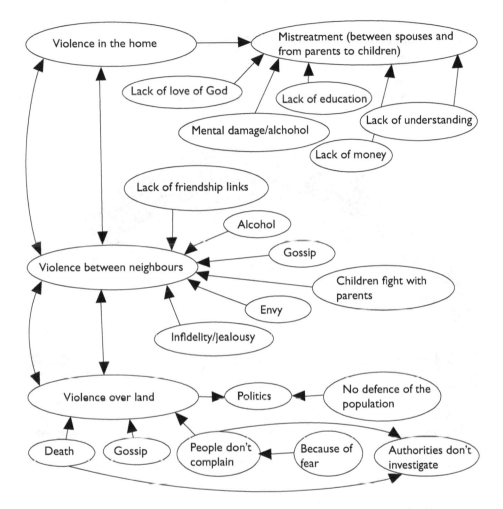

Figure 3.3 *Causal flow diagram of violence at the local scale in Aguazul, Colombia*

Source: adapted from Moser and McIlwaine (2006, p98, Figure 4)

respectful and non-violent society (see Figure 3.5). Their vision of a non-violent society includes honest and accountable individuals, responsible and egalitarian families, and tolerant and respectful communities within an environmentally conscious and economically fair society.

Based on work in another region with high rates of violence, Barbara Holtmann of the National Crime Prevention Research and Resources Centre of the South African Centre for Scientific and Industrial Research (CSIR) has developed a wheel-type model to illustrate the generational cycle of crime, violence

Figure 3.4 *The wheel of power and control*

Source: Minnesota Program Development Inc (2007)

and distrust (see Figure 3.6), which, like the previous models, ties individual and family dysfunctions to community and societal structural issues.

For Holtmann (2006) and the CSIR, the phenomenon of individual violence and dysfunctional families is related to structural community factors, such as mistrust between community guardians (e.g. the South African Police Services, or SAPS) and community members, exacerbated by few employment opportunities, entrenched poverty over generations, easy availability of guns, and poor services for individuals and legitimate businesses. In this environment, illegal trafficking of alcohol (shebeens) and illicit drugs become normalized, as does child abuse and neglect, low educational attainment, and health issues related to violence and prostitution, such as HIV infection. Midway through the cycle shown in Figure 3.6, the child loses his or her identity as a vulnerable victim and becomes identified with offending behaviour.

Holtmann contrasts this vicious cycle of crime, violence and distrust with a virtuous cycle of peace, safety and security (see Figure 3.7). In these latter communities, structural issues such as trust and cooperation between community members and police help to create an economic climate where job opportunities can be developed, local people can have access to these jobs, and substance abuse declines because there are licit businesses to provide income support and personal satisfaction. At the family scale, children are nurtured and supervised, and their parents or guardians have access to the basic Maslow necessities of shelter, food and security. Healthy and well-cared-for children become productive citizens. Figures 3.6 and 3.7 are overly schematic since every individual childhood is different. They also simplify the process as community–police trust and partnership, an issue that is complicated in South Africa by the police force having been an agent of apartheid and related institutional violence in the recent past (du Plessis and Louw, 2005). However, the model does provide a sense of linkages over the life cycle and between individuals, families and communities.

The previous theories on the causes of violence draw links between structures of exclusion and individual and family behaviours. The work of two more theorists further elaborates on these structures of economic and social exclusion within a HIC context. Iris Marion Young, an American political philosopher, discusses the relationships between violence and other forms of structural oppression, such as *exploitation* of both wage earners and people who take on the unpaid work of caring for children and communities; *marginalization* of 'people [whom] the system cannot or will not use', such as the disabled, older people and young people who cannot find first jobs; *powerlessness* associated with being a person with low status or ability to make changes in a society; and *cultural imperialism,* or being a member of a group that is 'stereotyped and inferiorized' (Young, 1990, pp48–60). Both Young and UK geographer Rachel Pain, whose research on fear of violence was discussed in Chapter 2, analyse the oppression of groups whose identities are 'marked as fearful', such as visible minority young

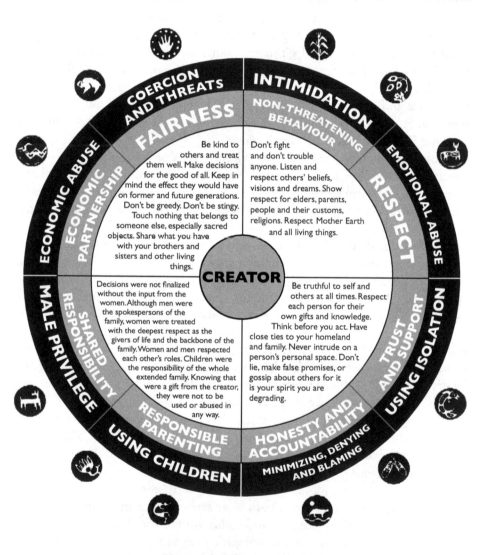

Figure 3.5 *The creator wheel*

Source: Minnesota Program Development Inc (2007)

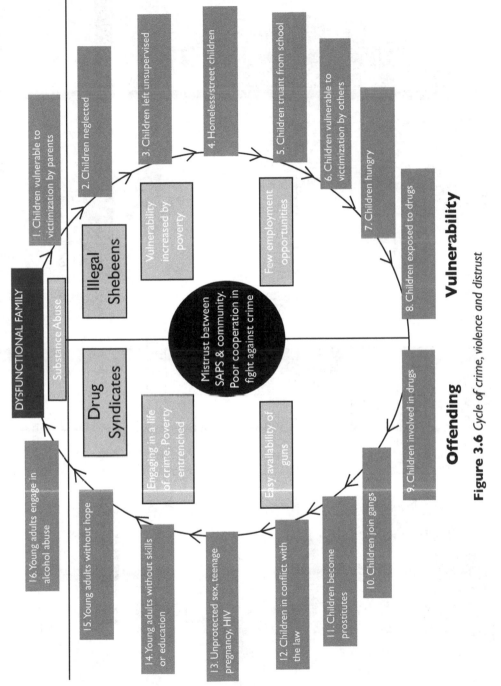

Figure 3.6 *Cycle of crime, violence and distrust*

DYSFUNCTIONAL FAMILY

Substance Abuse

Illegal Shebeens

Drug Syndicates

Vulnerability increased by poverty

Few employment opportunities

Engaging in a life of crime. Poverty entrenched

Easy availability of guns

Mistrust between SAPS & community. Poor cooperation in fight against crime

1. Children vulnerable to victimization by parents
2. Children neglected
3. Children left unsupervised
4. Homeless/street children
5. Children truant from school
6. Children vulnerable to victimization by others
7. Children hungry
8. Children exposed to drugs
9. Children involved in drugs
10. Children join gangs
11. Children become prostitutes
12. Children in conflict with the law
13. Unprotected sex, teenage pregnancy, HIV
14. Young adults without skills or education
15. Young adults without hope
16. Young adults engage in alcohol abuse

Offending

Vulnerability

Source: Holtmann (2006); copyright CSIR, 2005, www.csir.co.za

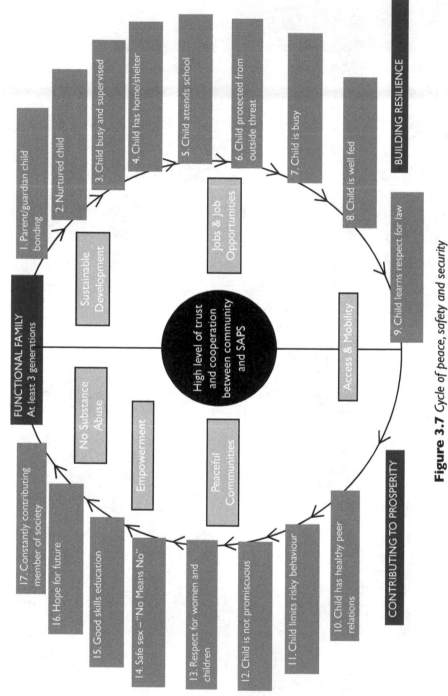

Figure 3.7 *Cycle of peace, safety and security*

FUNCTIONAL FAMILY
At least 3 generations

1. Parent/guardian child bonding
2. Nurtured child
3. Child busy and supervised
4. Child has home/shelter
5. Child attends school
6. Child protected from outside threat
7. Child is busy
8. Child is well fed
9. Child learns respect for law
10. Child has healthy peer relations
11. Child limits risky behaviour
12. Child is not promiscuous
13. Respect for women and children
14. Safe sex – "No Means No"
15. Good skills education
16. Hope for future
17. Constantly contributing member of society

Sustainable Development

Jobs & Job Opportunities

No Substance Abuse

Empowerment

Peaceful Communities

Access & Mobility

High level of trust and cooperation between community and SAPS

BUILDING RESILIENCE

CONTRIBUTING TO PROSPERITY

Source: Holtmann (2006); copyright CSIR, 2005, www.csir.co.za

men (Young, 1990, p11). Pain provides five categories of social exclusion as a result of violence and insecurity:

1 exclusion through direct experiences;
2 exclusion through sub-criminal but fear-inducing acts, such as street harassment;
3 exclusion through avoiding spaces because of fear;
4 exclusion through being constructed as a threat to community safety; and
5 exclusion through community safety policies themselves (Pain, 2001, p902).

While the degree of violence and exclusion varies greatly between cultural contexts – exclusion in a HIC such as the UK might mean widespread use of Anti-Social Behaviour Orders or moves to exclude all young men from public spaces after dark, while exclusion in a LIC such as Brazil might mean security forces extra-judicially killing young men identified as criminals – the theory behind it remains the same.

What all of these writers imply is that tackling the root causes of violence requires not only improving the life circumstances of people identified as potential victims of violence: women, children, youth and older people. It also requires an improvement in the lives of the people identified as being at high risk of being offenders: young people, particularly young men, who have limited life choices, respect for themselves or others, and easy access to mind-altering substances and weapons. Whether labelled as a victim or as an offender, both groups have human rights at the scale of the family (the right not to be violated, intimidated or economically exploited) and at the scale of the nation (the right to justice, which includes protection from summary imprisonment, torture or execution). Inclusive societies and communities, who are able to provide educational and employment opportunities to all, who promote respect and empowerment for all, and where a healthy childhood for all is treated as a top priority, will reduce the number of both victims and offenders. This is especially true since most offenders are themselves victims of violence and mistreatment.

An increasing number of researchers are finding evidence that backs up these theories regarding the linkages between different forms of violence. The *World Report on Violence and Health* (Krug et al, 2002) reports the common finding of links between exposure to violence in the home as a child (either as a victim of child abuse or as a witness to intimate partner abuse), and risks of being a perpetrator or a victim of violence in later life. Similarly, numerous studies have found associations between child maltreatment, intimate partner violence, sexual assault, abuse of the elderly and suicide (Krug et al, 2002, p15). According to the *World Report*, the fact that violence is so predictable makes it preventable: there is enough evidence at this point that child abuse and neglect leads to later criminality, or that the easy availability of weapons leads to increased impacts of violence in communities, to know that tackling these problems would have flow-on effects on a number of violence issues (Krug et al, 2002, p243).

How do these linkages work? Let us take the example of child physical and sexual abuse, in which the majority of perpetrators are parents or other family members. Not only does the abuse have potential immediate impacts on a child's physical and emotional development, it also provides an association to children between the expected love of a parent and the use of force; encourages the view that the more physically or socially powerful person has the right to subordinate a less powerful person; and teaches that feelings of anger and frustration justify violence (Ellison and Bartkowski, 1997, p46). It is thus hardly surprising that many researchers speak of an intergenerational 'cycle of violence', where lessons taught by parents are then applied by their children in their relationships with peers, intimate partners and, eventually, with their own children. Not all boys who are abused take on the message that as the more physically and socially powerful gender, they have the right to subordinate others by force, or that violence is an easy and acceptable way to resolve conflict. Not all girls who are abused receive the message that being the victim of violence is a normal and acceptable part of a loving relationship. But enough do to make this scenario a strong link.

Let us look at another strong association: between poverty and lack of educational and employment opportunities, on the one hand, and being a victim or perpetrator of violence, on the other hand. This association is usually seen as a simplistic case of 'poverty causes crime'. It is perhaps more accurate to simplify the relationship as 'crime causes poverty' (Vanderschueren, 2006, p2). Violence and insecurity, on the one hand, and poverty, on the other, can be seen as operating in a circular relationship. Poverty can increase the risk of being a victim or a perpetrator of violence; in turn, violence and insecurity impoverish and reduce opportunity. To give one example of this circular relationship, a study in Chile found that abused women had a lower probability of working and earning money outside the home, which in turn reduced their chances of escaping an economically dependent relationship with their assailant and increased their chances of being victims of violence (Waters et al, 2004, p34). Related to this issue is one of social networks: who you know and who you can turn to in a crisis. Violence limits your social networks, through self-imposed or abuser-imposed limitations on your mobility, and limited social networks can lead to negatively reinforcing peer relationships and few positive role models or sources of help. The *Multi-country Study on Women's Health and Domestic Violence against Women* reported a high correlation between physical and sexual intimate partner violence, and highly controlling behaviours by the abuser, including keeping her from seeing friends and family, insisting that he knows where she is at all times, and controlling access to healthcare (Garcia-Moreno et al, 2004, p34). A number of studies, both within the US and in multiple countries, show that a decline in employment opportunities, particularly in the area of low-skilled entry-level jobs, has led to upward pressures on rates of violent crime, particularly for young men (Waters et al, 2004, pp37–38). It is, however, overly simplistic to argue that unemployment causes crime (UNODC, 2005, p6). The issue, particularly among young men, appears to be not so much absolute poverty or unemployment as economic and social inequality: the sense of being shut out of the social, as well as economic, network of legal employment (Waters et al, 2004, p38).

The United Nations Office on Drugs and Crime has argued that societal and global inequalities are a strong causal factor for crime and violence. South America and Africa, the most violent regions in the world, have a much more highly skewed distribution of richest to poorest deciles: the richest 10 per cent in South America earn 40 times the income of the poorest 10 per cent, while in Africa, the ratio is 31. In contrast, the income ratio of richest and poorest deciles in Western Europe is 7, and in Asia, the income ratio is 13. The globalization of images of wealth from HIC breeds resentment and social tensions in poorer countries, which can lead to the belief that the only way to get rich is to commit crimes, usually against other poor people. The notion of 'frustration violence' vented against less powerful targets, such as women and children, has also been brought up by several African political figures, such as South African President Thabo Mbeki (UNODC, 2005, pp3–4).

Particularly at the community and societal scales, the causes of violent crime and insecurity should include the inability of the criminal justice system to respond adequately to violence and insecurity. Globally, only a small proportion of offences, less than 10 per cent, ever reach courts; policing has become privatized and distant from citizen control; and most prisons 'constitute technical schools for the training and development of criminal networks' (Vanderschueren, 2006, p2). In Africa, which along with South America has violent crime rates much higher than the rest of the world, there are only half the numbers of police officers per capita than in the much lower crime region of Europe (180/100,000 in Africa; 346/100,000 in Europe). There are only one sixth the numbers of judges: 3/100,000 in Africa versus 18/100,000 in Europe. All aspects of justice in Africa are seen as corrupt: almost 17 per cent of Africans said that they had been asked to pay a bribe to a public official, most commonly a police officer, while 70 per cent of Nigerians say that their police are corrupt. Only 11 per cent of murder charges in Africa lead to convictions, compared to 69 per cent in Europe. However, imprisonment rates are similar in the two regions: 141/100,000 in Africa versus 152/100,000 in Europe. While European prisoners have human rights protection and some access to rehabilitation programmes, one third of African prisoners are awaiting trial, some for periods in excess of five years, many in holding cells so overcrowded there is not room to sit down. When weak and corrupt law enforcement combines with high crime, the result is no trust in the justice system and outbreaks of vigilantism and other signs of societal despair (UNODC, 2005, pp10–14, 44).

A few anecdotal examples will provide illustrations of how these structural issues affect individuals.

Amartya Sen writes powerfully of his first personal exposure to murder, during the large-scale communal violence that occurred before, during and after the partition of India in 1947. A Muslim daily labourer was knifed in front of Sen's house in a Hindu section of Dhaka, now part of Bangladesh. While his father tried vainly to get medical assistance, the author, then an 11-year-old boy, talked to the dying man. The labourer knew he ran a risk in entering a hostile neighbourhood; but it was the only place he could find work. He died as a Muslim, but also as a poor person with limited choices for survival (Sen, 2005, p208).

When a group of colleagues and I interviewed women who had experienced homelessness in both urban and rural settings in the province of Ontario, Canada, low-income women with children spoke of how they stayed with violent partners in order to avoid losing accommodation and possibly losing custody of their children. A number of women who had been living in violent situations had experienced severe depression, compounded by social isolation, often imposed by their violent partners, and turned to drug and alcohol abuse as a coping mechanism. Several women had turned to prostitution as a way of supplementing their incomes, including the purchase of drugs. This, in turn, made it harder to find and keep rental or public housing accommodation, let alone find paid employment or childcare. Several of the women we spoke to had lost custody of their children as the indirect result of their leaving violent relationships (Hierlihy et al, 2003; see also Watson and Austerberry, 1986; Davies et al, 1998; Moe and Bell, 2004).

As part of his research on masculinities, Bob Connell spoke to several Australian young men who were on the fringes of the labour market, most of whom were also in conflict with the state and immersed in various forms of violence. One 17 year old, 'Pat', spoke of how his father would give him 'hidings' and his older sister would also punch him at an early age. He became aggressive towards his teachers and was eventually expelled from secondary school. At an early age, 13, he began sexual relationships with women, but had no idea of how to progress a relationship beyond casual sex. His father arranged an informal apprenticeship; but by then Pat and his friends were involved in both car thefts and breaking into homes. He was sent to a juvenile institution, escaped and was sent to a higher security institution, where he got into fights. Although on parole at the time of the interview, his future prospects for legal employment were extremely low. Connell also interviewed a 21 year old, 'Eel', who expressed anger at his mother, his stepmother, his mother-in-law and his wife: in fact, all the significant women in his life. He appeared to blame them for his constrained circumstances. Eel, like Pat a young man with more experience of correctional institutions than legal employment, was sleeping with two women when he made one pregnant. In his words, 'he just went absolutely berko on her' but kept around the 'bed-warmer' 'because of the kid' (Connell, 2005, pp103–104). Connell's interviews with these young men suggest a culture where criminality, violence and contempt for women are normalized. Their peer subculture provides few opportunities for positive role models, either as responsible citizens or as loving and non-violent family members. Their thefts were not even particularly remunerative. They provided a certain amount of excitement and fun in lives considered boring, as well as a quick way to make money for drugs (Connell, 2005, pp93–98). Connell describes their petty criminal careers 'as episodic and chancy as [their limited experiences of legal] employment' (Connell, 2005, p98).

The interrelationships between different forms of violence were illustrated in another PUA exercise by three young men in a youth centre in Bucaramanga, Colombia (see Figure 3.8). They saw intra-family violence as the basis of other types of violence, leading some young people to leave home and join gangs as alternative structures of support. Some young people also turn to drugs, which are linked with insecurity, as well as the related economic violence of robbery and delinquency. The impacts of these violent acts include fear, social disintegration, and erosion of both human and social capital. For these young men, as for many of the current generation of researchers, violence is not so much an individual act or set of acts as it is a web or cycle of violence and insecurity.

These anecdotes help to illustrate the linkages between three concepts that Moser provided – structure, identity and agency – and, more generally, the linkages between individual and societal causes of violence, and between public and private violence. In each case, the choices or agency that people had was constrained by limiting structures. The Muslim labourer had to find work to provide for himself and his family. He knew that he was at high risk of violence if he entered the hostile neighbourhood because of his identity as a Muslim; but that unsafe place was where he knew there was employment. The women living in violent relationships knew that they were at risk of further violence by staying with their intimate partners, but judged that they were at greater risk by separating from them, a judgement that may have been correct where women ended up in situations of prostitution, homelessness and/or losing their children. The young men whom Connell and Moser and McIlwaine interviewed were trapped in a vicious cycle of family violence, low educational attainment, little or no employment prospects, and despairing anger, leading to more violence and collective insecurity.

To summarize the information on the reasons for violence, no single cause explains why some people are more violent than others or why some societies become more or less violent. Instead, a range of social and economic factors

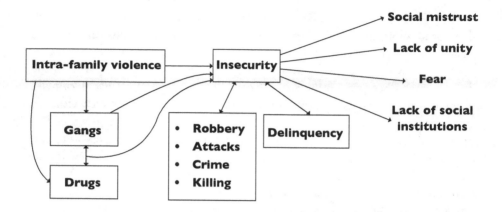

Figure 3.8 *Causal flow diagram of violence and insecurity, drawn by young men in Bucaramanga, Colombia*

Source: adapted from Moser and McIlwaine (2006, p95, Figure 2)

interrelate to create structures of violence that are iterative, multigenerational and operate across scales. These factors are often based on social and economic disparities grounded in individual and household income, gender, age, ethnicity and many other aspects of identity. They are also based on cycles of violence, exacerbated in regions where there is civil and international conflict, and cultures that see violence as a legitimate response to anger and conflict. These structural inequality and injustice factors combine with trigger factors such as alcohol, weapons and violent peers to create situations where violence appears predictable, if not inevitable.

The consequences of violence

Some consequences of violence and insecurity have already been touched upon. Aside from immediate health impacts, such as death and physical disability, individual impacts of violence include depression and other mental illnesses, and loss of economic and social opportunities, as well as direct loss of income. Female victims of physical and sexual violence may find themselves ostracized or at risk of further harm from their families and communities because of the supposed shame of exposing a 'private' issue or the supposed dishonour of having 'let herself' be raped (Pickup, 2001, pp102–103). Violence is more likely to be iterative, and the subsequent health and economic impacts greater, when the abuser and the victim share a legal relationship and/or a domicile. Substance abuse is a two-sided sword: not only is it a trigger factor in much domestic and public violence, but its abuse as a coping strategy by some victims further compounds health and economic impacts.

At the family scale, too, consequences of violence can be iterative and generational. Violence limits the possibility of economic independence, which, in turn, traps people in violent relationships: this is true whether the problem is child abuse, intimate partner violence or elder abuse, or membership in a criminal gang. Living in violent communities also limits the economic and social choices of individuals and families. Even if the violence is a one-off act committed by a stranger, the impact of violence can extend to the entire family, particularly where there are children involved. Violence can destroy trust in neighbours and in the ability of democratic local governance to assist individual and families, who in turn are further isolated from potential sources of help (Vanderscheuren, 2006, pp2–3).

Developing an economic costing of violence at the community and societal scales is a highly fraught enterprise. The World Health Organization released a report on *The Economic Dimensions of Interpersonal Violence* (Waters et al, 2004) two years after the *World Report on Violence and Health*, which, like its predecessor, is a meta-analysis of dozens of previous studies of violence. Other community and national studies have focused more generally on the costs of crime and the economic benefits of crime prevention (e.g. Waller and Sansfacon, 2000). However, there are a number of reasons why these economic analyses are limited in their reliability and comparability.

First, economic analyses use remarkably utilitarian measures that are more prone to subjective interpretation and are more limited in their understanding of the value of human life than health measures, such as death and disability adjusted life years (DALYs). To give one example, the idea of a universal economic value on a human life is absurd, as well as demeaning. Various economic studies, usually performed by US insurance companies, have calculated a value ranging from US$2.6 million (all figures in 2001 US dollars) to US$13.7 million, with a mean of US$4.2 million (Waters et al, 2004, p9). This figure is based on research into what is called wage–risk trade-offs: factors such as wage premiums for risky jobs, willingness to pay for safety measures and individual behaviour related to safety measures, such as using seatbelts. It is largely based on an adult male wage earner's potential in a HIC, and would provide lower values for the lives of women, older people, people with disabilities or, indeed, the vast majority of the world's population living in LICs and with low wage-earning capacity. Similarly, costing out the impact of violence on a nation's gross domestic product (GDP) is based at least partially on lost wages and earnings, which not only results in underestimating impacts upon the informal economies that dominate LICs (Waters et al, 2004, p14; UNODC, 2005, p68), but also undervalues the impact upon the lives of people who are completely excluded from economic life. While the impact of a violence prevention intervention could theoretically be measured by lives saved, disabilities prevented, violent acts averted or less recidivism (return to incarceration), Waters et al (2004) recommend a measure called quality-adjusted life years (QALYs). QALYs assign a utility score for a health rate, with 0 being death and 1 'representing perfect heath'; then the amount of time spent in a particular state is weighted by the utility score (Waters et al, 2004, p8). The problem, as has been amply demonstrated by US private healthcare providers using this cost-effectiveness calculus since the 1960s, is that an externally provided quality-of-life score may undervalue the lives of older people, people with disabilities or chronic illnesses, and other people whose lives are assumed to be of lesser value to themselves and society. The WHO and other health promotion organizations increasingly prefer the newer formulation of DALYs, developed during the 1990s (Gold et al, 2002), which simply measure death and disability impacts upon potential life years.

Second, the lacunae in information on violence are compounded by the even more underdeveloped state of economic analyses. As was the case in the data used in Chapter 2, sources for violence prevalence estimates include police crime reports, hospital statistics and household surveys, which all tend to underestimate hidden acts of violence, particularly intimate partner violence and sexual assault (Waters et al, 2004, p8). Most economic analyses rely on crimes reported to the police, the least likely of these three sources to accurately estimate hidden violence. In many LICs, there is a lack of public access to information on direct expenditures on police, courts and prisons, let alone privatized and informal security forces (Moser and McIlwaine, 2006, p98). There are no systemic economic studies on a number of violence issues, including elder abuse (Waters et al, 2004, p13). In order to estimate the costs and benefits of a particular intervention, an intervention that had been thoroughly and objectively evaluated would first be needed. As is discussed throughout this book, rigorous evaluations of violence prevention interventions are still extremely rare, particularly those performed by independent researchers, as opposed to the organizations providing the intervention.

Third, the measures of cost used in particular studies vary widely. Some studies only count costs over a one-year time period, while others, particularly those focusing on the costs to victims, use a lifetime approach (Waters et al, 2004, p9). As discussed in Chapter 2, since so many acts of violence are iterative, recurring within families and communities over time, the latter approach would be more suitable. Some studies only count the cost to victims, while others count the costs to perpetrators, third parties, such as families, and society at large (Waters et al, 2004, p9). Some studies measure only direct costs, usually (but not always) including the police, courts and correctional facilities; direct monetary losses to the victim; and direct medical and legal costs to victims and perpetrators. Indirect costs are potentially exponentially larger and include private security costs undertaken by the victim to prevent another offence; lost earnings and productivity; psychological costs; lost investments in human capital (e.g. suffering and foregoing opportunities because of violence or insecurity); indirect policing costs in communities with high rates of violence; increased life and health insurance premiums; and, at the community and society scales, lost domestic and foreign investment, particularly tourism (Waters et al, 2004, p6). Insidious and intangible impacts upon community well-being, such as the breakdown of local social institutions or the abandonment of public life, are almost impossible to cost out using existing economic forms of analysis (Moser and McIlwaine, 2006, p98).

Despite all of these weaknesses, governments and charities who fund services and advocacy want to hear about the 'dollars and sense of crime prevention', as one Canadian report put it (National Crime Prevention Council Canada, 1997). Economic cost–benefit analyses can allow more informed policy choices. For instance, massive increases in the number of police officers hired and the number of people incarcerated in prisons may have some impact upon reducing the numbers of crimes committed. But is this the most effective use of societal resources, and does this blunt instrument focus on the most destructive aspects of individual, family and community violence? In the US, increasing the incarceration rate by 250 per cent from 1974 to 2004 is estimated to have decreased the reported crime rate by 35 per cent, at a cost exceeding US$20 billion. This amount is enough to provide employment for every unemployed person in the US or childcare for every low-income family in need. Both of these upstream policy tools have been shown to have larger impacts upon crime rates when implemented, as well as more beneficial external impacts upon societies and economies (Butchart et al, 2004, p7).

In the UK, the Audit Commission assessed the costs of neglecting early intervention through a real case study of a boy they identify as 'James' (Audit Commission, 2004, pp115–122; see also Graham, 2006, pp22–24). James's father was rarely present in the household, and was violent and disruptive when he did appear. James lived with his mother and his older stepsister, who had a history of drug abuse and related criminality. Just after James started school at the age of five, his mother began requesting help in managing his behaviour and in addressing learning difficulties. Despite formal assessments at an early age for special educational needs, no educational help was forthcoming to James until he reached the age of eight, when he was sent to a special-needs school. Even then, no efforts were made to address his problems at home despite the fact that the school reported that his mother often left him alone in the house until 9 pm. A school psychologist reported that James had low self-esteem and would often hide from other children. By the age of ten, he had his first brush with the law over a case of arson at the local high school; but several requests for a positive adult role model in the form of a mentor came to nothing and his school attendance began to suffer. He was falling behind his peers in scholastic achievement and was getting into trouble at home, in school and in his neighbourhood.

James was not asked for his own views until he was 13, by which time he was rarely at school, either because he was playing truant or because he was under suspension for bad behaviour. James stated that he had never wanted to go to a special school but would prefer to go to his local school and wanted a mentor. A meeting of professionals was arranged, but no one directly involved with James, other than the principal of his school, attended, no social worker was assigned, and none of the plans drawn up to help James and his family was implemented. Within a short space of time, he was sent to a juvenile detention centre for an assault on a girl and several thefts. Upon release, there was another meeting of professionals; but again no services were received by James or his family. By that time, at the age of 14, he was no longer attending school and had made an allegation of abuse within his family that was not resolved. He was back in custody within a few months, and at the age of 15 was serving his second custodial sentence.

The Audit Commission estimated that the costs of family support at an early age, pre-school education, anger management, learning support and mentoring to James, all of which are proven to work in preventing crime and violence (see the following section), would have cost US$84,000 (all costs converted to US dollars) up to the age of 16. The actual cost of services he received was US$368,000, most of which were court and custody costs, with the highest likelihood that these costs will increase over James's life course since early incarceration does not work in preventing future crimes. If the appropriate interventions had been made 'upstream', when James was a young child, US$284,000 might have been saved in downstream costs for that one individual. If similar investments had been made in just one in ten of the over 8000 young people, mostly young men, sentenced to custody in the UK each year, more than US$200 million annually would be saved by the national government.

The majority of national-scale studies on the societal costs of violence have been undertaken in the US. There, in 1996, the direct and indirect costs of personal violence (domestic violence, sexual assault and child abuse) were estimated as US$507 billion per annum, or 6.5 per cent of GDP. A multi-country survey in 2001 found that interpersonal violence costs were equivalent to 5 per cent of GDP in HICs and an average of 14 per cent of GDP in LICs, even taking into account the underestimation of impacts upon the informal economy mentioned earlier. A further Latin American survey, which included the costs of collective violence, found that some countries such as Colombia and El Salvador were losing the equivalent of one quarter of their GDP to violence, while less violent and wealthier countries in the region, such as Mexico, only lost the equivalent of 1.3 per cent (Waters et al, 2004, p14–15). Other than individuals, it is national and local governments who bear the disproportionate share of costs of violence: aside from policing, courts and corrections, most health and legal costs are borne by the public sector, even in a largely privatized system such as the US (Waters et al, 2004, p26).

But the private and non-profit sectors suffer as well as governments and individuals. A recent Brazilian study modelled the relationship of violent crime (with homicide rates as a proxy) and GDP growth in a large number of nations, and found a causative relation (World Bank, 2006, p24–30). Studies focusing on political violence have found clear causation between high levels of conflict and decreases in tourism (Solimano, 2004) and internal and international investment (Blomberg and Mody, 2005). A Jamaican study on urban violence and poverty found that violence eroded both labour force potential and social capital, stigmatizing people and communities and instilling fear. This leads to reduced business investments in perceived high crime communities, residents who are unable to access jobs, and reduced community resources for local infrastructure and services such as schools. The report concluded that:

The costs of violence include weak investor confidence, higher health and police costs, the disaffection and migration of the urban middle class, higher morbidity and mortality rates, reduced access to social services, dysfunctional families, deeper oppression of women and an overall climate of fear that replaces a spirit of co-operation and participation in community life. (Holland and Moser, 1997, p2)

In Latin America and the Caribbean, as in other LICs, violence is increasingly recognized as a 'development problem', albeit one that is a 'new area of development enquiry' (Moser and McIlwaine, 2006, p89). The United Nations Office on Drugs and Crime (UNODC) summarizes three ways in which crime and violence hinders development in Africa and other LICs (UNODC, 2005, pp67–92). First, violence and insecurity destroy social and human capital, the norms and networks that support collective action. Death and disability of family members due to violence has an even larger impact in LICs due not only to high rates of violence, but to a lack of insurance and social safety nets. Even thefts take a larger toll. The average theft in Mozambique is of money or goods worth US$13; but when annual wages are only a little over US$1000, this represents a significant proportion of yearly earnings (UNODC, 2005, p71). Fear of violence stops children and teachers from going to school. The UNODC gives an example of a community in Zambia fundraising for a fence to go around their school, where there is limited access to clean water (UNODC, 2005, p72). A 2003 national crime survey in South Africa found that 24 per cent of respondents do not use public transportation for fear of crime, a serious issue in a country where the majority of blacks have no other means of accessing job markets. Over 26 per cent said that crime prevented them from starting their own business, 27 per cent said they feared letting their children walk to school, and over 30 per cent said they did not use public parks because of fear of crime. When quality of life declines to this extent, those who are able to emigrate do so, creating a 'brain drain', or the loss of money and skills. Over 80,000 highly qualified Africans leave the continent for Europe, North America and Australia every year, not including students (UNODC, 2005, p74). This skills flight has left Africa with only 20,000 scientists and engineers to serve a population of US$600 million. Ninety-six per cent of skills migrants from South Africa mentioned crime and violence among their reasons for deciding to leave the country (UNODC, 2005, p76).

Second, violence and insecurity drive business away and weaken businesses that stay. Forty per cent of private wealth in Africa is invested abroad, as opposed to 5 per cent in South Asia and 6 per cent in East Asia. Eighty per cent of South African business people in a recent survey said that crime and violence were a 'major impediment' to their business, and 84 per cent reported some crime, ranging from employee thefts to attacks on employees, over the previous year. The biggest global growth industry is tourism, representing 10 per cent of the world's GDP and 8 per cent of people employed. In Egypt, after a spate of attacks on tourists during the late 1990s, it is estimated that the country lost over US$1 billion in tourist revenues (UNODC, 2005, p77–86).

Third, violence and insecurity erode democracy. There are three times as many private security guards in South Africa than there are police, most of them armed and without any direct accountability to the public (UNODC, 2005, p78). The growth of vigilante groups has already been mentioned in many LICs. Combined with corruption in police and other governance mechanisms, a vicious cycle is created where legitimate responses to crime and violence seem useless, thus increasing widespread flaunting of the rule of law.

In HICs, too, 'safety' is the most commonly used criteria in developing quality-of-life rankings of cities for international business investment (Rogerson, 1999), while a number of studies have found a decline in town centre trading when fear of crime rates increases (Worpole, 1992).

The most holistic and, in many ways, the most satisfying summary of the costs of violence is based on recent work by Moser and McIlwaine (2006). Although based in a LIC (and, specifically, a Latin American) context, it combines a health, social, economic and environmental understanding of impacts, from the individual to societal scales. The model focuses on four categories of assets: financial, human, natural and social capital. *Financial capital* includes homes, businesses and savings. All forms of violence, but particularly interpersonal economic violence, are a drain on these resources, both through direct theft and robbery, and also through the use of scarce resources to pay for either individual responses such as high fences or alarm systems, or collective responses such as policing or increased prison costs. *Human capital* includes individual and collective investments in education and health. All forms of violence, but particularly family violence, cause long-term physical injuries and mental health problems, such as depression and self-harming acts, and limit access to education and consequent employment. *Natural capital* includes soil, atmosphere, forests and water. In cities, the main natural capital asset is land to live on; in rural areas, the main natural capital asset is land to provide a subsistence living. Especially in LICs, violence can be a cause of migration to cities, with subsequent battles over land. In HICs, insecurity can also be an indirect impetus for the misuse of natural capital, such as when people use cars rather than public transport because they are afraid using the latter, or when people retreat to suburban and ex-urban gated communities and shopping malls because they are afraid to use public spaces. Finally, *social capital* is the most intangible asset, consisting of rules and norms of behaviour, as well as reciprocity and trust in interactions with others. Collective and interpersonal violence erodes trust and cooperation, eats away at human rights and reduces membership in informal organizations. Women play a disproportionate role in informal organizations that make up civil society, and when women are afraid to use public space, or are constrained through intimate partner violence to limit their associations, these organizations decline (Moser and McIlwaine, 2006, pp99–100). Franz Vanderschueren (2006, p2) makes a similar point in relation to social capital: 'urban violence erodes the social capital of the poor and dismantles their organizations, thus preventing social mobility and particularly that of youth'.

The prevention of violence

Given that the causes of violence are complex, interrelated and often structural, and that the cycle of violence is often generational, knowing where to start is not a simple task. Dealing with violence appropriately begins with uncovering the full nature of its extent and prevalence, a topic that is often painful and controversial for individuals or societies to discuss. There is a culture of moral panic and collective anxiety over some of the manifestations of violence, such as terrorism or youth gangs. There is a normalized culture of denial over some other manifestations, such as child abuse or homophobic violence. It is extremely difficult to separate out the value of an intervention from the other factors that are influencing violence in an individual or family, let alone evaluating interventions in communities and societies. And any violence prevention initiative faces potential political and public opposition simply because it cannot offer easy quick fixes to an endemic and complex problem. For all of these reasons, 'knowledge of the causes and correlates of crime is substantial, but our understanding of crime control and prevention strategies remains rather primitive' (Rosenbaum, 2002, p172).

Let us take the example of intimate partner violence. It is one of the most prevalent forms of violence, and one of the most harmful in its impacts to individuals and families. It is also a form of violence that is destructive and costly to communities and societies, whether a health, economic, social or environment impact perspective is used. Yet, it is a perfect example of a form of violence surrounded by silence at every level, starting at the individual scale.

For between 10 and 68 per cent of the thousands of women surveyed for the *WHO Multi-country Study on Women's Health and Domestic Violence against Women* (Garcia-Moreno et al, 2004), depending upon the site, the interviewer was the first person they had talked to about their past and present experiences of violence. Between 28 and 63 per cent had disclosed the violence to a family member, between 18 and 56 per cent of women in most sites had spoken to friends, and with the exception of one site, Tanzania, less than 10 per cent had spoken to formal services, such as a health service, or to people in positions of authority, such as the police. Of the small proportion of women who spoke to formal services, the preference was to approach a service provider that was woman centred, rather than to trust in a government or religious-run service. In Tanzania, where 25 per cent of women said they had gone to local leaders, only 7 per cent said that leaders had then tried to help them (Garcia-Moreno et al, 2004, pp73–75). When asked why they didn't seek help, the most common response was that the violence was considered 'normal' or 'not serious'. Other common reasons were fear of consequences if she told anyone (e.g. threats of more violence from the abuser, fear of losing children and possibility of community censure) and being afraid of being blamed or bringing shame on her family (Garcia-Moreno et al, 2004, pp75–76).

Even in Australia, a HIC with a long history of public education campaigns on intimate partner violence and a relatively high degree of gender equality, the 1996 *Women's Safety Australia* survey found that only 58 per cent of women who had been physically assaulted in the previous year had told a friend, neighbour or work colleague (59 per cent in the case of sexual assault), and only 53 per cent of women had told a family member (32 per cent in the case of sexual assault). In the case of physical assault, fewer than 10 per cent of women had contacted each of the following services (which are relatively accessible in a HIC such as Australia): a doctor, counsellor, crisis service, financial adviser or religious leader (although slightly more women, 8 per cent, contacted crisis services in the case of sexual assault than in the case of physical assault: 4.5 per cent). Fewer than 20 per cent of women contacted the police in the case of physical assault, and only 15 per cent of women contacted the police in the case of sexual assault (Australian Bureau of Statistics, 1996).

What does that mean in terms of prevention? Simply that the first step is a broad-based public education campaign that educates both potential victims and offenders that intimate partner abuse is a crime, and that help from formal services as well as informal networks is available. But in order to ethically offer such a broad-based public education campaign, governments would need to ensure that an adequate social service safety net was in place first. After a high-profile Australian national campaign on violence against women that emphasized intimate partner violence, the 2005 *Personal Safety Survey* found that almost double the number of women who had been physically assaulted, 36 per cent, had reported the incident to the police, although sexual assault reporting rates had only increased to 19 per cent (Australian Bureau of Statistics, 2006). There appears to have also been an increase in family violence helpline calls, requests for emergency shelter and requests for family interventions, such as counselling. However, the national government had been simultaneously cutting funding to many of those services that would be taking the brunt of the increased response (Phillips, 2006).

Training for improved police, health services, financial assistance organizations, such as welfare bureaus or small-scale lending institutions (where they exist), and religious leaders is also a necessary response to the under-reporting of intimate partner violence so that all of these institutional actors can respond appropriately to identify and support victims of intimate partner violence. Even more importantly, workplace and neighbourhood based training for individuals who might be able to help as family members and friends is necessary since they are the people called upon for advice most often. But in order for victims and offenders to create pathways to safer lives, there must be long-term institutional support systems in place, as well as a general cultural shift.

There is also an important lesson for evaluation from those cases where campaigns have focused on increasing awareness and improving response to cases of intimate partner violence. In 1999, the new government in the Australian state of Victoria, where the author lives, set a goal of reducing violent crime over the first five years of its mandate. Instead of triangulating victimization, agency and police data, the new government relied solely on police statistics to measure the progress of this indicator. But unsurprisingly, the national campaign on violence against women, coupled with a new state-wide code of conduct for police in responding to family violence incidents, led to increased police reports of assaults. Unable to report 'progress' on the issue of violent assault, the state government quietly dropped this indicator in favour of a more generalized crime statistic dominated by property offences, and with it, dropped its commitment to its *Safer Streets and Homes* crime and violence prevention strategy (Whitzman, forthcoming).

This leads us to two politically unpalatable truths that must preface any discussion of violence prevention. First, *any comprehensive violence prevention initiative must aim to increase police-reported rates of previously hidden violence.* Ideally, if there were regular, comparable and reliable international, national and local victimization surveys, these results could be triangulated with service agency and police statistics to determine whether it was the actual prevalence of violence that was increasing, or simply reporting of previously hidden violence. But these types of victimization surveys are still in their infancy, and investment in these forms of research is low, partly because the results are so politically upsetting.

Second, *any comprehensive violence prevention initiative must expect and prepare for increased use of violence prevention service infrastructure as a measure of success.*

This would, in the case of intimate partner violence, encompass increased training for police in responding appropriately to complaints about violence (not necessarily a zero tolerance or mandatory arrest procedure, but not erring too far in the other direction of complete individual discretion); training for judges and lawyers and/or specialized court programmes; provision of emergency shelters and longer-term housing options; individual and family health and counselling services; emergency income support (from welfare or loaning institutions); and, possibly, school and other community supports. Ideally, these services would provide similar messages and would also be mutually supportive – for instance, the police referring to income, health and housing supports. This is why both local and national coordination of violence prevention initiatives is so vital.

Perhaps the best known and most influential report on crime and violence prevention is *Preventing Crime: What Works, What Doesn't, What is Promising,* often known as the Sherman report after its first author (Sherman et al, 1997; see also Sherman et al, 2002). The report was requested by the US National Institute of Justice in 1996 in order to better utilize its almost US$4 billion annual expenditures, with an emphasis on preventing youth violence and drug use at the local scale of governance. The report critically reviewed 500 evaluation studies, mostly from the US, in order to discern best practices. Its primary conclusion was that programmes funded by governments needed to be much more rigorously evaluated, with at least 10 per cent of funding provided for independent evaluation of programmes (Sherman et al, 1997, p4). Remarkably few of the programmes funded by the National Institute of Justice were judged effective, using reliable and statistically verifiable methods, such as those that compared before and after data with a similar control site where the intervention had not taken place (Sherman et al, 1997, pp3–5). The lack of good evaluation was a particular concern in relation to policing expenditures, which make up over half of the annual US crime prevention budget.

As the Sherman report recognizes, scientific evaluation of crime prevention is extremely difficult. Prevention is usually measured using reduction in number of crimes committed (or at least reported to the police), although sometimes the number of offenders, the number of offences or the amount of harm is considered as well (Sherman et al, 1997, p21). The report considers the minimum requirement for a strong evaluation, a reliable and powerful correlation test, a temporal ordering of cause and effect, and the elimination of major rival hypotheses. Moreover, the evaluation would have to focus on impact, not on process. To give one example, training police to treat domestic violence victims more respectfully, to provide better victim assistance and to gather better evidence at the scene could all be important objectives of police training. But it is an altogether different and more complex task to ascertain whether this training programme led to a reduction in repeat domestic violence (Sherman et al, 1997, pp28–29). Ideally, you would want to be working with a large enough sample size and one that was of sufficient stability to study impacts over time. But many programmes work with small groups of individuals who may live in unstable accommodation or otherwise are likely to disappear over time. You would want to have a comparison group, similar to the group receiving the programme in every respect but the intervention itself. In the real world, this is difficult to find, as well as ethically difficult to justify. You would also want to be able to prove temporal ordering of cause and effect: that the programme cause came before the prevention effect. But, again, individual, family and community lives are complex enough that it is difficult to control for external variables, such as declining or reviving economies, new or cheaper illegal substances, or a death in a family or community having a cascading effect.

Ideally, an evaluation would answer three questions. First, you would want to know whether the intervention had an independent effect on the problem identified. Second, you would want to know the comparative return on investment in the intervention: whether it was worth the money and time spent, or whether it was the wisest use of the money and time. Finally, you would want to know the interdependence factors: whether this intervention was affected by things happening in the setting, and whether it affected other things happening in the setting. Unfortunately, current social science can barely answer the first question (Sherman et al, 1997, p23). It also cannot answer related questions, such as whether it is better for a single causal mechanism (youth unemployment) to be pursued across multiple domains (schools, local businesses or housing), or whether it is better to pursue multiple causal mechanisms (inequalities between genders, lack of trust in justice and lack of financial resources) across one domain (communities) (Rosenbaum, 2002, p174).

The report emphasized the interrelationship of seven settings: communities, families, schools, labour markets, specific premises, the police and criminal justice. It pointed out, for instance, that the positive impacts of an intervention aimed at improving educational outcomes for children, or even a multi-agency coordinated strategy on youth violence, might well be undone at a later stage if there were no local employment available. It thus recommended interventions that focused simultaneously on these seven interdependent settings, while admitting that that the evidence that these coordinated interventions worked was lacking (Sherman et al, 1997, pp3–4).

The Sherman report's analysis of the causes and costs of violence was similar to theories and evidence previously discussed, although it emphasized the particular political, economic and social context of youth violence in the US. For instance, in the US, the concentration of inequalities and violence within African-American inner-city communities is particularly acute. However, its finding that the majority of community-based initiatives were not targeted to the communities most at risk of public violence (Sherman et al, 1997, p3) is applicable to other settings. In fact, the Sherman report found no interventions at the community scale that it could confidently say were proven to have worked, as well as several popular programmes in the US (gun buy-back programmes and neighbourhood watch) that were proven *not* to work in particularly high violence communities (Sherman et al, 1997, Chapter 3).   One of the few programmes that appeared to have substantial positive impacts in relation to expenditures was the family setting intervention of long-term home visitation programmes for at-risk children, combined with the provision of free pre-school programmes and family therapy with delinquent and pre-delinquent youth.   Other programmes that were proven to work included long-term school-based programmes, such as anti-bullying campaigns and anger and stress management; short-term vocational programmes for ex-offenders; directed patrols in high crime 'hot spots'; and focused multifaceted rehabilitation programmes with offenders. Although the Sherman report did not record the extent of the effectiveness of programmes, other summaries have indicated differences in reported crime and delinquency rates between test and control sites of between 33 per cent (for the US Job Corps youth training and employment support programme) to 70 per cent (for the US Quantum programme, which offers incentives for at-risk youth to complete school) (Shaw, 2001b, p6).

The Sherman report's matrix of 'what works, what doesn't and what is promising' was utilized in *Preventing Violence: A Guide to Implementing the Recommendations of the World Report on Violence and Health* (Butchart et al, 2004). Unlike the Sherman report, which focused on US national funding to the local scale of governance, *Preventing Violence* concentrated on national interventions within an international context. As a WHO publication, *Preventing Violence* also highlighted the role of health-related organizations, a sector that was largely absent from discussion in the Sherman report. The Sherman report emphasized youth crime and violence, while *Preventing Violence,* like the earlier WHO reports, looked at interpersonal violence, as a whole, within an injury prevention framework. While the Sherman report examined a variety of settings, *Preventing Violence* used the ecological model described at the beginning of this chapter, as well as the life cycle or developmental framework used in Chapter 2, a life-cycle approach that was unfortunately lacking in the *World Report on Violence and Health* (Krug et al, 2002; see Johnson, 2007, for another example of the life-cycle approach to categorizing interventions).

Despite these differences, the two reports, using somewhat different data sets, provided remarkably similar findings when it came to successful violence prevention. For instance, home visitation services, parenting training, therapeutic foster care and pre-school enrichment were identified as being of proven effectiveness in reducing violence against young children, while long-term social development training that emphasizes making positive choices and mentoring programmes were identified as successful with older children and adolescents. Since the scope of *Preventing Violence* went beyond the traditional definition of 'youth violence' as a problem in and of the public sphere, the report also was able to identify school-based dating violence prevention programmes and family therapy as successful interventions in preventing interpersonal violence. *Preventing Violence* echoed the Sherman report in reporting that drug resistance and gun safety education does not work, nor do repressive approaches such as 'shock' programmes with young offenders (e.g. boot camps and quasi-military settings) or trying young offenders in adult courts.

The largest category of possible prevention strategies in both reports consisted of those that were promising, but needed further evaluation. For young children, this includes reducing unintended pregnancies, increased access to pre-natal and post-natal support services, treatment programmes for children who experience or witness violence, and child protection services in general. For older children and youth, school-based child maltreatment and screening programmes, home–school partnerships, recreational programmes to extend adult supervision, 'safe havens' for children on high-risk routes to and from school, restricting alcohol availability, and metal detectors were found to be promising. For older youth, incentives for education or vocational training and temporary foster care for serious and chronic delinquents were promising. For adults, services for those abused as children, adult recreational programmes, incentives for post-secondary or vocational training, job creation programmes for the chronically unemployed, waiting periods for firearm purchases, shelters and crisis centres for battered women, mandatory arrest policies for intimate partner violence, and public shaming of intimate partner violence offenders were found to be promising. For older people, shelters and other services for victims of elder abuse were encouraging. Across the life course, screening for healthcare providers on the identification and treatment of violence; public education campaigns to increase awareness of violence and promote anti-violence norms; reducing media and sports violence; community-based policing that was informed by awareness of risk factors and by community participation; improving police and justice responses to violence; de-concentrating poverty and inequality; inclusive programmes for incarcerated perpetrators that targeted substance abuse and instilled acceptable norms of behaviour; and gun control were found to be promising. And like the Sherman report, *Preventing Violence* concluded that coordinated interventions were vital, yet evaluation mechanisms had yet to prove that they worked (or how and why some interventions worked and others did not).

A number of studies, again mostly from the US, have provided cost–benefit analyses of crime and violence prevention programmes. For instance, the Rand Institute estimated in 1999 that the per capita taxes required to reduce reported crime by 10 per cent would range from US$228 for extended incarceration options such as a 'third strike law' (whereby any third offence would receive a minimum 20-year sentence) to US$48 for intensive support for parents with young children or US$32 for incentives to keep young men in schools (Waller and Sansfacon, 2000, p8). Another economic analysis of the 'third strike law' as it was applied in the US state of California found additional costs of between US$4.5 billion and US$6.5 billion a year, with no proven effect. In contrast, a home visitor programme for every newborn baby in the US state of Michigan cost US$70 million, with a further universal parent education programme costing US$35 million; but these prevention costs were estimated as one nineteenth the annual cost of child abuse in that state. Cost–benefit analyses of intimate partner violence prevention are rare; but a study in the state of Arizona found that the provision of emergency shelters led to a net socio-economic benefit of US$3.4 million annually, with a benefit-to-cost ratio of between 6.8 and 18.4 (Waters et al, 2004, pp28–32).

The World Health Organization, like most health promotion organizations, distinguishes between primary, secondary and tertiary prevention. *Primary prevention* means broad-based universal programmes that seek to prevent violence before it occurs. *Secondary prevention* or *early intervention* focuses on at-risk groups, who may have already experienced violence. *Tertiary prevention* comprises intervention services to those already identified as victims and/or offenders, providing support and treatment intended to prevent re-victimization or re-offending (Krug et al, 2002, pp15–16; see also VicHealth, 2005). An example of primary prevention, using a mechanism that has been proven to work, would be a school-based programme for all secondary students that focused on appropriate dating behaviour and understanding that 'no means no'. Examples from James's story would have been maternal–child health nurses screening for the early warning signs of trouble in a family or the provision of early childhood education. Examples of secondary prevention that are known to work would be mentoring programmes and extra learning supports for children who are not doing well at school, family therapy and anger management: these would be particularly applicable to James's story. Promising examples pertaining to adults might include recreational, language training or vocational programmes for new migrants fleeing conflict in their home country, which might provide positive messages on healing from past violence and inclusion in the new country's economic and social fabric. Promising examples of tertiary prevention would be emergency shelters for victims of elder abuse or intimate partner violence, particularly when backed up by longer-term income creation and housing opportunities.

Generally, there have been stronger evaluations, including longitudinal evaluations, of primary prevention aimed at younger age groups, and these interventions do appear to provide greater cost–benefit savings at the societal scale. However, there is a need to develop prevention programmes that target individuals across the life course, particularly if the goal is to stop the generational cycle of violence, and to promote violence prevention across communities and societies. The Australian organization VicHealth, the Victorian Health Promotion Foundation, has developed a matrix of public health interventions to prevent violence against women (see Figure 3.9). This matrix focuses on seven strategies that have been commonly used to prevent violence, including research, monitoring and evaluation; direct participation; organizational development; community strengthening; communications and social marketing; advocacy; and legislative and policy reform. The interventions are mostly targeted at youth and adult risk groups.

This matrix differs from the Sherman report's sectoral approach, emphasizing the kinds of strategies that might mesh in an integrated model. It also implies a progression from universal primary prevention programmes to more focused intervention programmes as needs are clarified. Unlike the Sherman report, which is weak on comparative success (to what extent programmes 'that work' are successful), the VicHealth matrix assumes that primary prevention is more likely to be cost-effective than intervention further downstream. Furthermore, it extends the Sherman report's list of relatively formal sectors (education, job markets, police and justice), to incorporate other parts of civil society, such as sporting organizations, women-centred services, men-centred services, media and local government councils.

The 2002 United Nations guidelines for crime prevention, *Effective Community-based Crime Prevention* (UN Economic and Social Council, 2002, p9), argue that crime prevention considerations should be integrated within 'all relevant social and economic policies and programmes, including those addressing employment, education, health, housing and urban planning, poverty, social marginalization and exclusion'. The guidelines' definition of primary prevention includes social and economic development programmes that combat marginalization and exclusion, and promote positive conflict resolution and a culture of lawfulness and tolerance; situational crime prevention, such as improved environmental design, and target hardening, which does not limit free access to public space; and preventing organized crime through national legislation and protecting women and children who are vulnerable to trafficking. They also talk about preventing recidivism by facilitating certain police methods such as rapid response; courts using more diversionary schemes and mediation for less severe crimes or those involving youth; socio-educational support of offenders diverted from prison, in prison and after prison; and involving the community in the rehabilitation of offenders. Although these guidelines are rather general, they do acknowledge proven good practices.

Moser and McIlwaine (2006, pp102–104) extend the possible range of violence prevention interventions and organizations that could provide these interventions. They categorize seven forms of intervention. Some focus on what health promotion organizations would call tertiary prevention, supporting victims or seeking to change behaviours of offenders. Some seek to ameliorate context-specific problems, which would be categorized as secondary prevention. Others work on the peaceful resolution of conflicts (collective as well as

VicHealth

Public Health Strategies	Primary Prevention	Early intervention	Intervention
Research, monitoring and evaluation	A study explores whether there is a relationship between gender related income inequality and the prevalence of domestic violence	A long term study of young women at risk of domestic violence explores whether there is a link between unemployment and vulnerability to violence	An intensive job search assistance program to survivors of domestic violence is evaluated to determine whether it reduces their risk of further victimisation
Direct participation	A school based program is offered to young people exploring healthy and respectful relationships	Following evidence of forced sexual contact, a school nurse delivers a program targeted to young women focussing on their right to respect in relationships	A support group is established for young women who have been subject to sexual assault
Organisational development	A sporting club develops policies and procedures to ensure female participants and spectators have equal access to club resources and facilities and a safe and welcoming environment	The club develops a training program for its coaches to assist them in identifying and responding to player behaviour which is disrespectful of women	The club introduces and enforces penalties for players found to vilify or harass women
Community strengthening	A local council works with its community to develop a women's safety strategy covering a range of council activities from land-use planning to community services	Local men develop a mentoring program targeted to young boys who have been identified as behaving disrespectfully toward women and girls	The community attracts additional resources to provide emergency accommodation for local women and children fleeing family violence.
Communications and social marketing	Radio and television advertisements are developed advocating respectful relationships between men and women	After incidents of sexual assault, including sexual harassment and date rape, come to light local clubs develop a campaign warning male patrons of the legal consequences of their behaviour	The campaign urges young women to contact the police if they are subject to sexual assault
Advocacy	Women's groups lobby government to introduce a family violence policy asserting that this violence will be treated as any other criminal assault	This includes lobbying for a police code of practice which seeks to deter domestic violence by mandating police to arrest perpetrators	Women's refuges meet with senior police to urge them to adopt measures to ensure that the code is enforced so that perpetrators of violence are removed from the family home
Legislative and policy reform	Legislation is introduced making rape in marriage a crime. The law communicates a message to the community that violence against women is unacceptable regardless of the relationship	The legislation communicates to potential perpetrators that such behaviour is not acceptable and will be treated as would other violent crimes	The legislation improves protection for victims of rape in marriage

Figure 3.9 *Public health model for the prevention of violence against women*

interpersonal) and the promotion of human rights, what might be termed primary prevention.

The most common form of intervention, according to Moser and McIlwaine (2006), is the criminal justice approach. Unfortunately, policing, courts and prisons are quite often an ineffective, as well as a fiscally inefficient, use of resources in the struggle to prevent violence. In many communities and societies, the criminal justice system is perceived as being highly biased on the basis of gender, 'race' and class. However, Moser and McIlwaine point out that particular initiatives, such as women's police stations (see Chapter 6), have proven to be successful in Latin America. A second, and increasingly important, approach is the public health promotion approach used in this book. This multi-sectoral and evidence-driven approach has been employed throughout Latin America and has led to some clear successes. A third approach, which according to the Sherman report has not proven effective in the US context, is conflict transformation – for instance, training former gang members as negotiators. Another approach that is particularly popular in Latin America is education on human rights, especially in relation to empowering women. Moser and McIlwaine (2006) describe citizen security or coordinated efforts at the community scale as a fifth approach, although I would argue that this is a meta-approach that can encompass all mechanisms and settings described. Crime prevention through environmental design, or what the Sherman report would describe as interventions in the setting of particular places and the UN would term situational crime prevention, is a sixth approach. Finally, supporting local organizations that can increase the resilience capacities of individuals, families and communities is an approach that has been taken in Latin America to reduce violence.

Another PUA described by Moser and McIlwaine (2006) highlights strategies that individual women could take in the case of a wide range of community safety concerns, from dealing with drunks to flooding. In each case, the women described short-term individual strategies and long-term solutions, then identified particular organizations that might help with the long-term solutions. As is often the case when consulting with members of the public, a responsive and trusted police force was considered the most important element of prevention.

This division between short-term reactive protective 'coping strategies' and longer-term proactive 'solutions' bears a strong resemblance to a typology developed by an influential women's safety project based in Montreal, Canada (CAFSU, 2002). According to CAFSU (Comité d'Action Femmes et Sécurité Urbaine, which translates as Women's Action Committee on Urban Safety), successful women's safety strategies must support autonomy by increasing choices, assuming that women are rational actors, and taking a whole-of-community approach to eradicating violence against women in both public and private space, rather than making violence an individual responsibility.

CAFSU and its related international organization Women in Cities International have developed another typology of violence prevention initiatives. First, public education campaigns work to increase awareness of violence and to promote individual, family and community responses that can prevent violence. Second, community mobilization can improve neighbourhood and local governance responses. Third, safety planning can promote safer public spaces and develop public spaces where the concerns of violence in private space can be addressed. Fourth, coordinating programmes and organizations under an umbrella initiative can support research and sharing of best practices (CAFSU, 2002, p25; see also Whitzman et al, 2004).

Conclusion: From analysis to action on violence prevention

Whether focusing on health impacts, as Chapter 2 did, or economic and social impacts, as in this chapter, the costs of violence are onerous. This is particularly true in LICs with fewer resources to combat violence, as well as higher levels of

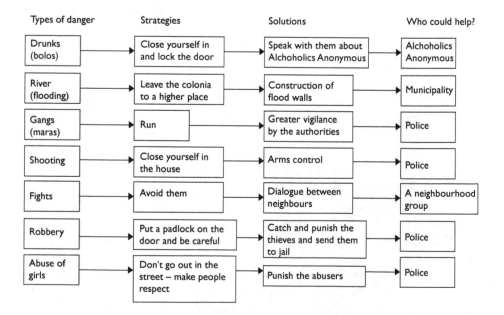

Figure 3.10 *Categorization of types of danger and solutions*

Source: Moser and McIlwaine (2006, p101)

violence. The scholarly consensus on causes of violence presents a complex and interrelated picture of a set of linked factors operating at the individual, family, community and societal scales. Structural inequalities and tolerance of violence combine with individual histories to create both risk and resilience factors.

Evaluating violence prevention programmes is in its beginning stages. However, there is a growing body of evidence that successful violence prevention can be enormously cost-effective in terms of government and charitable expenditures, as well as saving lives. Most recent reports on violence prevention focus on the importance of coordination: at the community/local governance, society/national governance and global/international governance scales. This is for two reasons: first, because risk factors are complex and inter-sectoral and, second, because of the need to develop an evidence base for violence prevention and to learn from what works.

There are several ways of categorizing violence prevention programmes or initiatives: by setting, sector, stage of life cycle, type of activity, stage of intervention (from before any violence to after an incident) and philosophical bent. I would like to propose a hybrid categorization model with ten categories, to be used in the next chapters of this book. First, there are *early childhood interventions* with pre-school babies and children from before birth to the age of six, as well as their families and other caregivers. Second, there are *school-age interventions*, centred on children from 6 to 16, primary and secondary schools, and on families and other caregivers. Third, there are *employment and income-generation* community-based economic development programmes, mostly aimed at young male and female school leavers between the ages of 16 and 30, but also applicable to low-income people in general. Fourth, there are *public awareness models*, aimed at the general adult population, age subgroups such as young people, adults and older people, or particular communities such as women, men or linguistic subgroups, and often emphasizing human rights and equality issues. Fifth, there are *community mobilization models* that work on improving capacity at the individual, family and community scales to respond to violence, including leadership development. Sixth, there is improving *direct service delivery* to minimize harm and prevent re-victimization. Seventh, there are *spatial planning strategies* that encompass both safer design of public spaces and the provision of a network of spaces and services where violence can be addressed. Eighth, there are *policing models* that respond to violence when it is reported. Ninth, there are *legal and justice interventions* that both educate the public as to what will and will not be tolerated in a society and also deal with offenders. For all of these nine strategies to succeed, there is an overriding need for *coordination strategies* at a wide range of scales: neighbourhood, city, state, nation, regional and global scales, which bring all of the preceding strategies together in a coordinated action plan.

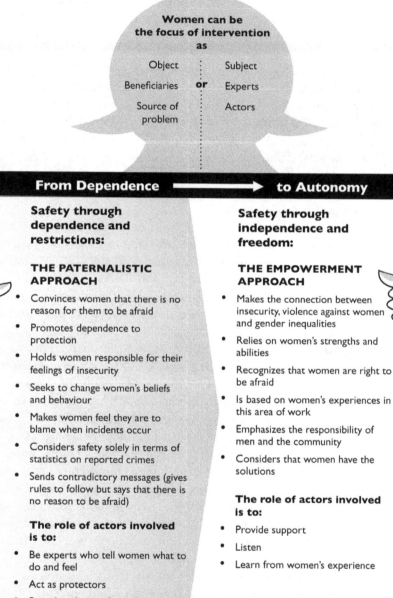

Women can be the focus of intervention as

Object	Subject
Beneficiaries **or**	Experts
Source of problem	Actors

From Dependence ➝ to Autonomy

Safety through dependence and restrictions:

THE PATERNALISTIC APPROACH

- Convinces women that there is no reason for them to be afraid
- Promotes dependence to protection
- Holds women responsible for their feelings of insecurity
- Seeks to change women's beliefs and behaviour
- Makes women feel they are to blame when incidents occur
- Considers safety solely in terms of statistics on reported crimes
- Sends contradictory messages (gives rules to follow but says that there is no reason to be afraid)

The role of actors involved is to:

- Be experts who tell women what to do and feel
- Act as protectors
- Provide solutions for women

Safety through independence and freedom:

THE EMPOWERMENT APPROACH

- Makes the connection between insecurity, violence against women and gender inequalities
- Relies on women's strengths and abilities
- Recognizes that women are right to be afraid
- Is based on women's experiences in this area of work
- Emphasizes the responsibility of men and the community
- Considers that women have the solutions

The role of actors involved is to:

- Provide support
- Listen
- Learn from women's experience

Figure 3.11 *Paternalistic versus empowerment approaches*

Source: CAFSU (2002, p12)

The purpose of this chapter and the previous chapter has been to contribute to a shared understanding of the links between different forms of violence: their causes, risk factors and the resources that can be called upon to prevent violence. This common understanding is a precondition of the coordinated approach outlined in Chapters 4 to 6.

4

Coordinated Community Safety:
From Local to Global

Now that we have a better sense of the prevalence of violence and insecurity, theories on their causes, their consequences and their costs, and what works to prevent violence and insecurity, we can turn to the 'how to' of community safety and violence prevention in the next three chapters. The Sherman report (Sherman et al, 1997) asserts the importance of neighbourhood and local government coordination in effective crime prevention within a report that focuses on the national role in funding and disseminating good practice. The United Nations has produced guidelines for urban crime prevention that stress the importance of coordinated action at the local governance level (UN Economic and Social Council, 2002). The World Health Organization (WHO) Collaborating Centre for Community Safety defines community safety as preventive action 'led by the community' (WHO Collaborating Centre on Community Safety Promotion, 2007). In contrast, the WHO's *Preventing Violence: A Guide to Implementing the Recommendations of the World Report on Violence and Health* (Butchart et al, 2004) emphasizes coordinated national plans of action to prevent interpersonal violence, and both the WHO and UN-Habitat have global and regional campaigns on community safety and violence prevention. Why is coordinated action at various levels of governance considered so important in community safety? What are the relationships between coordination at these five different scales of governance: neighbourhood, city, nation, region and globe? Who are the key actors in coordinated action at various scales and who are the potential leaders? And how exactly can coordinated action lead to an integrated and gendered approach to preventing violence in both the public and private spheres?

In order to explore these questions, we move from the health promotion and criminology literature that has thus far provided the basis for the analysis in this book and turn to theories on participatory governance and spatial planning. *Spatial planning* is a term associated with English planning theorist

Patsy Healey, who describes it as 'efforts in the collective management of shared concerns about spatial and environmental qualities, expressed in explicit policies which emphasize a strategic orientation to coordination between diverse actions' (Healey, 1997, p82). In other words, spatial planning goes far beyond an emphasis on traditional land-use planning, zoning and urban design to integrate social, economic, environmental and cultural policies that can accomplish particular societal aims in a coordinated fashion. *Governance*, or 'the management of the common affairs of political communities', goes beyond the formal institutions of government to incorporate all aspects of how people collectively govern themselves (Healey, 1997, p59). Work supported by the World Bank, the United Nations and the International Centre for the Prevention of Crime (ICPC) has begun to explore the interrelations between institutional and interpersonal violence, and has also started to develop ways of incorporating community safety within spatial planning and management policies, particularly at the local governance level. According to the United Nations Development Programme, good urban governance is 'efficient and effective response to urban problems by democratically elected and accountable local governments working in partnership with civil society' (Council of Europe, 2004, p14), and this problem-solving perspective is equally applicable to rural governance.

In Chapter 3, there was an emphasis on the four scales of intervention used in the *World Report on Violence and Health* (Krug et al, 2002): individual, family, community and society. However, the individual and family scales are not scales of political governance, the emphasis in this chapter. The 'community' scale includes both the 'neighbourhood' and 'city' scales of governance, and the 'society' scale includes both the 'national' scale of governance and subnational entities, such as states and provinces. Finally, the 'global' scale, which is absent from the *World Report*, can be broken into regional governance bodies such as the European Union and international governance bodies such as the United Nations and the World Bank.

Coordinated community safety initiatives have a short history. In the US, the late 1960s War on Poverty led to cities receiving federal money for crime prevention, particularly through neighbourhood policing and coordinated social development mechanisms (Sherman et al, 1997, p7). During the 1970s, the violence against women movement began in cities and countries around the world, leading to a number of coalitions that began to take a multifaceted approach to the problem (CAFSU, 2002, p1). In 1982, the Bonnemaison programme was established in France, a national government-led but locally administered programme that focused on coordinated action on youth violence, which was the forerunner of other nationally coordinated local governance community safety initiatives (Shaw, 2001a, p9). At roughly the same time, local governance-based 'women's safety initiatives', such as those in Toronto and Montreal (discussed in Chapter 5), began to be founded (CAFSU, 2002, p1), as were regional groupings, such as the European Forum on Urban Safety. It was only during the past decade, the 1990s, when publications, conferences, articles and guidelines on local governance of community safety began to appear in large numbers, and international bodies began to take note of the power of coordinated community safety and violence prevention. It is also only in the past ten years that crime prevention and community safety efforts have begun to encompass a gender analysis (Shaw and Andrew, 2005).

Over the next three chapters, there will be an emphasis on case studies of community safety initiatives. The case studies will follow a standardized format. Beginning with a brief description of the setting and the problems identified, the chapters will then move on to the partnerships developed (including sources of funding and other support), the stated objectives, the interventions and the outcomes of these interventions, and any lessons learned from the initiative. The criteria used for inclusion of these case studies are: a clear sense of the community safety/violence prevention problem being addressed; a coordinated approach that brings together government, community organizations and, in some cases, the private sector; some measure of programme success (attaining its stated objectives, which in many cases does not include a proven reduction in violence or insecurity) and longevity beyond an initial funding period of one or two years; the results having been written up in some format; and being influential in some way in other places. I have tried to include a range of problems, approaches and geographic settings. There is a preponderance of examples from sub-Saharan Africa, Latin America and several high-income countries (HICs) for reasons that will be explained in 'Coordination at the regional and international scales'.

Coordination and the question of scale

As Chapter 3 described, the causes of crime can range from an individual's characteristics to structural social and economic factors. Violence can be deeply embedded in families and societies. There is no single or simple measure to address these issues. Rather, there is a need for a mix of prevention measures that reinforce one another, along all stages of the life cycle and based in coordinated action at all levels of governance. The public health approach often talks about the interactions of different environments in creating risks or resilience to health and well-being problems (see Box 4.1). Like the Sherman report's discussion of settings, this notion of interlocking environments helps to conceptualize how to approach complex problems through partnerships.

Developing a consensus and a set of interactions between schools, health providers, police, businesses and community services is one reason for coordination. Keeping track of individual victims and/or offenders as they move

Box 4.1 *Environmental determinants of health*

The World Health Organization's (WHO's) health promotion approach to community safety discusses how any health problem is the product of a complex set of determinants found in natural, built, societal, economic, cultural, political, organizational and technological environments (Fifth World Conference on Injury Prevention and Control, 2000). The prevention of any health problem can only occur through developing approaches that address a range of environments. This classification of environmental determinants of health is largely drawn from a report on how to carry out municipal public health planning in Australia, *Environments for Health* (State Government of Victoria, 2001).

Natural environment

The natural environment comprises the quality of the air, land, and water in a settlement, and the environmental capital embodied in the surrounding forests, fields and water. The *viability* of these resources may have an indirect influence on violence. To give two examples, community tensions might be higher in an area where there are many conflicts over limited arable land or firewood; conversely, urban dwellers working together on a waste management issue or developing a community garden may learn to collaborate across diversity. The natural environment is influenced by international, national and local government policies, as well as by communities and the private sector.

Built environment

The built environment is composed of the roads, housing, shops, offices, transport systems, monuments and other amenities that people create, individually and collectively, in a settlement. The built environment's impact upon violence has traditionally been conceptualized as a very narrow issue of crime prevention through environmental design (CPTED), dealing with aspects such as adequate lighting or limiting public access to multi-unit housing (Newman, 1972; Poyner, 1983). However, the influence of spatial planning decisions – land use, transport, economic, and social planning – on the prevention of violence is much more complex. People are much more likely to use public spaces where there are streets and footpaths safe from the risk of traffic accidents, and communal spaces where people casually meet on a regular basis, including parks, recreation facilities, libraries, shopping districts and neighbourhood houses. Recreation facilities and other places where low-income youth and adult women can safely congregate have been seen as important in the prevention of youth violence, and the promotion of migrant inclusion, since the settlement house movement in the US and the UK during the late 19th century. The importance of establishing 'safe spaces', such as community centres where older people, lesbians and gay men and visible minorities can congregate, is a return to this notion of settlement houses. The provision of emergency and affordable housing is extremely important in providing options for people escaping violence within their families. The provision of a *liveable* built environment has traditionally been seen as a local government responsibility, with strong influences from the private sector, community organizations and senior levels of government.

Social environment

The social environment is generally seen as the demographic mixture of people of different genders, ages, incomes and backgrounds, as well as the social services that meet the needs of these people. *Equitable* environments are a function of strong and diffused *social capital*, the extent of trust and shared norms, and reciprocity between people living in an area. Schools, adult education opportunities and libraries are considered vital aspects of *social infrastructure*, the places that can help build social capital, and public events and socio-economic diversity in neighbourhoods are other factors that are felt to contribute to social capital. The social environment is generally seen as a community and private-sector responsibility, usually with local and senior government funding support and standards for services.

Economic environment

The economic environment is defined by who is employed where and in what jobs, and what other forms of informal economic activities and income supports are available. As in the case of the social environment, *equity* is a characteristic of a good economic environment, but so are *sustainability* and *resilience*. A local economy overly dependent upon a single resource or source of employment can be devastated by price changes in the resource or the loss of that employment provider, leading to increased community tensions and violence. At the individual level, the loss in job security caused by global economic forces can lead to depression, particularly among older men. Conversely, a local economy with a mixture of jobs, apprenticeships and business start-up opportunities, particularly for those who are lacking in formal training and education, can be an important factor in reducing youth violence and intimate partner violence. Community economic development is a private- and charitable-sector concern, often with the assistance of local or senior government funding or other fiscal mechanisms, such as tax remissions.

Political environment

The mechanisms by which people have a say in the decisions that affect them, and the extent to which these mechanisms are participatory and *democratic*, describe the political environment. Governments can be discriminatory and violent; but they can also initiate positive changes in society, including the prevention of violence. The *organizational environment* is closely linked to this concept – that is, which organizations are dominant and how they have a say. It is not so much the number of formal and informal organizations as their ability to form *partnerships* that is central to successful violence prevention.

Cultural environment

The cultural environment is the extent to which people feel that their language, artistic expression and culture belong to a larger society. Cultural mechanisms such as visual arts and music can be vital forms of public education on violence and its prevention, just as cultural expressions that promote violence and discrimination can be part of the problem. *Convivial* cultural environments are usually developed by civil society, sometimes with private-sector and governmental assistance in funding and patronage.

Technological environment

This environment is described by the degree to which technological innovation promotes or prevents violence. The internet, for instance, has been posited as a powerful source of both good and evil: the source of cyber-bullying as well as disseminating good practice in violence prevention and providing online assistance to those in need who might be otherwise isolated. It is important not to reify technology and to depend upon it as a quick fix. Closed-circuit television (CCTV) can never replace people keeping an eye on one another. Although sometimes useful in solving crimes that have been filmed in progress, CCTV does far less to prevent violence or the fear of violence. Similarly, the use of new and expensive biometric technologies, such as iris scanning at public school entrances or facial scanning at US airports, is financially unfeasible for most settings and exceedingly troubling in terms of civil liberties, and will do nothing to address the root causes of violence.

through housing, health, legal, employment, education and other services to meet often complex needs makes sense, as does the ability of one service to refer people to other available facilities. A coalition at any scale is more likely to get a truer sense of the magnitude and characteristics of violence, and identify existing local resources and gaps, than any one-off audit. Not having one intervention

cancel another out (a summer job creation programme for young people without further job opportunities available after the programme) is another reason to
plan prevention activities together. Mutual learning from different backgrounds
and approaches can lead to better services and programmes through particular
disciplines, such as public health or policing, 'thinking outside the box'. A sense
of common purpose and vision is important for a violence prevention initiative to
be sustainable over time, and coalitions around violence prevention can develop
a steady political pressure to keep prevention programmes and services funded.
Last, but not least, coordination can lead to more efficient use of scarce monetary
and human resources (Shaw, 2001a; Rosenbaum, 2002).

What has been described above can be broken down into three separate
aspects of coordination. First, there is *case management* at the individual or family
level: keeping track of what services are needed and what has been received. The
anecdote of 'James' in Chapter 3 showed poor case management in action, where
James and his family were not consulted on their needs, and recommended social
services were not forthcoming. However, if case management is properly managed,
it is the best way of meeting the complex needs of victims and offenders. Second,
there is the spatial aspect of *co-location*: where services are located in relation to
one another and the populations whom they serve, and whether it is easy to access
them. Sometimes, it helps to have related services located in a *hub* – for instance,
family health services can be developed near early childhood education, which
in turn can be provided near primary schools. Some police stations have specialized medical staff to help victims of violence located either within the station or
nearby in a hospital setting. Third, there is the question of a *coalition*, a working
alliance that might accomplish peer education, research or advocacy aims in the
most effective and efficient way possible. Coalitions might draw upon public,
private and non-profit organizations, and also engage in consultation and other
participatory practices to gain ideas from as broad a range of people affected as
possible.

Rosenbaum (2002, p177) summarizes the advantages of coordinated partnerships as issues of quantity and quality. In terms of quantity, multiple interventions
can be assumed to be more effective than single interventions, multiple sources
of funding better than single sources, and multiple ideas from disciplines more
effective than single perspectives. In terms of quality, there is the issue of synergy,
or the whole of a coordinated initiative being more effective than the sum of its
parts. But he also warns that working together requires time, clarity of intent
and a spirit of cooperation, elements that are difficult to establish and maintain.
Successful partnerships are able to obtain long-term funding, have a clear organizational structure and engage in activities that have attainable short-term and
long-term outcomes. However, it is difficult to develop easy 'rules' to ensure that
these good things happen, especially since sites vary so widely in terms of culture,
history and resources.

At every scale, successful partnerships require both *horizontal integration* (coordination of initiatives located in a particular place) and *vertical integration* (coordination of initiatives that may operate or be funded across different scales of governance). Successful partnerships also require *strategic integration* of groups whose speciality is primary prevention (such as health and education sectors), victim services, law enforcement and research (Council of Europe, 2004). These aspects of integration have been given a number of names – whole-of-government approach, place management, integrated service delivery; but all require the breaking down of 'silos' between levels of government, governments and the private sector, and between governments and civil society.

The question of who is involved in partnerships varies considerably and is related to questions of scale. Generally, there are three types of coalitions (Rosenbaum, 2002, pp201–202). *Leadership* coalitions include political, social and/or business leaders. These coalitions are generally associated with the local and national levels. *Grassroots* coalitions usually consist of citizens affiliated with informal organizations. They are generally associated with the neighbourhood level, although there are examples of grassroots coalitions at the national scale (such as the National Congress of Neighborhood Women in the US) and the global scale (such as Slum Dwellers International). *Professional* coalitions bring together organizations representing government, for-profit and non-profit sectors, often including researchers as well. These coalitions are associated with every scale. In practice, coalitions often include a combination of all of these types of people and organizations, which can lead to a clash of assumptions and working styles.

When looking at potential scales for action, there are two potentially opposing principles at work. The first is *subsidiarity*: the notion that the primary responsibility for defining an issue, ascertaining needs and assigning resources should be as near as possible to the people most directly affected by the issue. This principle would lead to a focus on small-scale neighbourhood-based interventions. An opposing principle is *accountability* to structures and norms that are generally produced at a higher scale. The funding for any kind of socially transformative work rarely comes from the smallest scales of governance, either neighbourhood or local. It would hardly be fair for this to happen since the areas or communities with highest needs are usually least able to afford this kind of work. The responsibility of higher scales of governance are to ensure that both public and charitable funding is well used, that small-scale efforts are capable and interested in consulting all stakeholders, and that lessons learned from one place are transferable to other places (Healey, 1997, p307). This does not, however, imply that *standardization* is the best approach since the needs and resources of each place will probably be different.

Coordination at the neighbourhood scale

At the most micro-community scale, there is coordination in a neighbourhood or small village. Of course, most neighbourhoods do not operate as villages once did in an earlier era of pedestrian transportation and limited social mobility. In some rural areas, people still spend their lives dwelling, working and playing in the same small area of a few square kilometres and a few hundred people. Their immediate vicinity is where they meet their friends and, quite possibly, their spouse, who may be part of an extended family network. But in an era when over half the world's population lives in cities and the pace of urbanization is growing, most people move several times in their lives and do not work and play in the immediate proximity of where they live. Their social range is much greater than the neighbourhood of a few hundred or a few thousand people, and is much more diverse. Having said that, neighbourhoods, even if they are only the place where we sleep, are central to our physical and mental health. Urban neighbourhoods can be dominated by high-rise buildings, narrow one-room shacks or sprawling single-family homes, and one architectural form is not necessarily better than the other in terms of community building. Of far more importance is the mixture of land uses, the local amenities and the way in which cultural and economic diversity is managed. There is a huge difference between neighbourhoods where shopping, good schools and community services such as libraries and parks offer destinations for a pleasant stroll and an opportunity to talk to neighbours, and neighbourhoods where there are more places to buy illegal alcohol or drugs than food, where violence is a constant threat, or where gender or ethnic no-go areas are found. While some jurisdictions have neighbourhood governance, structures by which people can be involved in neighbourhood decision-making, this is still relatively rare. Two successful neighbourhood-level projects are described in Boxes 4.2 and 4.3.

Box 4.2 *Neighbourhood capacity-building in the barrios of Buenos Aires, Argentina: Improving community safety through the provision of basic infrastructure*

A number of reports (Sherman et al, 1997; Rosenbaum, 2002) have discussed both the importance of coordinated action for community safety at the neighbourhood scale and the difficulties of establishing and evaluating these initiatives in the most disadvantaged and marginalized neighbourhood. This case study is chosen because of its longevity and positive impacts in a slum community with interrelated problems typical of the informal settlements where over 1 billion people in the world currently live. However, there has been no evaluation of this neighbourhood development project's impacts upon violence and insecurity.

In 1961, Barrio San Jorge, located in the municipality of San Fernando, north of Buenos Aires, became a 'temporary' resettlement site for families living in areas with frequent flooding. Over the years, the *barrio* grew, despite being located on the banks of a polluted river that was also prone to flooding. According to a census taken in 1990, there were about 450 households and 2400 inhabitants in the *barrio*, over half of whom were under the age of 20. Only 46 per cent of adults had completed primary school, unemployment and poverty were high, two-thirds of the housing was classified as substandard, and there was little access to clean water and sewers. The lack of paved roads was used as a rationale for the refusal of police cars, ambulances, fire trucks and municipal waste disposal vehicles to enter the neighbourhood. Unsurprisingly, there were severe health problems, such as high infant mortality and prevalence of infectious diseases. Also unsurprisingly, there was a high level of violence and insecurity, with identified problems including drugs, youth gangs and extremely high levels of burglary. The individual responses were for parents to keep their children indoors, and for most citizens to avoid using streets and services, particularly after dark (Schusterman and Hardoy, 1997, pp92–98).

In 1987, residents working with the local Catholic church decided to develop a mother and child centre in the *barrio*. The aim was to improve child health, nutrition and development, and to provide childcare for working mothers. An architect associated with the parish was asked by a charity organization, Caritas, affiliated to the church, to plan and coordinate the construction of the centre. Funding was obtained by that charity, as well as the Canadian embassy and private Argentine donors.

In 1989, the Dutch branch of the charity Save the Children provided a donation to support three part-time professionals – an architect and two social workers – to assist with developing further community infrastructure. A derelict building located near the childcare centre was repaired by local men to create a new community centre, which housed several income-generation projects and provided a meeting place for residents. A multidisciplinary forum began to emerge, including researchers from the Latin American Faculty of Social Science (FLACSO), the health centre, the school, the kindergarten, the childcare centre, and religious groups, architects, doctors and social workers. The network coordinated initiatives, shared expertise and pooled resources.

This led to the launch of the Integral Improvement Programme in 1990, which supported housing improvements, access roads and land regularization, including tenure rights, provision of water and sanitation, and child health and education efforts. The programme was supported by the International Institute of Environment and Development (IIED Latin America), along with municipal and provincial governments. Following the *barrio*'s first municipal election, 16 municipal councillors and other leaders underwent leadership training and developed the cooperative advocacy group Nuestra Tierra ('Our Land'). The cooperative focused on formalizing tenure and improving housing through negotiations with the municipality of San Fernando, and launched successful campaigns for waste collection, water and sewer provision and public lighting. The childcare centre obtained continuing funding for 100 spaces, including a programme to assist 70 primary school students with learning difficulties. They also consulted with youth aged 8 to 16, and developed sewing, football and artistic expression activities. By 1996, the municipality of San Fernando had donated a 7 hectare site to lower density in the *barrio* (Schusterman and Hardoy, 1997, pp100–110).

At this stage, the IIED expanded its efforts to five other low-income neighbourhoods in San Fernando, each with between 500 and 2000 households, and all containing a relatively high proportion of indigenous people. The first stage involved community consultation with the following four 'vulnerable groups': people over 60 with low incomes; women heads of households with children under the age of 14; young people between the ages of 14 and 24; and people with a disability. The next stages were prioritization and programme development, in conjunction with over 20 organizations representing these communities. While the overall aim was poverty reduction, the relationship between violence, low educational outcomes, unemployment, social isolation, health issues related to lack of infrastructure and poverty was acknowledged. There were differences in the emphases of the organizations representing vulnerable groups. Seniors developed initiatives focused on improving social connectedness and health through dance and yoga classes, movies and games, and a newsletter. The women's organizations focused on awareness-raising on domestic violence and reproductive rights, employment generation through a catering company and provision of childcare. The young people developed a school work assistance centre to prevent dropping out, training of 120 youth to be 'community promoters' and peacemakers, and employment training related to new construction. The people with disabilities were hardest to consult with (owing to there being no pre-existing community organization); but eventually a new organization was created to promote awareness of rights and resources, both among families and the larger community. The new organization also developed training in prevention and detection of disabilities among infants. Youth and women's groups collaborated on computer training, women and seniors groups collaborated on assistance in formalizing tenure and getting housing repairs, and seniors and people with disabilities collaborated in training 35 home helpers. All four sets of organizations collaborated on the construction and running of a community centre (Schusterman et al, 2002).

Outcomes from San Jorge after ten years included the emergence of grassroots leadership and neighbourhood governance mechanisms, which in turn were able to create an avenue for neighbourhood-based identification of problems and resources to deal with these problems, and then broker for improved housing, water, sewerage and social infrastructure with the municipality. Outcomes from the other neighbourhoods after two years included greater collaboration from organizations and the development of a number of programmes; but it was too early to say after two years whether these partnerships and programmes were sustainable. Lessons from all of these initiatives include the importance of long-term investment in community leadership and capacity-building. Efforts to obtain regular water and sanitation, regularize tenure and provide social infrastructure in San Jorge took almost ten years of effort and flexible funding from international agencies. The total cost of these efforts in San Jorge was not large, however: under US$800,000 over the period of 1987–1996 (Shusterman and Hardoy, 1997, p98). Efforts to improve housing, employment and health outcomes were linked to the prevention of violence and insecurity. A focus on particular vulnerable groups in San Fernando, as a whole, helped to develop a diversity of integrated neighbourhood-based initiatives, including a focus on gender. It would have been difficult to obtain a baseline estimate of insecurity and violence in these neighbourhoods due to police and social service neglect prior to the community development work. There was no initial victimization survey. However, several of the community programmes developed (services for youth to stay in school, public education on violence against women and training of youth as 'peacemakers') have been identified in other contexts as promising practices to prevent violence.

Box 4.3 *Tastrupgardsvej Estate: Reducing youth crime and violence in public housing in Copenhagen, Denmark*

The Tastrupgardsvej Estate in Copenhagen, Denmark, was built during the 1970s. It is a set of high-rises comprising 912 flats, with 2500 residents. Seventy per cent of the residents were born outside Denmark, with one third from Turkey. There is a large youth population (47 per cent) and the average household income on the estate is less than two-thirds of the national average. Unemployment is high among the youth on the estate, particularly those with limited knowledge of Danish. When the project began, there were concerns about crime and violence among the young men on the estate, as well as anti-social behaviour associated with alcohol and drug abuse. These concerns had been expressed by the tenant association, dominated by Danish-born residents, as well as by the police and the housing authority.

Denmark has a programme of providing tenant counsellors on public housing estates, co-funded by the local housing authorities, municipalities and the national housing service. Stig Christenson has worked under the direction of the tenant association in Tastrupgardsvej Estate since 1995. His work consists of consulting with residents, assisting in the development of pilot programmes to address their concerns, then helping to develop funding proposals to continue programmes that are successful.

One of the first priorities was to create a community centre on the estate. Eight ground-floor flats were redesigned into a 'one-stop shop' for community services, including welfare benefits, an employment service and Danish-language classes. Twenty-three clubs meet there, including one for youth with special needs. Specialized Danish-language classes included one for young Muslim women, publicly supported by the local imam.

Links with local sporting associations have led to trips and outings for children. There is a go-cart club called Burning Rubber for under 18s, with five soldiers who act as 'father figures' or mentors to young boys, many of whom have little interaction with their own fathers. Job Express is an organization based on the estate that furthers contacts between local businesses and migrant youth aged 18 to 24. It has found employment for 320 people in the last few years, including several youth who have previously been in trouble with the law. Strong links with local social services and the police have led to successful re-integration of several young people previously convicted of non-violent offences, including, in several cases, providing small flats to youth who have been rejected by their families.

The aim of these programmes is to 'cut off the supply of young men passing from school to crime', according to Kristenson. Between 2000 and 2005, reported crimes and anti-social behaviour on the estate declined by 20 per cent, and complaints about fear of crime no longer dominate tenant council discussions and the tenant counsellor's time (Capobianco, 2006, p12).

Some lessons from this initiative appear to be similar to the Buenos Aires neighbourhood case study. First, a long timeframe (ten years in both cases) is necessary to see substantive results. In this case, positive results appear tied to the longevity of one community development worker embedded in the neighbourhood, who over time was able to know and be trusted by the local individuals, businesses and agencies. The process of identifying a problem, developing a pilot to deal with the problem, and then obtaining long-term funding once the pilot has proven successful can work only when there is a highly skilled and knowledgeable coordinator. It also helped that this case study focused on a particular group's needs (in this case, young men) within a relatively resource-rich environment.

Who might be involved in community safety partnerships at the neighbour-hood level? The two case studies presented in Boxes 4.2 and 4.3 suggest a range of partners: locally based organizations such as youth services, women's serv-ices, seniors' services and services for new migrants and people with disabilities; community development workers (whose wages would almost certainly be paid for by a higher level of government or a charity); faith-based organizations (the local church in Buenos Aires and the local imam in Tastrupgardsvej Estate); local businesses; sports associations; police in the Copenhagen example, but not the Buenos Aires example; and various local and senior government departments. People not directly involved in organizations could access resources and become involved in projects, through public meetings in the Buenos Aires example and through the one-stop shop in the Copenhagen example.

In both cases, creating a community centre for groups to meet was a first crucial step. There was also a certain measure of leadership and organizational development, particularly in the case of Buenos Aires: creating a neighbourhood governance structure where none previously existed. There was a previously exist-ing neighbourhood governance structure in the Copenhagen example; but the implication is that it was not very representative or effective.

Buenos Aires can be characterized as a grassroots coalition despite its profes-sional staff being drawn from international aid organizations since its aim was to develop neighbourhood-level leadership. Tastrupgardsvej Estate can be charac-terized as a professional coalition. Both examples used local human resources in innovative ways: the sewing and catering enterprises built on individual skill sets in the Buenos Aires example, and the use of soldiers as mentors in the Copen-hagen example (a situation inconceivable in Argentina, with its recent history of brutal military dictatorships). Local employment in service delivery was devel-oped in both cases.

There are problems inherent in almost all neighbourhood-based initiatives. One is the relative fiscal and political powerlessness of individual neighbourhoods, particularly when compared with higher levels of governance. Rosenbaum (2002, p185) discusses neighbourhood-based community action teams in Salt Lake City, US, who met weekly to engage in local problem-solving around crime and insecurity. They were initially comprised of a police officer, a probation officer, a city prosecutor, a community development worker, a youth/family specialist and a community relations coordinator – in other words, a classic professional coali-tion. The neighbourhood teams were able to bond with one another and the local community. However, they faced bureaucratic obstacles due to the formal nature of many of the entities that they represented. As departments, the police and justice bureaucracies were not able to implement many of the innovative ideas generated at the neighbourhood level because of rigid hierarchies and distrust among the parent agencies. This suggests a problem also evident in the story of San José: that neighbourhoods, particularly poor neighbourhoods, often have to fight larger entities, such as police forces and local and senior government, to obtain their rights.

Rosenbaum (2002) provides a slightly different lesson on neighbourhood partnerships arising from the large-scale US effort Operation Weed and Seed, which operated in 200 neighbourhoods with high levels of drug-related violent crime. They were intended to develop comprehensive and coordinated strategies that would involve both more effective policing and criminal justice responses, and longer-term community-led prevention strategies. Evaluations indicated that while inter-agency cooperation among local and federal police was improved in almost all sites, the prosecutors' offices did not necessarily develop effective interaction with the police; in most cases, preventive social services were slow to develop. Reasons for these results were not difficult to find. First, the budget for social services was less than one quarter the budget for increased policing. Second, the diversity of viewpoints, the biggest source of potential success, was also the partnership's greatest weakness. Various stakeholders brought very different politics and organizational cultures, with no neutral observer to facilitate or lead the group.

Perhaps most importantly, there was widespread criticism by the groups most affected (young men and poor residents) that they were not involved or, if involved in a limited fashion, were not listened to. There was little leadership development, and both community organizations and social service agencies felt that they were outnumbered and overpowered by various arms of policing and prosecutions. In turn, government officials charged that it was difficult to find community leaders, given feelings of hopelessness and despair, fear of gang retaliation, deep-seated distrust of government agencies and the police, in particular, and the impacts of poverty and lack of education on the ability to lead. Those community members who participated were not necessarily representative since they were more likely to be isolated 'do-gooders', and there were various community factions competing for legitimacy, making it difficult to decide who should be invited to the partnership. Having professionals and grassroots representatives at the same table was problematic because of their different styles of work, with professionals able to spend more time preparing for, attending and following up from meetings. Professionals also tended to dominate the discussion and be more aware of the unwritten 'rules' of meetings. Involving the community made for slower meetings and delayed the ability to act – 'lean and mean' being seen as more efficient. It also meant that certain confidential information about individuals, families and addresses could not be shared (Rosenbaum, 2002, pp185–188).

This two-way criticism is common within neighbourhood-scale community safety partnerships. Because this is the scale closest to 'the community', which, of course, is never a unitary group, community members feel that they should be treated as the experts on identifying neighbourhood problems and resources. They are *grassroots experts of local experience*. On the other hand, police officers, social workers and urban planners, to name three professions, can all have many years of experience in many neighbourhoods working on a particular issue. They are *experts of professional experience*. The potential conflicts between these two notions of expertise will come up many times in the next two chapters, and there is no easy resolution. To give one anecdotal example, I was interviewing a neighbourhood leader who was a new migrant to Melbourne, Australia, from the Horn of Africa. I asked her about violence prevention services to this rapidly growing group of new migrant women, who generally were clustered in several public housing sites. She said that the state government had funded a number of public health nurses to provide information on the prevention of female genital mutilation in 'the community', which actually consisted of several ethnic, religious and linguistic communities, some of whom did not practice female genital mutilation. In several cases, the nurses brought translators, and the women, relieved to be speaking in their language to a government representative for the first time since their move to Australia, complained about encounters with racism in attempts to obtain housing and employment, and family conflicts that were not classified by them as intimate partner violence, but were related to reunification or separation after years of collective conflict and living in refugee camps. This was how they defined their own violence problems; but the public health nurses did not necessarily know how to assist them. For instance, they might know of a domestic violence service, but not a service that could provide culturally sensitive family counselling (there is such a service for people affected by torture in their home countries; but it was not known to several of the nurses). Furthermore, the initiative was being evaluated on the ability to prevent female genital mutilation, not to assist in more general settlement issues, and the public health nurses had large case loads and a limited amount of time to spend on what they saw as side issues.

At first glance, this might seem different from the problems affecting the Weed and Seed sites; but it was not. In Weed and Seed, a problem was defined by the national government as 'drug-related violent crime'. The partnership and policy mechanisms to combat the problem, as well as the ways to evaluate the problem, were largely standardized across neighbourhoods. In the Australian programme to eradicate female genital mutilation among new migrant women, the problem, mechanisms and evaluation criteria were also being decided in a top-down fashion. This top-down decision-making facilitates easier cross-site evaluations of effectiveness, and also improves the efficiency of a focused programme. However, by not putting the time and money into leadership development at the neighbourhood level, related problems and innovative solutions that might come out through a bottom-up process were being neglected, and the community affected was not being empowered as they were in the Buenos Aires example (see Box 4.2). In the Copenhagen example (see Box 4.3), although there was little mention of leadership development, at least there was an involved worker who got to know neighbourhood problems and resources over a long period of time and whose remit was wide enough to encompass a range of violence-related issues. The ongoing tension between subsidiarity and standardization is an issue of democratic governance and can be found even at the theoretically most democratic scale of the neighbourhood.

It is perhaps easier for neighbourhood-scale organizing to be flexible and innovative than initiatives at the larger scales; but neighbourhood initiatives have to interact with these more powerful scales for support and action. As discussed earlier, the tension between working styles of the grassroots, leaders and professionals can be difficult. Again, I can give a personal anecdote to illustrate this tension. Although I began my work life as a community organizer, I went on to work for the City of Toronto for many years. Part of my job duties at one point was to evaluate grant proposals and reports. I was talking to a grassroots activist, involved in setting up and managing a community recreation centre, about her report on a grant. 'It says here that Julio got his running shoes stolen, and he came to you, and you talked to Antonio because he was caught stealing at the centre before, and he didn't say anything at the time; but Julio's sneakers were returned to the centre the next day', I read out to her. 'Yes: you asked about impacts of this grant on community safety', she replied. 'Do you have any statistics as well?' I asked. 'Because this is a great story, but the politicians will want to see some numbers before they give you any more money.' This anecdote illustrates the problem with what is paradoxically the greatest strength of the neighbourhood scale: when everyone is treated as an individual with individual concerns and needs, it becomes difficult to generalize trends within and across sites.

Coordination at the city scale

The next level, and there is quite a jump, is to the local governance scale. In current '100 mile cities' with millions of inhabitants (Sudjic, 1992), some cities have very large and powerful metropolitan governments covering most of the built-up area of cities, while other cities are divided up into smaller jurisdictional entities with weak local governance structures. Local governments are sometimes, although not always, responsible for policing, public transport, welfare, public education, public housing and public health services (which, in turn, may or may not have separately appointed boards of management). In most cases, local governments are responsible for day-to-day spatial planning decisions, ranging from the location of physical infrastructure, such as water and sewage lines, to social infrastructure, such as libraries and community centres, to zoning decisions governing the location, size and design of housing, offices and shopping areas. They also tend to be responsible for enforcing building, fire and health code infractions, provision of public parks and playgrounds, and the maintenance of local footpaths and roads. In this era of economic globalization and urbanization, local governments have often taken on additional responsibilities, either because of downloading by senior governments or because of bottom-up pressure from citizens. However, the fiscal situation of local governments is often limited by their powers of taxation and their ability to make by-laws by senior government legislation. Most local governments are dependent upon property taxes (necessarily lower in areas of higher need) and transfer payments from senior governments. Local governance also encompasses the decision-making power of neighbourhood groups, business coalitions, developers, agencies and other actors in the political process. Two examples of local governance-based community safety initiatives, domestic violence coalitions in Duluth, US, and London, UK, and a violence prevention campaign with a broad mandate in Bogotá, Colombia, are described in Boxes 4.4 and 4.5. Box 4.6 describes two rural violence prevention campaigns in Canada and Ghana.

Box 4.4 *Community safety begins at home: Coordinated intimate partner abuse prevention in Duluth, US, and London, UK*

Some of the most successful long-term local-scale initiatives to prevent violence have focused on the prevention of intimate partner abuse from a feminist perspective. One of the first examples, and perhaps the best known, is the Domestic Abuse Intervention Project in Duluth, US, a mid-sized city of a little under 200,000 people (Sheppard and Pence, 1999).

The project began in 1981 as a response to a mandatory arrest policy for all people accused of domestic violence. The choices available to the police and courts were jail, community service, probation, fines or marriage counselling. There were concerns by women's service agencies that while marriage counselling would allow further intimidation of the female victim, leading to dropping of charges, jail might also lead to negative economic consequences for the woman and children victims of domestic violence. None of these choices focused on the prevention of recidivism or further abuse by the offender, and the choices also did not prioritize the needs of the victims.

Several agencies began to work together to develop an integrated response, including police, the public prosecutors' office, the probation department, the local women's shelter, and physical and mental health services. They developed a shared framework for intervention, emphasizing the victims' right to protection from further harm. Protocols, policies and programmes followed, including training for police, courts, public health nurses and other appropriate actors on how to refer to one another in supporting adult and child victims. The philosophy of the Duluth Domestic Abuse Intervention Project was that to make fundamental changes in a community's approach to violence against women, individual practitioners must work cooperatively, guided by training, job descriptions and standardized practices that all reflect desired changes. The project has also stressed continual evaluation and enhancement to meet not only the needs of the general 'community', but of 'people of colour, the lesbian/gay/bisexual community, and low-income people' (Minnesota Program Development, 2007). A 24-week batterer intervention treatment programme was developed during the early 1980s that has been used across the US and more than a dozen other countries. Several offshoot programmes, including the Native American-led Mending the Sacred Hoop Project (see Chapter 3), followed in the 1990s and the present decade.

A number of evaluations have been carried out of the Duluth coordinated model of service delivery. Eighty per cent of the female victims who have encountered the services are happy with the approach, and 69 per cent reported that they had not experienced further physical abuse after one year (Shaw and Capobianco, 2004, p40). The introduction of a domestic violence screening protocol for public health nurses, such as maternal and child health nurses who undertake mandatory post-natal visits, increased the number of victims supplied with information and, consequently, using more domestic violence prevention services (Sheppard et al, 1999). While a number of previous evaluations had proven the effectiveness of the batterer intervention programme as it is practised in Duluth, a 2003 National Institute of Justice study appeared to suggest that the Duluth model applied in other places without an adequate service network in place was not effective in preventing repeat victimization (Jackson et al, 2003; this study will be discussed further in Chapter 6).

The Duluth example has inspired dozens of local governance initiatives, including the London UK Domestic Violence Strategy. When metropolitan governance was restored to London in 2000, one of the first priorities of the new Mayor Ken Livingstone (who had also been head of the Greater London Council at the time of its abolition by senior government in 1986) was addressing the issue of domestic violence effectively. The first strategy, entitled *One in Four* and published in 2001 (Association of London Government, 2001), was followed by a second strategy published in 2005 (Greater London Authority, 2005), which involves a greater range of partners and powers. A number of specialized reports have been published, including reports of projects on the role of faith organizations in preventing domestic violence and the links between domestic violence and substance abuse. There have also been annual reports published since 2001, measuring progress on the strategy's priorities, and awards for neighbourhood- or interest group-specific best practices (e.g. Greater London Authority, 2006).

The priorities include development and strengthening of new services, as well as better coordination across this metropolis of 7.5 million people. Like Duluth, services involved include courts, police, women's advocacy and support services, the health sector, schools and community-based children's services. The project's vision includes coordinated services for women and children experiencing domestic violence, an approach that encourages self-determination and empowerment, and clear public messages to men, women and children that society will not tolerate domestic violence. For practitioners, the emphasis has been on a central information bank that disseminates good practice, training and support for all relevant staff, and standard criteria against which services can be assessed and compared. For funders and government organizations, the priority is better data to ensure that future services can be more effectively targeted. The benefits for Londoners will be a safer community, the upholding of human rights, a reduction in the severity of domestic violence and an increase in service user satisfaction. As the mayor of London says, in the introduction to the latest progress report, 'community safety must begin at home' (Greater London Authority, 2006, p5).

The strategy has been successful in unlocking new sources of government and charitable funding to develop domestic violence advocacy services in all 33 London boroughs (sub-metropolitan local governments), increasing the number of specialist or integrated domestic violence courts, improving primary healthcare identification of and responses to abuse, expanding services that enable abused women to stay safely in their homes, and improving service provision to abused women from disadvantaged groups, such as new migrants, racial minorities and people with disabilities. Community-based services for children affected by domestic violence have been improved, as has school-based domestic violence prevention education. Protocols for information-sharing, referrals and risk assessments have been developed between agencies, and monitoring systems have been established with quarterly reports.

Lessons from these two initiatives are applicable to all local community safety strategies. They include broad membership from as wide a range of services as possible; examining the needs of minority cultures, as well as the majority culture; the need to develop a shared vision that leads to shared protocols, information-sharing and policies; and perhaps most importantly, an emphasis on the needs of both victims and offenders to access as broad a range of services as is possible.

Box 4.5 *Bogotá's integral plan on security and co-existence*

Bogotá is the capital and largest city of Colombia, one of the most violent countries in the world. Its population is 6.5 million. During the 1980s and 1990s, Colombia was going through a painful process of civil war and social and economic turmoil, leading to calls for decentralization and democratization at the national level that resulted in a 1991 constitution devolving policing and other powers to cities (Rojas, 2002, p3; Acero, 2006). In 1993, Bogotá's murder rate was the highest it had ever been: 80 people per 100,000. For the first time, the city had a higher murder rate than the rest of the country despite being untouched directly by the political violence of other regions. An account by a local writer of Bogotá's metamorphosis gives a vivid impression of the city in 1991:'A dirty city, disorganized, with a chaotic system of transportation, parks covered with garbage and wild grass, a nobody's land with a police force that it was better to avoid' (Andres Guerera, in Rojas, 2002, p5).

In 1995, under the leadership of new Mayor Antonus Mockus, the former rector of Colombia National University, the City of Bogotá developed a comprehensive and integrated community safety action plan. The first step was to establish an observatory, associated with the Colombia National University, with technical assistance from Georgetown University in the US. This group developed and analysed local data on causes of violence and insecurity, where violence occurred and what appeared to be triggering violent interactions. The resultant plan had a number of principles: strengthening police, while making them more accountable to the city administration and to citizens; evaluating progress by monitoring every programme and developing indicators; developing 'civic culture' from tolerance of everyday violence to rejection of violence; and making public spaces more lively through a combination of increased enforcement of crime and traffic violations, and special events. There was an emphasis on changing the life circumstances of those who are vulnerable, including the homeless and slum dwellers, aboriginal people, young people, prostitutes and those displaced from their homes by violence (both internal refugees and women and children in violent homes). The safety action plan was tied to a larger city development plan, which also addressed slum conditions, access to primary education and public transportation issues.

There were two hallmarks of this approach. First, a combination of short-term initiatives with longer-term social development helped to placate citizens who needed to see quick action, while continuing to address root causes of violence. Within the first year of the plan, at least three short-term actions were taken. First, access to guns and gunpowder was severely restricted, particularly for children. Second, establishments that served alcohol were regulated to close at 1.00 am and establishments that sold alcohol were more closely monitored – measures nicknamed the Squares Law, but popular nonetheless. Third, the transit police, who were widely believed to be a hotbed of corruption, were abolished.

Longer-term social development and urban design campaigns worked on instilling a civic culture of civility, reinforcing pedestrian use of public space and including people in local decision-making. Community leaders in Bogotá's ten local districts were trained in conflict resolution techniques, and neighbourhood conflicts were referred by police to these leaders. Seven thousand police–community partnerships, or 'local security fronts', were established. Over 350,000 'thumbs up/thumbs down' cards were distributed so that people could comment silently on traffic and other minor neighbourhood conflicts, rather than yelling or using their fists. When Mockus decided to run for president and was replaced by Enrique Penalosa, another independent candidate, as mayor in 1997, the new mayor established nearly 1000 new parks, 600,000 metres of new footpaths, and 120 kilometres of bicycle trails. He also continued to support Mockus's plan for an ambitious new public transport system, *Transmilenio*, which did much to improve traffic congestion and safety. Two of the most violent areas in Bogotá – Avenida Caracas and the Cartucho zone – underwent urban renewal to reduce car use and make them more walkable and public transportation friendly. From 2000 onwards, a consultative priority-setting model was used to engage citizens. At public meetings, citizens were urged to recommend 'hints' for local government action at events such as the International Book Fair. These would then be developed into 'how to' initiatives and priorities decided at further public meetings, through newspapers and surveys. For instance, 'valuing children as educators of adults' was followed by a campaign that hired and trained young people who had previously been gang members or prostitutes as 'civic guides', who work at high-accident intersections, at public events, and in libraries and heritage buildings (Rojas, 2002, p24). Five years into its implementation, almost 40 per cent of Bogotáns said that they were at least 'somewhat' informed about the development plan (Rojas, 2002, p14)

The second hallmark of Bogotá's community safety plan was a highly imaginative set of public campaigns and events that ensured that people were actively engaged in strategies, and spread out responsibility to challenge cultures of violence.

Both mayors used symbolic public events and campaigns to reinforce the right to both traffic and personal safety. In 2000, Penalosa declared a Car Free Day, which has been repeated annually after a referendum where citizens give 'permission' for this event to take place. A trial programme, where 20 mimes were hired to tease car drivers and pedestrians who flouted traffic laws, was extended to hire 420 mimes at problematic intersections, a pacifist and employment-generating solution to an ongoing problem. Fifteen hundred white stars were painted by public works officials where pedestrians had been killed.

Alarmed at the incidents of violence and intimation by taxi drivers, Mockus asked people to call the city hall if they found a friendly taxi driver. One hundred and fifty people did so, and Mockus held a party for them at the city hall, dubbing them Knights of the Zebra (Bogotá's taxis are black and white), and also using the opportunity to consult with them about repercussions for less tolerable drivers. Approximately 50,000 people participated in two Vaccination against Violence campaigns, which asked people to speak with a psychologist or social worker, to draw a picture of someone who had hurt them as a child, and to then pop the balloon (Rojas, 2002, p23). Another campaign, Let Arms Rest in Peace This Christmas, which encouraged the voluntary handing in of firearms in exchange for a teaspoon made of molten metal with the legend 'I used to be a weapon'. Twenty-five hundred guns were turned in during this campaign (Rojas, 2002, p23). Mockus told the story of a three-year-old girl who had asked to meet with him as a birthday present. Her mother told him that every time she threatened to hit the child, the child would say she was going to call the mayor (Caballero, 2004).

Mockus's best-known symbolic event is perhaps the annual Women's Night Outs, which commenced in 2002. At the first Women's Night Out, 70,000 women danced in streets, received discounts at local restaurants, and attended all-night parties and concerts held throughout the city, including the central boulevard of Bogotá, which was closed off to traffic. Men were urged to stay at home with their children, and Mockus himself was photographed reading to his four-year-old daughter. In the weeks preceding the event, men were urged to stay at home that night, and if they had to be out, to present 'safe conduct passes' signed by a woman. The safe conduct passes could be clipped from newspapers, downloaded off the internet or picked up at local police stations. The male chief of police resigned for the night in favour of a female deputy, and the city was patrolled by 1500 female police officers and fire fighters. The event, which was intended to bring attention to both street and domestic violence against women, was widely covered locally and internationally. Some of the 200,000 men who ventured onto the street were openly contemptuous of the assembled women and criticized Mockus in the media. In turn, there were incidents of women catcalling men, as well as applause for men who were waving from windows. There were only six felony arrests that night, a much lower than average arrest rate for a Friday night. The event was repeated annually, with growing attendance each year (Caballero, 2004).

It is difficult to separate out the impact of these cultural approaches from broader educational, employment generation and housing improvement programmes undertaken in Bogotá over the past 12 years. The murder rate in Bogotá has fallen by over 70 per cent, from 80/100,000 in 1993 to 22/100,000 in 2005 (Acero, 2006). The murder rate is now half the national average, and much lower than in Medellín and Cali, both of which cities had previously established violence prevention campaigns (Rojas, 2002, pp20, 23). Traffic fatalities have also decreased dramatically, from 23.5/100,000 in 1995 to 8.7/100,000 in 2004 (Acero, 2006). The police have improved in efficiency and honesty, with arrest rates increasing by 400 per cent, without an increase in numbers (Shaw, 2006, p11). The city's credit rating has increased, and the city was able to collect three times the property tax revenues in 2002 than it did in 1990. In fact, when Mockus asked people to pay a voluntary 10 per cent surcharge on their property taxes if they were happy with increased services, 63,000 people did so (Caballero, 2004). The improvement of particular crime hot spots would appear to have had an impact as well, with reported robberies decreasing in the improved Cartucho district by 70 per cent between 2000 and 2003 (Shaw, 2006, p12). However, perceptions of security have not improved, a somewhat puzzling and discouraging result that appears to be related to continuing high unemployment rates (Rojas, 2002, pp24–25). There are continuing concerns about corruption and lack of transparency in local government, and about social exclusion of homeless youth (Rojas, 2002, p28).

Why has the community safety action plan had such impressive results? Strong leadership by both Mockus and Penalosa is undoubtedly a strong factor. Another factor is the political and social consensus that was built up: three successive mayors have supported an integrated strategy over 12 years, with strong public support. But that consensus would not have occurred without a combination of quick visible measures such as the Squares Law and broad-based symbolic campaigns. The programme was thus able to be institutionalized both within the local government and within the imaginations of a large proportion of residents. More than any one campaign or symbolic event, the linking of programmes and issues within the integrated plan and the commitment to keeping violence prevention as an issue in public consciousness appear to have resulted in a significant positive change in the city.

Box 4.6 *Local governance for community safety in rural areas:*
The cases of rural British Columbia, Canada, and Kadjebi district, Ghana

Rural areas are often assumed to be safer than urban areas; but this may not be true (Panelli et al, 2004). Small towns often have large numbers of unemployed and out-of-school young people with alcohol and drug issues and the casual violence associated with these substances, and family violence can thrive in isolated areas without appropriate services. Rural problems are often compounded by poor economic and social conditions leading to few options for employment and higher education; poorly funded health, social and emergency services that are spread out geographically; low provision of public transportation and roads in marginal condition; no access to telephone or internet services; local decision-making processes that are inaccessible because of distance and transportation factors; and increased vulnerability and fear of exposure and retaliation in small communities where everyone may be related or know other people's business (Dame and Grant, 2002, p2; Panelli et al, 2004). Moreover, newcomers, whether new migrants drawn to employment in farming and resource extraction or people seeking a rural lifestyle, create much more diversity than is commonly attributed to rural areas (O'Malley, 2000; Panelli et al, 2004). However, there are advantages to organizing in order to prevent violence in a rural setting: people may be accustomed to working together for the common good with limited resources; long-term residents may know and care for one another in a way that is rarely possible in an urban community; residents may wear many hats and personally know the people in positions of authority (O'Malley, 2000, p6).

British Columbia is the westernmost province of Canada. Aside from the third largest city in Canada, Vancouver, and the provincial capital, Victoria, much of the population is based in small towns that were founded based on mineral and forestry resources, and which are often isolated from one another by mountains, rivers and the Pacific Ocean. Cowichan Valley is a rural farming region, found in the middle of British Columbia's largest island, Vancouver Island. Its population is 75,000 people, spread across 373,000 hectares, and its largest town, Duncan, has only 5000 residents.

In 1979, the Cowichan Violence against Women Society began in Duncan as a part-time service dedicated to helping female victims of sexual and physical assault. In 1996, the Cowichan Valley Safer Futures programme was developed by the society to advocate for local government action on violence against women. The project began by organizing a number of women's safety audits in the region (see Chapter 5), focusing on places that were known by the police and by community organizations to be 'hot spots' for crime and insecurity: a bus terminus in one town, a rural recreation centre in another small community area, a commercial area with several bars and a public park in a third town. They then worked with the local authorities, businesses and community organizations to improve these spots. For instance, the recreation centre had additional lighting installed near the parking area and around entrances; signage was improved in relation to access for people with disabilities; an information kiosk was built at minimal cost for information on local events and services, including violence prevention programmes; staff procedures and training were improved for their own safety and the safety of recreation centre users; the staffing area was relocated closer to the changing rooms; and programming was expanded to encourage non-athletic forms of recreation since the centre was used almost exclusively by young men (Dame and Grant, 2002, pp92–94).The group also advocated entrenching planning for safer communities in their municipal policies and guidelines. For instance, one village development plan developed an objective to 'provide a safe, accessible and clean community ... where all segments of the population, inclusive of race, ability, income and gender, are able to live and work without fear of their personal safety', supported by a policy that 'the Regional Board shall encourage the development of initiatives which promote cooperative efforts between residents, business and community groups to improve women's and children's safety, in particular, and the public's safety generally', and involving a programme to improve street lighting and reduce speed limits on the main street, leading to the development of a youth centre in the local elementary school and a seniors' residence near the local shops (Dame and Grant, 2002, pp112–113). The Safer Futures programme and its parent organization, Cowichan Violence against Women Society, continued to advocate for better funding for local service provision, improved education and awareness about violence against women, and for increasing the number of women at all levels of governance (Cowichan Safer Futures Program, 2003).

Over the next ten years, the Cowichan Valley Safer Futures programme developed tools that have been used throughout rural British Columbia, as well as internationally: a rural safety audit guide, a planners' guide to incorporating safety in rural planning, a checklist for planning departments and commissions, a checklist for local governments, and videos and a well-used website. Another rural region in British Columbia, the Boundary District, also developed a community plan to prevent relationship violence and sexual assault in 1998 in the face of lack of service infrastructure, implemented over the next three years (O'Malley, 2000; Dame and Grant, 2002, pp49, 114).These two regions formed the basis for a province-wide coalition on rural women and community safety that has provided training workshops and disseminated resources (Cowichan Safer Futures Program, 2007).

Safer Futures has been successful in terms of programme evaluation — that is, their projects, such as safety audits, have led to specific public space improvements, and they have been successful in obtaining funding from government to produce and disseminate training materials. They are also a successful example of *scaling-up*, an initiative at one scale of governance (local), which has gone on to influence a larger scale (provincial/national). They have not undertaken an impact evaluation, either in terms of increased use and satisfaction of the particular sites that have been transformed due to safety audit recommendations or changed policies, or violence/insecurity data in the Cowichan Valley. Reasons for their success appear to include being based in a long-serving agency with a good reputation within the region, having one dedicated staff person (Terri Dame) and one long-term consultant (Ali Grant) who have worked on the initiative for over ten years, and relatively harmonious relationships with local political leaders, service providers and funders, all of which took time to develop.

A very different form of organizing around women's safety issues can be seen in Kadjebi district, a rural province in western Ghana with a population of 52,000. Poverty, unemployment and illiteracy were higher than the average in the rest of the country, and family violence was also believed to be high, although information on incidence was limited. Across Ghana, the district level of governance is a focus for development activities; but gender-disaggregated statistics from the 1990s revealed that fewer than 10 per cent of district assembly members were women (IULA, 2001, p9). In 2000, the Kadjebi District Assembly embarked on a series of activities to address women's empowerment and the reduction of violence. This included using queen mothers, female elders in rural areas, to promote positive messages about educating girls and to take a more formal role in the district's economic and social development through the formation of an association; training and financially supporting women to seek positions in local government, which increased the number of female councillors from 1 to 14 in the course of a single electoral cycle; using drumming and ululating (yelling in a specific way) in local markets to disseminate information about crimes against women; and providing training to women selling in local markets on health, fire hazards and how to respond in all forms of emergencies, including violent incidents. The district was judged most gender sensitive by the National Association of Local Governments in 2003, and was awarded two computers and two fax machines as prizes (*Modern Ghana*, 2003; Whitzman et al, 2004, p26).

In some ways, this example is the complete opposite from Cowichan Valley: directly supported by local government, with formal goals and benchmarks (e.g. increasing the number of elected women in local government at the next election), and using cultural, educational and economic development

> approaches, rather than planning approaches. However, the two initiatives share a commitment to consultation and empowerment of grassroots women who have not previously been involved in governance issues, and a perspective that combines improvements to public space with an acknowledgement that the majority of violence takes place in homes and within families.

Local governance models do not have to be led by local government. The Duluth and Cowichan Valley projects were not managed or even particularly associated with local government, despite the involvement of services that were funded and administered by local government. However, when local government is involved in a violence prevention campaign, the list of potential key partners is much greater than at the neighbourhood scale.

Because directly elected politicians are more common at the city than the neighbourhood scale, they assume a greater importance. The mayoral leadership of Antonus Mockus and Ken Livingstone has been noted in the case studies of Bogotá and London (see Boxes 4.4 and 4.5). Not every mayor is interested in, or capable of, leading a violence prevention initiative. And the risk of a political champion is that when that politician is voted out, all of the policies that he or she was associated with are relegated to the dustbin as well. But a popular mayor can serve effectively as a public face for a campaign, which, if popular enough, can survive a change in mayoralty, as it did in Bogotá.

The entirety of a local government bureaucracy can be engaged in an anti-violence initiative. If policing is part of city governance, and in large cities it may make sense for this public service to be directly accountable to the local level, they can form police–community partnerships in particular neighbourhoods and on particular initiatives. What makes a successful police–community partnership has already been touched upon in the previous section on neighbourhood governance, and will also be discussed further in Chapter 7. Public health nurses, who are usually locally accountable, are another obvious example; but so, too, are researchers such as epidemiologists often associated with a public health department. Both land-use and social planning are usually associated with the local level of governance. As has already been discussed in the Cowichan Valley case study and will be elaborated upon in Chapter 6, they can be engaged in creating welcoming and secure public spaces day and night, and also in decisions that release appropriate land for social infrastructure, such as health services and community centres, which can then become 'safe spaces' for people seeking assistance with violence in the private sphere. Public transportation schedules and driver training can be improved in response to safety concerns. For example, a 'request stop' programme, allowing women to get off between bus stops after dark if it is possible for the driver to safely stop, started in Toronto Canada in

1991 and was then adopted by a number of public transportation authorities (CAFSU, 2002). If there is an economic development office, they can work with local businesses to not only make commercial areas safer from violence and theft, but also to distribute public information. If there is a public housing authority associated with local government, it can model improvements to the physical design and social infrastructure of neighbourhoods, and policies can be amended to facilitate victims of violence receiving preference on public housing waiting lists. Licensing offices can be used to enforce safety standards, such as codes of practice around the serving of alcohol and responsibility for violent incidents taking place in the vicinity of bars, or the Bogotá example of using good taxi drivers to identify what can be done about shifty or abusive taxi drivers (see Box 4.5). Building, health and fire inspectors have often worked together to close down 'problem properties' where drug dealing or other criminal activities thrive. Recreation centres and workers can provide safe and supportive activities, not only for children and young people, but for other vulnerable groups such as new migrants, older women and men, and people with disabilities. Libraries and community centres can become information distribution places, and their meeting rooms used for community organizing. In the example of Toronto, which will be discussed in Chapter 5, waste and road maintenance workers acted as extra 'eyes on the street' during the night, after they were trained to recognize and report suspicious activities in public spaces.

Local government can also be an ideal place for large-scale public education efforts. The example of Bogotá showed how the entire bureaucracy can be mobilized to close off streets for a gigantic street party, use the police to protect partiers and distribute information publicizing the party. In the example of Charlottetown, Canada, discussed in Chapter 6, local government took on a public education campaign on violence against women where a flag with the symbol of the campaign flew over the city hall, every vehicle used by the city carried the symbol of the campaign, and every information point, from kiosks where property taxes and parking fines were paid to public libraries, carried information on the campaign. Local governments can also model both education for staff on how to respond to family violence concerns of their colleagues or members of the public, and personal safety policies for staff who are particularly vulnerable because they work alone (building inspectors), work at night (waste collectors) or deal with irate members of the public (parking fine collectors). Whether it is a city of several million or a rural area with a few thousand people, citizens often primarily identify with their local area, rather than their nation, and their local government employees and services may be the most public 'face' of government.

Other than local government politicians and bureaucrats, possible actors include those already identified within the neighbourhood scale: service agencies that deal directly with violence, policing and justice; agencies that support at-risk populations (women, men, children, youth, older people, new migrants, aboriginal people, ethnic and linguistic minorities, people with disabilities, sexual minorities, drug and alcohol abusers, prostitutes, victims of crime and offenders); faith organizations; health organizations; service organizations, such as the Rotary Club or Scouts (as a potential source of volunteers or funding); housing providers; businesses; charities; education providers; sporting organizations; the media; and other levels of government that provide services or funding. Individuals or organizations representing residents or citizens, as a whole, may be identified, although direct grassroots involvement in steering committees often falls off at higher scales than the neighbourhood. While all of these actors can and should be consulted with, the actual steering committee for a community safety network should be manageably small: no more than a dozen key players. While at the neighbourhood scale or in a rural area, this number may be large enough to encompass all relevant partners, city-scale partnerships may require difficult decisions about who to exclude and include. Similarly, while the range of issues covered by a neighbourhood or rural initiative may be extensive, particularly if the initiative focuses on a particular issue such as youth violence or violence against women, it is sometimes difficult to limit the potential issues and initiatives that can be undertaken at the local scale. The issues and initiatives chosen will, in turn, determine the players around the table.

The great advantage of the city governance scale is that so many actors work at the local level, whatever their jurisdiction or source of funding (Vanderschueren, 2006, p6). However, the boundaries of particular catchment areas for policing, public health, hospitals, courts and boards of public education may bear little relation to municipal borders. This creates problems for data collection and also for programme implementation. Another advantage is that city-scale governance is seen as proximate: not only close to where people live and work, but relatively accessible in terms of human-scale governance mechanisms. The policy mechanisms controlled by city governance – land-use and social planning, education, health, public transport and roads – are often seen as directly relevant to people's lives. On the other hand, the city governance scale is often too large and seen as too powerful and impervious for grassroots involvement, certainly at the decision-making level. Despite city governance being perceived as overly bureaucratic and remote in terms of individuals and families (as expressed in the popular saying: 'You can't fight city hall'), the local scale is often powerless in comparison to senior scales of governance. Property taxes are usually the main form of financing, which are much more regressive than income taxes – that is, a disproportionate burden falls on lower-income households. City governments usually have to depend upon senior scales of government, upon charitable funding or upon partnerships with business to provide programmes and new or improved services. Cities usually do not have the capacity to create laws without senior government approval, and in the worst case scenario, such as London in 1986, the city scale of governance can actually be abolished, programmes discontinued and elected officials summarily dismissed by senior government. While subsidiarity is an excellent principle, city-scale coordination requires support and commitment from senior scales of governance.

According to UN-Habitat's Safer Cities Programme (Vanderschueren, 2006, p6), cities need four preconditions in order to work effectively on community safety and violence prevention. First, they need an adequate institutional framework and resources to address the issue. As discussed above, this support needs to come from senior scales of governance. Second, they need to develop a role that does not completely delegate the responsibility of a safer community to the police or to specialized organizations. Third, they need mechanisms to ensure participation of as wide a range of citizens as possible, such as consultation practices, public education and neighbourhood-scale initiatives. Fourth, they need measures of transparency, such as anti-corruption initiatives, regular reports updating progress on initiatives and the ability to change course over time in response to changing concerns.

Coordination at the national scale

Moving on to senior levels of government, almost all nations with larger areas or populations are subdivided into states or provinces, which, in turn, can be split into districts or counties. Funding and provision of services can sometimes be provided by four or five different scales of governance, with policing, education and health being common examples. This can be a real barrier to coordinated efforts. Depending upon the history and constitution of the country, state governments may have more powers over health, education and welfare issues than national governments, particularly in the case of federations of previously independent states. There are inherent tensions between local, state and national governments over who is responsible for which services, and these tensions are often exacerbated by different political parties being in power at each level. In Canada, for instance, the province of Quebec, which is dominated by Francophone residents, as opposed to the rest of Canada, has had a very different approach to crime and violence prevention, and what has worked there is rarely adopted by the rest of the country (Shaw and Andrew, 2005). At best, senior levels of government can offer funding, training and capacity-building; broad-based public education, advocacy, and legal and policy supports; and research, including dissemination of relevant information and lessons from best practices.

Generally, national governments are responsible for justice, employment, economic and defence policies, and most have ultimate say over education, social welfare and policing matters. National governments generally have greatest access to a range of taxation mechanisms and thus can offer transfer payments to lower forms of governance in return for their contribution to national goals. As we move up the scales of governance, they become more powerful, but also less directly accessible to citizens. While a political representative at the neighbourhood or local level might represent 5000 to 10,000 people, a political representative at the national level might represent tens of thousands, often over a large area. The opportunity for grassroots involvement in decision-making at the national level is limited. An example of a city initiative 'scaling up' to the national level is provided in Box 4.7, while an example of a small nation with an excellent reputation for top-down community safety coordination is provided in Box 4.8.

Box 4.7 *Tanzania: An example of local to national up-scaling*

Tanzania is a nation with 38 million inhabitants, located in East Africa. Like many of its African neighbours, it is in economic transition from a socialist to a market economy, and political transition from a one-party state to multiparty democracy (Andersson and Stavrou, 2000, p11). While substantial populations of Asian, Arab and European origin have left since independence, often under duress, Tanzania's religious make-up still reflects its historic position as a trading centre for the region, with approximately one third of the population being Muslim, one third Christian and one third adhering to traditional religious beliefs. Dar es Salaam is the largest city and commercial centre of Tanzania, with 2.5 million inhabitants in the city region and an extremely high annual growth rate of over 4 per cent (Mtani, 2007, p69). Despite Tanzania's relative wealth and stability in comparison with its immediate neighbours, it is beset by many of the problems found in countries of the developing world. Lack of basic infrastructure, poor health and deteriorating social conditions plague its informal settlements, which now house 75 per cent of the population. One quarter of young people are unemployed, and they represent close to two-thirds of the urban population (Andersson and Stavrou, 2000, p9). There is widespread violence and corruption and few government resources to tackle these problems. During the 1990s, the annual reported crime increase was 8.1 per cent, and these crimes were felt not only to affect urban economic and social development, but also national security, tourism, foreign investment and resultant employment (Andersson and Stavrou, 2000, p9). Over one quarter of the crimes were recorded in Dar es Salaam, despite the fact that the city's population is less than one tenth of the national population of 38 million (Andersson and Stavrou, 2000, p11). It was thus a national priority to prevent violence and crime in Tanzania's largest city, and Dar es Salaam became one of the first cities to be funded under UN-Habitat's Safer Cities Programme in 1998. The International Centre for the Prevention of Crime (ICPC) provided technical assistance, while the Dutch government provided funding.

A number of diagnostic surveys were undertaken in 1999 and 2000 to help clarify problems and suggest approaches. A survey of elected ward leaders suggested that the biggest problems were property and drug offences committed by young people (Andersson and Stavrou, 2000, p15); but a victimization survey revealed that 71 per cent of women had been physically abused in their lifetimes and 45 per cent of women had been sexually abused (Mtani, 2002, p2). A survey of 100 young offenders, mostly young men between 12 and 18, revealed long remand times before trials in Dar's lone youth court, and lack of employment or educational support to those sentenced to jail (Andersson and Stavrou, 2000). Actions thus focused on preventing criminality among young people, particularly young men, and reducing victimization among women.

One of the first actions of the Dar es Salaam Safer Cities Programme was to carry out a women's safety audit in the Manzese ward, one of the most densely populated parts of the city, as well as a regional business focal point. The audit involved both local female residents and municipal authorities. The audit identified problems such as streets once wide enough for vehicular circulation encroached upon by structures to the point that emergency and other vehicles could not enter; a large number of abandoned buildings; no street lighting or street names adding to night-time insecurity; no sewer system leading to back-ups and health hazards; no waste collection; high unemployment; use of private houses to sell 'local brews' with accompanying prostitution, loud music and fights; and widespread domestic violence exacerbated by the prevalence of alcohol and drugs. The audit recommended enforcement of local by-laws on construction blocking roads and tearing down abandoned buildings; a 'self-help' approach to street lighting where households would be encouraged to put in a light bulb in the fronts and backs of their houses, as well as the municipality providing lighting where there were no occupied houses; improved sanitation and waste disposal as a top health priority; job creation for women and youth, such as subcontracting municipal waste collection; and regularization of community security groups called 'sungusungu' who sometimes veered into vigilantism. A team consisting of a land-use planner, an economic planner and a city engineer then responded to the audit, including a repeat site visit with some of the women who had conducted the initial audit (Mtani, 2002). Street lighting was improved using the low-cost recommendation; closed streets were opened up by demolishing several illegally constructed buildings; the local authority sent warning notices to abandoned buildings and several were fixed or auctioned; and local tribunals were set up to deal with petty crimes. The women engaged in home brewing and prostitution successfully shifted to selling flour and prepared lunches instead, with business start-up funds provided by the local government (Mtani,

2007, p76). Crime in the neighbourhood was said to have decreased, although there was no formal before and after victimization survey (University College London, 2007), and audits were then replicated in several other of the 79 wards in Dar es Salaam.

The project on youth delinquency led to partnerships with non-governmental organizations (NGOs) on supporting legal income-generating activities for young people. The role of the *sungusungu* was enhanced through guidelines, training and developing institutionalized relationships with the regular police. Ward tribunals were developed to deal with petty crimes, reducing the pressure on youth courts. Training on planning for safer communities was developed through a partnership with the national planning school (Mtani, 2007).

From the beginning, there was interest expressed by other municipalities in Dar es Salaam initiatives, and with the help from the Swedish government, a national programme was developed in 2004. This programme had the twin aims of building national capacity and frameworks to support local community safety, and transferring knowledge and tools from Dar es Salaam to other locations. Eight other municipalities engaged in a pilot project in 2004 and 2005, with coordinators and potential youth and women leaders trained by Dar es Salaam staff to undertake victimization surveys, create job development programmes in partnership with local organizations, and institutionalize programmes such as the ward tribunals and *sungusungu*. The national government established a new Ministry of Public Safety and Security in 2005, with a mandate to further community policing, develop enabling legislation for local governance initiatives, support ward-level tribunals and support *sungusungu* initiatives. The Dar es Salaam coordinator became the national programme coordinator, and one of the sub-coordinators became the city coordinator. The national programme's current phase-three plan involves engaging more NGOs in developing support services for victims and offenders; public awareness campaigns on violence prevention; and improving juvenile justice programmes, such as alternative sentencing. Quarterly meetings, local-to-local and international 'twinning arrangements' with other safe city programmes and participation in regional forums are also intended to improve national capacity for local community safety initiatives. They also wish to expand their activities to other vulnerable groups, such as orphans, people living with HIV/AIDS, youths addicted to illegal drugs and the elderly (Safer Cities Tanzania Programme, 2006).

The national steering committee consists of the lead Ministry for Local Government, the City of Dar es Salaam, the national police, the justice department, the Association of Local Authorities of Tanzania, a legal and human rights NGO, the planning school, the International Labour Organization (ILO), the United Nations Development Programme (UNDP), and UN-Habitat (Safer Cities Tanzania Programme, 2006, Annex 5). Significantly absent is the World Health Organization (WHO) despite Tanzania being one of the ten countries participating in the *Multi-country Study on Women's Health and Domestic Violence against Women* (Garcia-Moreno et al, 2004) and potential synergies with the Global Campaign on Violence and Health. The national programme would benefit from a baseline and follow-up victimization survey, as well as from an external evaluation of the impacts of Dar es Salaam's work. However, the Dar es Salaam programme has accomplished remarkable success, considering its limited human and financial resources (the total budget is not publicly available; but figures from the latest phase suggest a national budget of approximately US$100,000 per year, including salaries, with this amount being the highest level of support since the programme began in 1998). The ingredients of success appear to be a low level of conflict and high degree of consensus between the six layers of government involved (nation, district, metropolitan government of Dar es Salaam, city government, directly elected wards and street-level sub-wards known as 'mtaa'); the longevity and skills of staff people such as Anna Mtani, the Dar es Salaam coordinator who has become the national coordinator; building on existing organizations, such as the *sungusungu*, and existing people resources, such as elected ward councillors; and a commitment to consultation and some measure of grassroots leadership development among youth and women.

Box 4.8 New Zealand's Crime Prevention Strategy:
A successful top-down approach

While in the Tanzania example (see Box 4.7), a successful local initiative led to national adoption of a community safety initiative, in New Zealand, local government community safety initiatives have benefited from a top-down but decentralized national programme since 1993. It was during that year that the national government created a Crime Prevention Unit, reporting directly to the Office of the Prime Minister and Cabinet, which would fund local community safety councils in return for adherence to national priorities and standards (Gauthier et al, 1999, pp23–24). New Zealand is a small, English-speaking Pacific high-income country (HIC) with a little over 4 million inhabitants. It has a relatively large proportion of indigenous Maori inhabitants (15 per cent, as opposed to less than 3 per cent in equivalent settler colonies such as Australia, Canada and the US) in a population that has been predominantly

European in origin for the past 100 years, but now has growing numbers of migrants from Asia and other Pacific islands. Although it is not a high crime or high violence society in comparison to others in the world, there were increasing concerns about family and community violence, particularly within the Maori population.

Between 1993 and 1999, approximately 60 safer community councils (SCCs) were created through memorandums of understanding with local governments and indigenous councils. Each SCC had the following roles: identifying and prioritizing local crime prevention issues; coordinating crime prevention activities; sharing crime prevention information with stakeholders; and supporting and monitoring specific projects through funding, developing and/or managing them. There were seven national priority areas for action: improving support to 'at-risk' families; reducing family violence; developing preventive programmes for 'at-risk' young people; minimizing formal involvement of minor offenders within the criminal justice system; developing a coordinated and strategic national approach to drugs and alcohol in relation to crime and violence; reducing white collar crime; and addressing the needs of victims. In addition to this network of local initiatives, demonstration three-year pilot projects on encouraging teenage parents to complete school, coordinated community safety initiatives in high crime neighbourhoods, support workers to children, and mentor programmes were developed and evaluated. Three pilot programmes on diversion of adult offenders from the court system were initiated and evaluated, as were a number of employment and education programmes for 'at-risk' youth (Gauthier et al, 1999, pp23–24).

An independent evaluation of the SCC programme in 1999 found many successful initiatives where there was extensive participation of community leaders and authority figures, commitment of people and monetary resources, strong leadership, a shared purpose, a positive community profile and activities that addressed local needs. In most cases, the relationships between police, local governments and indigenous councils had improved. However, there were problems with a large number of initiatives. These problems fell in three categories. First, some SCCs were not able to retain members from government, NGOs or the private sector with sufficient authority to attract funding and sustain efforts. Second, in some cases SCC coordinators lacked support and access to local government resources. Third, up to one in three SCCs was stockpiling senior government funds with no future tag for specific projects. Local governments complained that the national government did not allow sufficient funding for adequate coordination and innovative approaches to local priorities (Local Partnerships and Government Unit, 2003).

The national government responded to this evaluation by shifting their priority issues somewhat, reallocating funding to target locations with significant problems and prioritizing approaches that had already been proven to work. In 2001, the Crime Prevention Unit was moved to the Ministry of Justice, and the Crime Prevention Strategy renamed the Crime Reduction Strategy. Youth offending and family violence remained as priorities, while white collar crime, drug and alcohol abuse not directly related to community or sexual violence, support to families with young children, and support services to victims were reallocated to other departments, thus freeing up more money to be spent in a focused fashion. Theft of and from cars, burglary, organized crime, community violence, sexual violence and serious traffic offending were added to the list of priority concerns. The amount of discretionary special funds was reduced in favour of increased funding to SCCs and focused interventions. In addition to renewed guidelines and training for SCCs, 31 provider groups now run restorative justice programmes across the country, which is further discussed in Chapter 6 (New Zealand Ministry of Justice Crime Prevention Unit, 2007a). A stand-alone family violence reduction strategy, *Te Rito*, is committed to tackling intimate partner abuse, child abuse, elder abuse, parent abuse and sibling abuse through local and national partnerships (Government of New Zealand Ministry of Social Development, 2002). Another successful programme has been the local council's use of safety audits as a community engagement tool, coupled with utilizing crime prevention through environmental design (CPTED) principles in reviewing new applications and redeveloping problem sites (McCauley and Opie, 2007). In 2001, the national government commissioned a victimization survey, which was intended to provide baseline data for an outcomes-based national policy.

The New Zealand example provides a comprehensive national policy for local delivery of crime prevention, coupled with a commitment to programme evaluation and consequent modification. The Crime Prevention Unit has weathered several changes in national government to become one of the strongest national crime prevention programmes in the world, measured by proportion of government funding (over US$3 million per year in 1993, rising to close to US$7 million in 2007) and the extent of its local partnerships (65 of its 74 local authorities) (New Zealand Ministry of Justice Crime Prevention Unit, 2007b). Although New Zealand's success has been facilitated by the fact that it is a small, relatively homogeneous and high-income nation, its practices could well serve as a model to other nations.

The two examples outlined in Boxes 4.7 and 4.8 provide an illustration of both the strengths and weaknesses of the national scale in providing community safety and violence prevention initiatives. On the one hand, policing, justice and local government legislative reform all rely on senior government scales, as was the case in both Tanzania and New Zealand. National governments are used to tying junior government transfer payments to national goals. On the other hand, innovation in both Tanzania and New Zealand has come from local pilot projects, which, if successful, can form the basis for other local programmes. According to a study of successful national initiatives by the International Centre for the Prevention of Crime, senior governments work best at elaborating a national (or state) plan of action, influencing policies through legislative and monetary levers, and stimulating or sustaining local action. They do so through greater capacity to analyse national trends (through data generally available only at a national level, such as the census), identify risk factors and supervise evaluations; through providing funding for pilot projects, training and information dissemination of successful projects; through ensuring cooperation among different scales of government; and through changing laws and policies if necessary (Waller and Sansfacon, 2000, p15). However, it is the community scales of neighbourhood and locality that are most likely to be the source of innovation and the place where community safety policies and programmes succeed or fail.

The World Health Organization focuses on a similar six roles for national government in violence prevention. First, it can develop, implement and monitor national plans of action, as was the case in both Tanzania and New Zealand (see Boxes 4.7 and 4.8). Second, it can enhance both national and local capacity for data collection, an issue in almost all of the case studies I have discussed thus far. Third, it can define priorities for, and support research on, the causes, consequences, costs and prevention of violence. Fourth, it can promote primary prevention responses, as was seen in the Danish national programme of appointing community development workers to low-income housing estates, such as Tastrupgardsvej (see Box 4.3). Fifth, it can strengthen response for victims of violence, a feature of the National Domestic Violence Strategy in New Zealand. Last, it can integrate violence prevention within social and educational policies, and thereby promote the gender and social equality that is a precondition for a less violent society (Butchart et al, 2004, pp2–3).

National governments have access to legislative frameworks that go beyond the criminal justice system. Legislation related to land and property rights, family courts, health policy, social, economic and educational policy, and the powers and responsibilities given to state and local government are all related to possible mechanisms for reducing violence and insecurity. National public figures, from the head of government to sports heroes, can be effective spokespeople for violence prevention, and national public education campaigns can also be powerful social change tools. National standards can be enforced, for instance, for domestic violence perpetrators' programmes or aged care establishments. The private sector and charities can be mobilized most effectively at the national level to supplement national government funding for violence prevention. Thus, national plans of action that involve national NGOs, government ministries, national cultural, sports and religious institutions, charities or donor agencies, national media, and national health organizations can be effective in framing and supporting local action (Commonwealth Secretariat, 2003, Chapter 2).

It is both particularly difficult and necessary for nations to develop violence prevention campaigns and policies in the wake of collective conflict. As discussed in Chapter 2, both family and community violence tend to be increased during civil and transnational conflicts, and it is important to stop the cycle of violence, particularly with young people. In Fiji, the Towards a Culture of Peace Project was developed by the Ecumenical Centre for Research, Education and Advocacy in the wake of a coup in 2000. A research study on inter-ethnic and inter-religious perceptions in the Fiji Islands was followed by training-the-trainer activities. These led to national workshops with national and local governments, security forces, churches, NGOs and faith-based groups. The documentary film *Mothers in Dialogue*, produced by fem'LINK, a women-run NGO, featured local women talking about the coup's impact upon their lives and the ways in which mothers contribute to peace and reconciliation in that country. A training manual was produced for Pacific peace-builders (Commonwealth Secretariat, 2003, p109).

Coordination at the regional and international scales

Regional groups of nations, such as the European Union and the Organization of African States, are becoming more powerful over time. Box 4.9 provides a case study of Raising Voices, an organization's developing capacity at the regional level. The ultimate scale is the international level, where organizations such the United Nations, the World Bank and the World Health Organization develop policies and resources that seek to serve the world's 6 billion inhabitants.

The European Forum on Urban Security (EFUS) is another regional NGO which works with local governments to prevent crime, violence and insecurity. Founded in 1987 by the French politician Gilbert Bonnemaison (see below), EFUS brings together about 300 local authorities in over 16 European countries. To join, a local authority must prove that it has a coalition for urban safety in a place that includes public-, private- and voluntary-sector organizations. Local safety policies must be built into a social development framework and respect human rights (i.e. policies must not lead to greater social exclusion). EFUS has published dozens of publications, mostly in English and French, on topics ranging from the cost of crime to jobs in safety, and from drug abuse to terrorism. Several vulnerable groups have been highlighted in their research and

Box 4.9 *Regional coordination and capacity-building:*
Raising Voices in Africa

Raising Voices was founded in 1999, in Kampala, Uganda. Like Duluth's Domestic Abuse Intervention Project and British Columbia's Cowichan Safer Futures programme, the project was an agency-led approach to preventing gender-based violence. Like all the case studies described thus far, Raising Voices wanted to shift the burden of responsibility for combating violence from the individual person and service to recognize that violence prevention is a community responsibility that can only be addressed effectively by comprehensive long-term efforts to address the root causes of violence. Like many of the case studies described in this chapter, Raising Voices was also committed to a bottom-up grassroots empowerment approach that stressed community ownership of ideas and initiatives, and saw violence as an issue across the entire life course, not as a single event that could be prevented simply by a harsher response from the criminal justice system.

Raising Voices began in a densely populated slum community north of Kampala, called Kawempe district. More than 230,000 people live on just 25 square kilometres, and like the residents of San Fernando in Argentina, most lack basic infrastructure, such as sewers and rubbish collection. The project began by training 33 local women and 33 local men to lead violence prevention education projects. Raising Voices' innovative use of comic books, games and other popular education materials is described further in Chapter 6. Its work expanded to include training police, social and healthcare services, media outlets, religious communities, school teachers and political leaders from the village to the district level on their potential role in preventing domestic violence. In its first three years, the project trained hundreds of community activists, helped to develop new legislation and improved coordination of community services in Kawempe. Some men were resistant to being involved; the project emphasized the benefits of non-violence for men and ensured that the focus was problem-solving rather than blame. Some women were afraid to 'raise their voices' as well; in this case, the project needed to ensure that it would be a sustained effort and that women would be supported in their actions. The overall emphasis was to remove domestic violence from its previous status as a hidden 'private' issue for women and move it to the 'public' sphere of discourse and collective responsibility (Michau and Naker, 2004, pp16–17; Whitzman et al, 2004, p20).

Its work soon led to interest from other localities, and with the help of the United Nations Fund for Women (UNIFEM) and several private donors, it developed a resource guide and a learning centre to disseminate its training materials (Michau and Naker, 2003). It was also funded by UN-Habitat to develop a regional conference on 'sharing experiences and breaking new ground', which led to a documentation and analysis of 20 good practices in the prevention of gender-based violence in the Horn of Africa and East and Southern Africa (Michau and Naker, 2004). For instance, the Kivulini Women's Rights Organization in Tanzania used Raising Voices materials to train 300 community volunteers, including leaders at the street and ward levels, to organize local activities and speak out in public forums on violence. It also provided training to police, social welfare officers, healthcare providers, journalists and religious leaders on how they could integrate violence prevention within their personal and professional lives. The project provided direct services to female victims of violence as well, including life skills and employment readiness training, counselling, mediation and legal aid to women who decided to pursue their cases through the criminal justice system. The organization's analysis of what worked for them included the following tips: identifying allies who were supportive and working with them at first, rather than trying to convince the most resistant; focusing on a culturally or religiously sensitive 'entry point' to discussions with leaders – for instance, a positive tradition of a particular group; keeping local authorities informed and involved, and giving credit to them whenever possible; and creating opportunities for local leaders to speak out at meetings, which built their confidence and added to their community status (Michau and Naker, 2004, pp18–19).

In 2004, Raising Voices expanded its mandate to explicitly include violence against children, and its efforts in that campaign are described in Chapter 6. Raising Voices shows how a relatively small organization can make a huge impact through a number of key interventions. By working with all potential actors, including men, local authorities and media, the project has made violence a public issue. It has done so, paradoxically, by 'making it personal', focusing on changes that individuals can instil in their personal and professional lives. Its belief that all people – women and men – are essentially good and capable of change informs its work on promoting equitable relationships, not only between intimate partners, but also between grassroots and professional organizations, colleagues and institutions. Aside from an excellent organizational website (Raising Voices, 2007), Raising Voices has also developed an African network website, with links to its newsletter, member and non-member resources, and ideas for posters, buttons and T-shirts (Gender Based Violence Prevention Network, 2007).

networking activities: new migrants, youth, elderly people and women (EFUS, 2007).

UNIFEM has funded a project in Latin America that seeks to coordinate gender-based violence prevention from a 'safe cities' perspective. The Centre for Exchange and Services in the Southern Cone (CISCSA) began in 2004, with pilot projects in the three cities of Rosario (Argentina), Lima (Peru) and Bogotá (Colombia), and is now being expanded to other cities in the region through a training manual (Rainero et al, 2006) and a series of regional workshops. A Spanish-language guide to using media has recently been published (Red Mujer, 2007).

There are also Combating Violence against Women regional initiatives in the Caribbean, Asia, Africa and the Pacific, supported by the Commonwealth Secretariat, representing 53 countries that used to form the British Empire (Commonwealth Secretariat, 2003).

Why do regional initiatives appear to flourish in Europe, Latin America and in sub-Saharan Africa, as opposed to North America, Asia and the Pacific? There are at least three reasons for the plethora of these initiatives. First, since regional data has demonstrated much higher levels of violence in Latin America and sub-Saharan Africa, international funders, and local and senior authorities, have given a high priority to violence prevention in these regions. The issue of need may be less acute in Europe; but perceptions of insecurity are still an important issue, and there are enough resources to provide relatively generous assistance to crime and violence prevention.

Second, the relative linguistic unity of Latin America (with Spanish and Portuguese as the main languages) and sub-Saharan Africa (with English and French as primary or secondary languages) have made links much easier with HIC resources and forums. Although European countries operate in many countries, at the European Union level English and French are the common languages. Asia has such a plethora of languages and cultures that multi-country initiatives are difficult to coordinate. Although a number of North African and West Asian countries use Arabic, and there are more speakers of Mandarin than there are of English, these are not official languages used by the UN and other international organizations, which makes written and online resources more difficult to access. Even if we were to focus on one Asian country, India, the population is as large as sub-Saharan Africa and considerably larger than South America, and the languages and cultures are as diverse as anywhere in the world. Almost as many people speak Bengali and Hindi as English and Spanish.

Third, the Organization of American States, the Organization of African States and the European Union have created opportunities for dialogue that do not exist in the Asia-Pacific. For instance, the Organization of American States developed its own Inter-American Convention on the Prevention, Punishment and Eradication of Violence against Women in 1994, with a review process that began in 2000 (Commonwealth Secretariat, 2003, p45).

Fourth, Latin America and sub-Saharan Africa have both been experimenting with participatory governance in the wake of relatively recent multiparty democracy. Many countries in North Africa, and in West, South, East and South-East Asia, have not yet attained this level of democracy, and the notion of mass-based movements, particularly those which challenge established norms such as violence, is threatening to authorities.

The notion of an international crime prevention effort is hardly new. The settlement house movement in the US, the UK and several other HICs during the late 19th century was one example of a network that indirectly worked to exchange good practices on social development approaches to reducing delinquency. However, the current wave of international initiatives dates only from the mid 1990s.

From the establishment of the United Nations in 1948, there have been international meetings on the control of crime. In 1955, the First United Nations Congress on the Prevention of Crime and Treatment of Offenders in Geneva set minimum standards for the treatment of prisoners. A congress five years later in London focused on the prevention of juvenile delinquency, although the emphasis was still on a criminal justice model. Further congresses during the 1960s through to the 1980s began to discuss technical training, data analysis and regional assistance to countries developing crime prevention policies; international rules on juvenile detention, police use of firearms and the use of torture, and extradition; and the relationship between crime and development planning (UNODC, 2007).

National programmes on crime prevention were established in Denmark in 1972, in Sweden in 1974, and in many other European countries by the early 1980s. Two European conferences on the role of urban policies on crime prevention, in Strasbourg in 1986 and Barcelona in 1987, led to the foundation of the European Forum on Urban Security. The Canadian government, and particularly the French-speaking government of Quebec, became interested in these European initiatives and hosted the First European and North American Conference on Urban Safety and Crime Prevention in Montreal in 1989, in collaboration with the Federation of Canadian Municipalities, the US Conference of Mayors and the European Forum on Urban Security. The City of Montreal, which was just beginning its *Femmes et Ville* (Women and the City) initiative on prevention of violence against women at the local government level, developed a proposal for establishing an international crime prevention organization based in that city. This led to the foundation of the International Centre for the Prevention of Crime in 1994, which was supported by the national governments of several HICs (ICPC, 2007).

In the meantime, the Ninth United Nations Congress on Crime Prevention, held in Cairo in 1995, developed guidelines for urban crime prevention that stressed the importance of the local level of governance (UNODC, 2003a), which were revised in 2002 (UN Economic and Social Council, 2002). The Safer Cities Programme was established in 1996 to build capacity among low-income country (LIC) local authorities in carrying out urban crime and violence prevention. It is based in UN-Habitat, the agency charged with promoting socially and environmentally sustainable human settlements and the achievement of adequate shelter for all (UN-Habitat, 2006a). A recent (unpublished) evaluation of the Safer Cities Programme found that while it had been successful in establishing and networking with 16 African cities, its role in Latin America, the Asia-Pacific and Eastern Europe was limited, and it required further resources and a strategic plan if it was to have a global impact. UN-Habitat has approached community safety as an issue of good governance (UN-Habitat, 2005a, 2006a). Its Global Campaign on Good Urban Governance has three platforms: transparency and inclusion; fighting crime and corruption; and including the previously excluded and marginalized, particularly women, in urban decision-making (UN-Habitat, 2006a, p7). Its goal is 'the Inclusive City, where all urban inhabitants, regardless of economic means, gender, race, ethnicity or religion, are able to fully partici-pate in the social, economic and political opportunities that cities have to offer' (UN-Habitat, 2005a, p4). A related Secure Tenure Campaign recognizes that good housing in secure neighbourhoods is an essential mechanism for providing safer communities, particularly for women, seniors and children (UN-Habitat, 2006b, p8). As Ana Falu, a professor of architecture and one of the advocates for gender equality in housing tenure, has said, housing is more than mere shelter, it is a precondition to the right to the safe and secure enjoyment of neighbour-hoods and cities, and the right to health and well-being (Women and Peace Network, 2002, p8).

There are two other UN agencies working directly on this issue. The United Nations Office on Drugs and Crime (UNODC) was founded in 1997, with an initial focus on transnational organized crime. UNIFEM, the United Nations Fund for Women, has made prevention of violence against women one of its four priority areas since 1995, along with the related issues of prevention of poverty, HIV and gender equality in governance (Heyzer, 1998; UNIFEM, 2007). Until recently, these UN agencies did not tend to work together on collaborative projects.

The UN has also developed an international legislative framework on human rights, which often informs community safety initiatives, particularly in relation to public awareness. For instance, the International Convention on the Rights of the Child, adopted in 1989, specifically bans physical abuse of children, including as a means of parental punishment, and also bans the use of children as soldiers and their imprisonment. The *Declaration on the Elimination of Violence against Women*, adopted in 1993, bears a similar message. There are several limitations, however, to the effectiveness of these instruments. First, some countries have not signed these conventions and declarations, and other nations have signed with significant reservations. Second, few nations have taken the additional step of creating action plans or specific laws to enforce these instruments. Third, the international treaty bodies that monitor implementation have no way of enforcing compliance, and simply publish periodic reports to measure the state of progress (Commonwealth Secretariat, 2003, p13).

The World Health Organization was founded, like the UN, immediately after World War II. Its mandate is to prevent disease and to promote health and well-being. The WHO's Community Safety Programme began in 1989, with an emphasis on the prevention of both unintentional injuries (road and other accidents) and intentional injury, through coordinated action at the community level. In 1996, the WHO officially recognized violence as a major and growing health problem and began to organize a Global Campaign on Violence Prevention as part of its renamed Department of Injuries and Violence Prevention (WHO, 2007a). Aside from extensive research, the global campaign provides regional training and publishes public education resources in six languages. Its 2005 activities report (WHO, 2005) suggests that the WHO is very active in Europe, Africa and South America, but somewhat less active in Asia. Another international organization, the World Bank, has funded considerable research and action on crime and violence prevention, particularly in Latin America (World Bank, 2007a). While the World Bank has worked with both the WHO and the UN, there is surprisingly little collaboration between the WHO's Global Campaign on Violence Prevention and UN-Habitat's Safer Cities Programme.

Also, as previously mentioned, there have been locally based coordinated initiatives on preventing gender-based violence since the early 1980s. At the 1989 international crime prevention conference in Montreal, a small number of feminists, mostly based in local Canadian initiatives in Toronto, Montreal and Ottawa (including myself), met to discuss why gender and gender-based violence was absent from the discussion of the conference and to advocate for some mention of domestic violence in the final declaration. After this conference, an informal network of local activists continued to support one another's initiatives through the internet. In 1994, an Organisation for Economic Co-operation and Development (OECD) conference on women and cities brought together European and North American women who were working on safer cities in Paris, and the decision was made to organize an international conference on women's safety, which eventually took place in 2002 in Montreal (First International Seminar on Women's Safety, 2002). The informal group of Canadian and international feminists decided to take on the name of the Montreal initiative, *Femmes et Ville*, which was translated into English as Women and the City. Women in Cities International has built upon and promoted the gender mainstreaming work of UN-Habitat (Smaoun, 2000) and the International Centre for the Prevention of Crime (Shaw, 2002; Shaw and Capobianco, 2004), and in 2004, organized a Women's Safety Awards competition that focused on international good practice (Whitzman et al, 2004). Also in 2004, UNIFEM organized a Second International Conference on Safer Cities for Women and Girls (2004) in Bogotá, Colombia, and further networking events have been organized in relation to the World Urban Forum in Vancouver in 2006 (WICI, 2007a). The Commonwealth Secretariat (2003) has organized regional workshops on eliminating gender-based violence for English-speaking countries that were formerly British colonies.

Conclusion: Coordination at different scales and the question of good governance

Part of the reason for including such a large number of case studies in this chapter is that I wish to argue that there is no single path to effective community safety. As we have seen throughout the chapter, successful community safety initiatives have operated at the neighbourhood, city, nation, region and global scales. One element that is true of most successful initiatives is their ability to work at several scales simultaneously: a national programme that involves projects at the neighbourhood scale, as we saw in Denmark and New Zealand, or a programme that starts in one neighbourhood or rural community and expands upward, as was the case in Dar es Salaam and Cowichan Valley. The ability to carry out effective action at different scales is a hallmark of successful initiatives, as is the ability to 'jump scales' and influence higher levels of governance. When there is coordinated action occurring at all scales of governance, then there is the greatest possibility for synchronicity and success in tackling the complex root causes of violence.

Some successful programmes discussed in this chapter were initiated and led by governments: London, Dar es Salaam, Kadjebi district and New Zealand. Other successful programmes developed out of, and continued to be led by, community-based agencies: the Duluth Domestic Abuse Intervention Project, Cowichan Valley Safer Futures and Raising Voices. Whether led by governments or by community organizations, both involved government–community part- nerships, sometimes with significant contributions from the private sector and private charities. The ability to develop and sustain strong leadership is an element that underscores both types of coalitions, whether that leadership is shown by popular mayors (as in Bogotá and London), administrative staff (as in Dar es Salaam and Cowichan) or by developing grassroots leadership (as in Buenos Aires and Kadjebi). While leadership is vital, the challenge is for an initiative to remain sustainable beyond the first generation of leadership, as has been the case in Bogotá and New Zealand.

Some of the initiatives described took a top-down approach, such as the Danish programme of locating community workers in public housing, or the New Zealand Crime Prevention Unit's conditions for funding safer community councils. Others were focused on bottom-up organizing, such as the initiative in

Buenos Aires or Raising Voices. There are arguments in favour of both bottom-up and top-down approaches. On the one hand, if the goal is for recognition of endemic violence and subsequent change at the individual and family scales, then a bottom-up strategy that engages and gives ownership to as many people as possible is necessary (Michau and Naker, 2004, p6). On the other hand, we know that interventions have a better change of success if designed and undertaken as a set of closely linked measures involving all scales of governance, a task that may be easier for national governments to enforce (Homel, 2004, p1). An approach that includes both legislative interventions and widespread community engagement, such as the one undertaken in Bogotá, may integrate both vital aspects of coordinated action. In any case, flexibility in types of partnerships, depending upon setting, culture and scale, may make more sense than arguing about the traditional divisions between 'top-down' and 'bottom-up' processes (Shaw, 2006, p8).

Several initiatives had a well-defined plan of action and annually measured milestones towards achieving goals. The London Domestic Violence Strategy is an exemplar of this approach. The evaluation and subsequent changes to New Zealand's Crime Prevention Unit show a different aspect of evidence-based community safety work. However, other approaches took a far more developmental and almost improvisational approach. Raising Voices stressed working with whoever was willing, and the work in Buenos Aires progressed as funding partners became available, as leadership developed and as needs became known. Some of Bogotá's public awareness initiatives took existing ideas a step further: Women's Night Out was an elaboration of Take Back the Night marches that have taken place internationally since the 1970s. However, the Knights of the Zebra initiative with Bogotá taxi drivers or the street warden/mimes are the sort of ideas that only occur when a government or community organization is willing to take a chance on a dramatically new idea. Ideally, there would be a balance between a clear plan of action and the readiness to incorporate good ideas as they bubble up in the course of implementation.

While none of the initiatives profiled in this chapter had an evaluation plan that would pass the standards of the Sherman report, a point that is discussed more fully in Chapter 5, they all had a sense of their ultimate vision of a safer society. Again, these visions varied widely. Some of the initiatives focused on a general goal of reducing reported crime and violence, such as the Bogotá initiative and New Zealand's Crime Prevention Unit. Some initiatives wanted to end tolerance of a particular form of violence, such as preventing intimate partner violence in the case of the Duluth Domestic Abuse Intervention Project or preventing gender-based violence (particularly physical and sexual violence) in the case of Raising Voices. Some worked to cut off the supply of potential offenders, as in the case of the Tastrupgardsvej Estate. Others did not focus directly on community safety, but worked on related health and urban development issues, such as provision of basic infrastructure (Buenos Aires), education and employment opportunities (Tastrupgardsvej Estate), or women's involvement in local governance (Kadjebi). As the Sherman report argues, crime prevention is a matter of results, not intentions or methods, and some of the interventions that are most effective in preventing crime are not developed or labelled as crime prevention (Sherman et al, 1997, p4).

Despite their diversity, all of the initiatives described in this chapter had three hallmarks, which I will call the three 'L's: leadership, longevity and a lateral approach. The aspect of leadership has already been discussed, as has the related aspect of working simultaneously on top-down issues, such as administrative and legislative reform, and on bottom-up issues of developing individual capacity to make non-violent choices and to influence others to do so. Longevity also has two aspects. In almost every case, it took at least three to five years to set up institutions that could work effectively together to tackle the root causes of violence; in many cases, such as London and New Zealand, it took at least two action plans to get it right. Because developing institutions and tackling the root causes of violence take time, it is important to simultaneously work on short-term initiatives that can demonstrate intent to work effectively and simultaneously act as capacity-building actions. The development of that first childcare centre in Buenos Aires led to many other successes. The Squares Law in Bogotá showed the intent of local government to enact positive change. Doing a first safety audit can hone people's skills in identifying safe and unsafe environments, as was the case in both Cowichan and Dar es Salaam, and when governments respond to these audits, it can help to develop trust between communities and governments. Finally, the lateral approach can be demonstrated both horizontally, as in the huge range of partners brought together by almost every initiative described, and vertically, as in the question of action on all scales, a successful pilot project scaling-up, and senior scales ensuring that potential leaders are trained and that good practices are disseminated.

It is possible to generalize about the strengths of various scales. The neighbourhood scale is best at grassroots leadership development and at using local resources to meet local needs. The local governance scale is best at coordinating all local actors, ensuring equity across neighbourhoods and promoting civic awareness and engagement. National (and state) governments can provide resources for training, evaluation and dissemination of good practices, as well as enabling legislative changes to health, police, justice, education and local governance systems. Regional and international programmes can create a global movement towards safer communities. These strengths are complementary, and strategies that engage all scales are most likely to create societal change.

This chapter has introduced the ideas behind coordinated action on community safety. In the next chapter, we will take a more developmental approach to the stages of establishing a community safety strategy that is applicable to any scale

5

The Process of Community Safety Planning

The last chapter described a range of effective community safety initiatives at various scales of governance. The case studies presented suggested a set of process criteria that ideally would be met for maximum effectiveness and success. However, very few of these community safety initiatives in the last chapter met all of these ideal criteria: broad-based partnership-building; thorough diagnosis; an analysis that encompassed all forms of violence; comprehensive strategies that galvanized available resources and met identified needs; and an evaluation of strategies that was able to prove a causative relationship between interventions and impacts. While many of the case studies implicitly recognized gender differences, such as Bogotá's Women's Night Out (see Box 4.5) or providing positive role models to young boys in the Danish housing estate (see Box 4.3), very few met the criteria of gender mainstreaming defined by the Irish National Development Plan, which suggests integrating gender in programme governance, data collection and needs analysis, project design and implementation, and evaluation (National Development Plan (Ireland) Gender Equality Unit, 2002).

Successful community safety coordination can only happen through sharing information, resources and ideas among as many potential actors as possible, including politicians, administrators, community organizations, the general public and researchers. These actors must develop a shared perspective on what is the problem to be addressed. Together they should discover and develop data sets that will allow some sense of the prevalence of the problem, analyse the root causes of this problem, and decide upon the most effective concerted actions that would maximize the levels of safety available under given conditions. If they focus on violence prevention and all people's right to a safe community, they must recognize and address violence in both public and private space, and acknowledge that there are significant gender differences in both experiences and perceptions of violence. They must negotiate tensions in allocating resources and resolving conflicting interests in order to be equitable and just, as well as sustainable over the long term. They should involve as many people as possible in the planning, design, implementation and evaluation of activities designed to affect their safety and well-being under the assumption that these people are 'experts of experience'. Groups who are discriminated against, such as visible minorities and indigenous people, and groups who are particularly vulnerable, such as children or low-income communities, may require increased efforts to ensure their involvement in programmes and improve their benefits from these initiatives. Eventually, social changes must be entrenched in law and policy. Finally, the accountability of those organizations and governments working on community safety should be ensured through objective evaluation, the results of which are available in the public domain (this list is based on Fifth World Conference on Injury Prevention and Control, 2000, and Sixth World Conference on Injury Prevention and Control, 2002, which does not, however, include a gender analysis).

This chapter will focus on this process of developing, implementing and maintaining coordinated community safety initiatives. As the list above demonstrates, there are a number of challenges involved, from defining the problem, to developing partnerships, discovering the prevalence of the problem, agreeing upon a shared perspective, creating a set of policy and programme interventions to meet a set of goals, and ensuring that conflicts over implementation are resolved equitably. Perhaps the most difficult task is evaluating these complex initiatives. Even under the most harmonious and resource-intensive circumstances, within the smallest scale of the neighbourhood, this kind of work cannot be accomplished in one or two years. Not one of the initiatives described in Chapter 4 took less than five years to demonstrate significant progress, and five years is the minimum amount of time recommended by the Council of Europe (2003, p17) for partnerships dealing with 'everyday violence'. The initial stages of the process described in this chapter – developing partnerships and defining the problem, diagnosing prevalence and developing a strategy – usually take at least six months, and it is rare for any positive results to be seen in less than a year. However, most of the initiatives took heart from initial short-term 'wins', which would sustain their energy over the long-haul work of making communities safer.

Models of community safety planning processes

Most literature on problem-based crime prevention and community safety agree that there are four steps involved, often referred to as SARA: scan, analyse, respond and assess (Cherney, 2006). The first step is scanning, or a diagnostic of the prevalence of the problem and the forms that it takes. The second step is analysis, not only of causative factors, but also of potential resources and actors. The third step of responding to the problem includes partnership building and

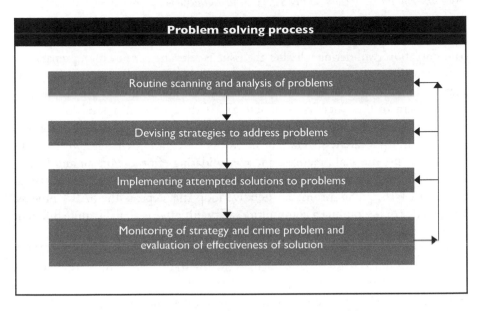

Figure 5.1 *The SARA problem-solving model*

Source: Cherney (2006)

the implementation of a coherent strategy with so-called SMART goals (specific, measurable, attainable, realistic and timely). The fourth stage of assessment involves monitoring progress on specific policies and programmes and some means of discovering whether the programmes have had an impact on the problems (see Figure 5.1).

However, these four steps leave a great deal out. It should be clear by this point in the book that identifying the problem to be addressed and establishing a partnership that can tackle it is a stage in itself and will influence all other aspects of the process of prevention. Mainstream crime prevention has assumed that the problem is self-evident 'crime' and 'fear of crime'; but feminist violence prevention initiatives have questioned assumptions behind the definition of this problem and have called for a wider range of partners to define the problem, as well as respond to it (Smaoun, 2000; Shaw, 2002). The partnership that is initially mobilized will determine the definition of a problem, the types of diagnostic data gathered, the resources and needs identified, and the evaluation of success. It is for this reason that groups such as the Cowichan Valley Safer Futures Project add a preliminary stage, which they call 'defining the problem and the partnerships' (Dame and Grant, 2002, pp49–50).

At the other end, sustaining partnerships past an initial plan or funding period is essential for the kind of long-term change processes we have already seen are necessary. Raising Voices uses a five-stage social change model that at the individual level moves from pre-contemplation (being unaware of the issue), contemplation (wondering whether the issue is relevant to one's life), preparation for action (finding out more information and resolving to change), action (new ways of thinking and behaving) and maintenance (finding benefits that lead to commitment to these new ways of acting). At the community level, this model moves from a community assessment of attitudes and beliefs, as well as actions, through raising awareness, building networks, integrating changes within individual and institutional practices, and consolidating efforts (Michau and Naker, 2004, pp9–10). It is important to be explicit about the maintenance or consolidation stage, rather than assume an iterative loop that repeats the SARA process. The practice of assembling a community safety initiative is actually quite different from the process of maintaining one.

Intriguingly, the United Nations Guidelines for Crime Prevention (UNODC, 2003a) leave out the assessment stage, as do the models used by Raising Voices (Michau and Naker, 2004) and the Cowichan Valley Safer Futures project (Dame and Grant, 2002). Evaluation of community safety partnerships is still in its infancy; but it is a necessary step. Criteria for assessment need to be decided upon at the very beginning of the partnership; evaluation cannot be left to the end of a project.

This chapter thus outlines six consecutive stages of the community safety process. First comes defining the problem and developing initial partnerships. Second is the question of diagnosing needs and available resources, using a triangulation of police statistics, victimization surveys and agency information, as well as diagnostic tools such as safety audits as a form of community mobilization. The third stage is developing a comprehensive plan that includes both short-term SMART goals and longer-term social change goals, which might include a vision of a safer community, and certainly incorporates specific lines of responsibility and interim indicators of progress in implementing recommendations. The fourth stage is realizing the plan, consolidating the partnership and monitoring the strategies as they develop. The fifth stage is evaluation, which has already been acknowledged as the most difficult aspect of community safety work and which needs to be planned for from the onset of an initiative. The sixth stage is sustaining the partnership beyond an initial plan and evaluation, and consolidating and mainstreaming the policies and processes to an everyday part of governance at all scales.

Throughout this chapter, I will be referring to the ten-year history of the Toronto Safe City Committee, created in 1989 and disbanded in 1999. I use this case study not because it is a particularly stellar example of a community safety process (although it was very influential within Canada and internationally), but because it is known intimately to me as the coordinator during those ten years; I can thus refer to aspects of 'the real world' of community safety processes that are rarely written about.

Stage one: Developing partnerships around a problem

Community safety initiatives sometimes begin with a *top-down impetus*, such as national governments legislating mandatory local government community safety strategies (as was the case in England and Wales) or creating a funding stream that provides senior government funding in return for local government crime prevention or safer community strategies that meet particular goals (as was the case in the US, France, New Zealand and through the UN-Habitat Safer Cities Programme). More often, community safety initiatives begin with bottom-up advocacy, which, in turn, often originates in a *galvanizing event* (Shaw, 2001a, p15). The mass murder of seven people along a busy street in Melbourne in 1987, the Hoddle Street Massacre, was just such a galvanizing event, leading to an Australian National Committee on Crime and Violence in 1989 (Egger, 1997, p89). Similarly, the killing of 14 women at the University of Montreal in 1989 gave impetus to a number of Canadian national and local initiatives on violence against women, including a national panel on violence against women (CAFSU, 2002, p1). Both mass murders were committed by young men with access to legal guns, and led to changes in gun control laws in these two nations. In the case of Canada, the Montreal massacre galvanized action among a small group of women, including a survivor of that massacre, to begin a campaign that successfully advocated for better gun control in Canada (Coalition for Gun Control, 2007). The same event led to the formation of a national organization called Men against Violence, which expanded into the international White Ribbon Campaign (White Ribbon Campaign, 2007).

As this anecdote shows, even in the fall-out from a single galvanizing event, the interpretation of a problem can vary widely. A national focus on violence is not the same thing as a national focus on violence against women; in fact, both Australia and Canada had parallel national task forces on 'public' crime and violence and 'private' violence against women during the early 1990s (Egger, 1997; Whitzman, 2002a). A single issue, even one as complex as gun control or changing men's attitudes and behaviours in relation to violence, is not the same as an integrated initiative on violence prevention. However, these two campaigns might well be elements of a broad-based campaign on violence prevention, or they may be the first projects of a campaign that then expand to include other campaigns. Other than a top-down impetus or a galvanizing event, a third mechanism that can start a community safety partnership is a *small-scale campaign* that grows because it is successful in mobilizing people. We have seen examples of this in Buenos Aires, rural British Columbia and Kampala.

It is the perspective of this book that preventing both 'public' and 'private' sphere violence ought to be the primary emphasis of any national campaign on crime prevention or community safety, whether it is focused on improving a population's health and well-being outcomes or providing better urban or social development. However, the actual priorities and components of such a community safety initiative might well depend upon the resources and perspectives of the neighbourhoods and localities that are most at risk. Recently, I analysed the community safety priorities of the 31 local governments in metropolitan Melbourne, Australia, finding a remarkable diversity of emphases on 'problems', from graffiti, family violence and car theft, to traffic safety and emergency management. Part of the problem with defining the problem was a series of contradictory policies from successive state governments, coupled with a lack of ongoing training for community safety officers. The most recent state government did introduce indicators of success, related to decreases in police-reported crime and traffic accident rates. However, it changed its indicators of success midstream: once successful work on improving police reporting of intimate partner violence led to increases in recorded rates of violent crime, the state government decided to report on the general crime rate since it was apparently concerned about increases in the reported rate alarming the public. But there was seemingly little effort to tie local government funding of community safety initiatives in with support for a set of local indicators that could link to state indicators. In the absence of a strong set of priorities from the state government, the composition of local community safety committees had the greatest impact on the priorities and programmes undertaken by local government (Whitzman, forthcoming). This example points to the importance of leadership, both at the local and senior governance levels, in determining the problems to be addressed, which, in turn, determine all other aspects of the community safety process.

A fourth way that a community safety partnership can begin is when an ongoing problem is brought into public discourse by a political or community organization *leader*. The examples of mayors Antonus Mockus in Bogotá and Ken Livingstone in London (see Boxes 4.4 and 4.5) have already been discussed, as have the organizational examples of the Duluth Domestic Abuse Intervention Project and Raising Voices in Kampala (see Boxes 4.4 and 4.9). Leaders set the tone and parameters for public discourse on a problem. Politicians can use the power of their office to convey messages to their community. Both political and organizational leaders play an important role in shaping the process, including using leadership skills to build trust, improve communication and resolve conflicts (Shaw, 2001a, p17). It is rare to find a single person who embodies all of these attributes, and often it is best to have one person as leader and another person or people as *champions*. The leader is the person who has the time and patience to set agendas and to chair long meetings, who has wide connections, and excellent communication and team-building skills. The main problem with political leaders is that if the initiative is overly identified with him or her, the initiative can fail once they are voted out of office. Leaders can be consensus builders or autocrats: generally, if the leader is an autocrat, it is probably better to have a separate consensus-builder doing the everyday work of chairing meetings and follow-up between meetings.

Champions are the people who ensure that the key messages reach community members. Champions do not need to be political leaders; but they do need to be people within organizations respected by a broad cross-section of the community. These may not be organizations with violence prevention as a primary mandate, but might be sporting, religious, health or community service organizations. Champions can also be articulate and respected public figures who are considered to be above partisan politics, such as heads of large foundations, media stars or royalty. Queen Rania Al-Abdullah of Jordan, who has a long history of supporting child abuse prevention initiatives, has been effective as the official patron of the World Health Organization's (WHO's) Violence Prevention Office in the Eastern Mediterranean region, which consists of 22 predominantly Arabic-speaking countries in West Asia and North Africa (WHO, 2005). Sometimes when leaders or champions come from the police or justice systems, their prevention message will be listened to more readily since they are considered experts on crime prevention. Similarly, when victims of well-publicized crimes speak out in favour of prevention, they often are listened to more readily as experts of experience. This was true of Heidi Rathjen, the survivor of the Montreal massacre who co-founded the Canadian Coalition for Gun Control.

Both champions and leaders require a minimum amount of experience and organizational skills, most commonly acquired through previous successful campaigns. Part of the problem in low-income neighbourhoods or in communities of identity that are particularly vulnerable to violence is that there is a shortage of experienced leaders with successful campaigns behind them. We have already seen through the examples of Buenos Aires, Cowichan Valley, Raising Voices, and Dar es Salaam that success breeds success. Successful campaigns, no matter how small, build up community capacity, momentum and optimism. Conversely, many communities begin with negative social capital, developed through a tradition of top-down ineffective campaigns that barely make a pretence of participation and community ownership, and often result in further stigmatization of individuals and communities (Rosenbaum, 2002). Perhaps a place to start is allowing neighbourhoods to define their own violence prevention immediate priorities though some of the diagnostic strategies described in the next section. These immediate priorities might include the provision of basic physical and social infrastructure, combating social and economic stigmatization, or making streets safe from traffic accidents as a precondition to making them lively. As we saw in Buenos Aires and Dar es Salaam, even a small step forward like creating a childcare centre or lighting a residential street can develop grassroots leadership if the process successfully mobilizes the community.

Whether the lead organization is a government or a non-profit organization, the third element of a successful start-up team, after a leader and/or champion, is a staff person devoted to the administrative aspect of the process. This would be the person who arranges meetings, takes minutes and acts as a liaison between people doing work for the partnership and the steering committee. Ideally, there would be a trained community safety officer in charge of this aspect. Realistically, most non-profit organizations and many local governments cannot afford a full-time staff person devoted to a community safety initiative, unless the funding to hire such a person can be found in a start-up grant. It is also realistic to assume that this officer is fairly junior, lacking in skills and experience in organizational development and equally lacking in knowledge of violence prevention. If this is a national campaign, ongoing training of these officers should be a priority, as it was in the case of Tanzania. Even if this is a grassroots partnership, a realistic assessment of the time involved in supporting a partnership (usually at least a half-time commitment for a year) should be made and the managerial support provided for training. The investment in supporting and training administrative support is crucial in order to avoid a revolving door of uncommitted administrators who have no sense of the organizational history or people involved in the initiative, or how to move it forward.

Whether the process starts with a senior government providing conditional funding or some form of organizational leadership starting a campaign, a problem is usually defined at the onset. The problem may be subject to modification as the process continues and it certainly will be subject to elaboration, depending upon what happens during the search for *partners and allies*. The search is necessarily informed by who the lead organization knows and trusts, which again is determined by human and social capital. For instance, let us take the example of a notice for a new violence prevention programme fund that goes out to several groups. One organization has an experienced fundraiser who immediately knows what kind of programme will probably get funded. A newly formed and unincorporated organization, such as one serving a new migrant community, might not know someone at a larger or more mainstream organization and be able to negotiate so that the two work together on a funding application. A third organization might hear about the fund, or if they do hear about it, not know the reason for the new fund or who to ask for help in filling out the application form. The third organization might not apply, or they might apply and not be successful in getting funding for their equally worthy project. This story is true not only of non-profit organizations, but also of local governments. Some local governments are extraordinarily savvy at attracting senior governmental or charitable funding, while others have a legacy of failure at developmental initiatives. While the lead organization must have some experience in partnership building (or an individual leader who is a genius at it), the potential partners whom they approach can be 'trained' as they go along.

Another factor influencing the search for partners and allies is how the problem has been identified and to what extent the partners can influence defining the problem. For instance, a women's organization might not think it is eligible for a youth violence prevention fund even if it works with girls. A police-led initiative on community safety might reach out to a neighbourhood watch organization but not to a social service working with young offenders. A health service-led initiative on the prevention of gender-based violence might contact a rape crisis centre, but not an ethno-specific organization or one working with people with disabilities. Politicians might be approached to join an initiative based on their membership in a particular political party, or certain media outlets may be approached for publicity, but not others. While it is sometimes difficult to reach consensus across political lines, it is important to engage as wide a range of political perspectives as possible in order to ensure sustainability in case of a shift in the political parties in power. Similarly, it is important to scope out as broad a range of interest groups as possible to ensure that the most vulnerable and/or hard-to-reach individuals are being touched by an initiative.

A breadth of organizations and individuals brings a diversity of opinions, which has both positive and negative aspects. There is always a tension about how widely to draw the boundaries around an issue without losing focus. On the one hand, the more that violence prevention issues are explicitly related to one another, the more it is possible to draw the largest possible range of ideas and initiatives to reach a common vision. On the other hand, the time spent on conflicts over vision and prioritizing ideas might doom the initiative if there is too much diversity of opinion and not enough willingness to compromise, particularly if the leader does not know how to reach consensus across difference. No matter how consensual the process appears at first, it will always take time and patience to manage inevitable confrontations based on dissimilar working styles and perspectives. Limiting an initiative to a small group of like-minded individuals almost guarantees that it will not be able to achieve a consensus in the community in which it works.

Partial lists of potential partners at the various scales have already been provided in Chapter 4, but they bear repeating (see Box 5.1).

As for the optimum size of a partnership, there needs to be a balance between lean and efficient, and inclusive of a range of perspectives. Quite often, a 'rule of 12' applies. While six representatives would be the minimum to get a diversity of perspectives, a dozen people is the maximum number to ensure that every voice is heard in a meeting. That does not mean that only 12 organizations should be involved, but that 12 or an absolute maximum of 18 individuals should be on the steering committee of a partnership. There are many other ways to ensure involvement of other groups, ranging from subcommittees on various issues, to making each organization on the steering committee responsible for reporting back to a set of other organizations, to consultation activities, such as focus

Box 5.1 *Potential partners in community safety and violence prevention*

1   Government/public sector:

- Politicians: individual leaders (e.g. mayors) and associations of local government.
- Education: individual schools, school boards, tertiary education (colleges, vocational institutes and universities), departments and ministries of education, adult education and vocational services.
- Social services: childcare centres and other services for children, such as pre-schools, family services, women's services, men's services, youth services, and community and recreational centres; government services for people with disabilities, indigenous people, new migrants, visible minorities and sexual minorities; welfare and emergency income support, emergency and public housing services, and departments and ministries of social services or social development.
- Health: hospitals, health centres and clinics, public health nurses, including child and maternal health nurses, individual doctors, medical organizations, health promotion organizations, departments or ministries of health.
- Policing: individual police–community relations officers or domestic violence liaison officers, police divisions, police forces, and state and national police, including civil defence and disaster management, and ministries of police.
- Public information and communications offices: information kiosks in shopping areas and tourist areas, libraries and community information centres.
- Planning and public space management: social and health service planners, land-use and transportation planners, economic planners, including those working with commercial areas and business development, urban designers, parks designers and managers, and public works departments or ministries.
- Researchers: strategic planners and local government research offices, individual universities or research centres, research consortiums and statistics bureaus.
- Inspectors, regulators and law-makers: health, fire and building inspectors, other by-law enforcement officers, taxi and liquor licensing offices, and ministries that develop and enforce legislation.
- Justice: neighbourhood justice or conflict resolution centres (if they exist), individual judges, public prosecutors, probation officers, legal aid clinics, and ministries of justice.

2   Non-governmental organizations and agencies:

- Educational, health and social service organizations and agencies not directly managed by government, especially those dealing with children, youth, women, men, older people, people with disabilities, new migrants, visible minorities, and sexual minorities.
- Non-profit housing and other social service providers.
- Sports and recreation organizations: from professional sporting clubs to neighbourhood recreation providers.
- Advocacy and service organizations that work in particular communities, with particular at-risk or marginalized groups (including visible minorities, sexual minorities, indigenous people, homeless people, low-income people and slum dwellers, drug users, prostitutes and alcoholics).
- Service organizations such as Rotary International and other business organizations; Scouts, Guides and other well-established youth service groups.
- Religious organizations: religious leaders, particular houses of worship or congregations, religious charities such as the Salvation Army (particularly those who work with at-risk groups), and national religious bodies.
- Neighbourhood-based groups, both directly involved with crime and violence prevention (e.g. neighbourhood watch) and indirectly involved in grassroots advocacy or service.

3   Private sector:

- Individual business leaders, individual businesses or corporations, commercial district or shopping centre managers, local or national business organizations.
- Trade unions and professional associations.
- Private charities and individual donors.
- The media, ranging from neighbourhood and ethno-specific to national sources of information, and encompassing newspapers, magazines, radio, television and the internet.

What are the advantages of the various sectors? Governments can entrench programmes and policies in laws and the everyday mechanisms of governance. Community organizations can contribute considerable expertise of experience, as well as professional expertise. The private sector, as well as providing resources, can increase the amount, the quality and the outreach to individuals and communities. To give one example, private-sector organizations are often better at marketing, including social marketing and public education, than most governments or community organizations.

groups, surveys, public meetings, and informal phone and email exchanges. An organization may decide to share information on their client base, or attend a public meeting, or review a draft document without committing to being an ongoing member of a steering committee or subcommittee.

How then might the initial members of a steering committee be chosen? Ideally, you would want senior, experienced and well-connected people, representing key organizations, from a variety of perspectives but willing and empowered to commit significant time resources to such a committee, energetic and optimistic, and capable of acting as articulate spokespeople. All too often, junior people are assigned to a community safety or violence prevention initiative, either because frontline staff people are felt to be 'more in touch' with problems, or because prevention is simply accorded a lower priority than immediate service delivery. With rare exceptions (a junior person who is unusually knowledgeable or respected), it is both fair and strategic to insist on a high-level representative who can make decisions on behalf of the organization at the meeting itself (as opposed to taking it back to the leadership or board of the organization). Making the steering committee smaller rather than larger might encourage competition among organizations to be on the steering committee, which, in turn, might improve the quality of the representatives. Each high-level representative can consult with their frontline staff and, possibly, other organizations as well.

At the neighbourhood level, a steering committee might include the head of a religious organization, a political leader, heads of agencies working in the neighbourhood, especially those working with groups who are at risk of being victims and/or offenders, the local chief of police, and at least two or three community leaders. At the local governance level, it might include a mayor; the heads of several major community agencies providing violence prevention services, particularly to vulnerable groups; either the chief of police or the head of the police crime prevention unit; senior officials from the education and health sector; perhaps a well-respected judge; and perhaps the head of a business association. At the national level, it would be helpful to have a senior minister or well-respected champion as leader, along with the heads of several national-level violence prevention organizations, one or two other ministry heads (drawn from health, education, justice or social services), and perhaps the head of a research institute or a major charity. At any scale, a gender balance of members would be crucial to providing a range of perspectives, as would a critical mass of people and organizations from minority cultures and representing children and youth, as well as adults (i.e. not just a token woman, visible minority person or young person). If the initiative is to focus on private and public violence, a balance between organizational mandates must be sought as well.

Some potential partners will be more experienced in working within partnerships than others. Rosenbaum (2002, p182) suggests that, in the US context, most police–community partnerships are dyadic, or made up of only two partners, and the schools, business organizations and neighbourhood organizations that work with police may traditionally defer to their authority. As organizations with a strong hierarchy, both police and justice systems (and, quite possibly, local governments) may need to undergo some form of organizational reform before becoming effective members of partnerships. Similarly, some community organizations representing visible minorities, homeless people, street prostitutes or victims of violence might have a well-established oppositional way of relating to governments or police, which could get in the way of working as partners. Each organization must determine whether and how a community safety or violence prevention initiative fits in with their mandate before they respond to an invitation to a partnership and should commit to being able to acknowledge and respect other perspectives in the inevitable conflicts that will arise.

The clearer the lead organization is about the *rules of engagement*, the more likely it is that the initiative will attract and retain a diversity of partners, and make decisions in a fair and democratic manner. The lead organization needs to be able to answer a number of questions when approaching potential partners. Developing a draft *terms of reference* will assist. The terms of reference will include the purpose of the partnership; the stages of the process and approximately how long they will each last; the proposed structure and management, including who will chair the partnership; the resource commitments of the lead organization; resources and responsibilities required from the organizations you are approaching; what level of partner organizational representative is being requested (a senior staff member or a frontline staff member); how often (and possibly when) meetings will take place; and whether a representative or delegate must be there at every meeting or arrange for an alternative representative. There should be some form of timeline and work plan, and a sense of whether there will be subcommittees, as well as a steering committee; how communication between partners and to the general public will take place (including rules for spokespeople); and what are the key decision points. The form and structure of meetings are important, including the rules used for decision-making and resolving conflicts. Setting up a meeting schedule at the outset, either a regular monthly or bi-monthly meeting (e.g. the first Monday), or a set of key dates and times, is important for people with busy schedules. Two-hour meetings are ideal, and it is important to set realistic agendas and to ensure that meetings start and end on time. There is no perfect time for meetings, and much depends upon the balance of professionals and volunteers involved. An initial canvass of good times for meeting is an essential step when setting up a partnership. Agendas and background materials should be sent out at least a week in advance of the meeting to encourage preparation and effective use of meeting time, as well as to ensure that additional items can be added by partners. Meetings should include a short period at the end for sharing information that is useful to members, but non-essential to the process. All items on the agenda should result in clear decisions unless they are for information only.

At the first meeting, it is important to set out a *code of conduct*. The code will include clauses such as the following:

- Criticism of ideas is allowed; but criticism of people is not.
- Be willing to share information.
- Be willing to compromise.

It is also important to be clear about the degree of collaboration expected. Are groups getting together to share information on their clients, and, if so, is the information they share going to remain confidential? Is there any chance that organizations will be asked to merge services or create new joint services? What benefits will accrue to the organization through involvement? Will it potentially lead to better services for their clients or their community? Will there be training, co-funding or other development opportunities as part of the partnership process? It may make sense to invite organizations to be the member of a partnership to develop a work plan, a commitment of between six months and a year, and then revisit the question of membership once the work plan is developed. It is perhaps most important to be clear about what the end product of this initiative will be. Although this may seem like a very long laundry list before the partnership begins to meet, the literature on partnerships suggests that the higher the degree of formalization, the more likely it is that a partnership succeeds. In fact, a signed memorandum of understanding (MOU) or *partnership agreement* might be developed for each partner in order to signal the seriousness of the commitment on both sides (WICI, 2007a, p31–32; Dame and Grant, 2002, p49–51; Rosenbaum, 2002, p206–208). The partnership agreement would include matters already discussed in relation to the terms of reference, but might also comprise financial arrangements if necessary (i.e. a research-based organization may commit to undertaking the diagnostic in return for a fee), the amount of work required between meetings, the information that will be requested from organizations, the decision-making processes and, possibly, the arrangements should an organization withdraw from the partnership.

An organization's willingness to become involved in a community safety partnership may range along a continuum, from interest in collaboration, through cooperation, consent, indifference, passive protest, defiance and active opposition to the initiative (Rosenbaum, 2002, p203). A steering committee would want to involve as many organizations as possible at the collaboration end of this continuum simply because it makes consensus-building easier if a critical mass of groups have a shared commitment. It is nearly impossible to involve an organization that is actively opposed to the idea of a partnership. To give two examples, it is difficult to involve police or the judiciary in an initiative that looks at institutional racism in the justice system unless the benefits of such an initiative to these stakeholders are clear, and it is difficult to involve anti-poverty groups in an initiative that examines problematic behaviours, such as drinking, doing drugs or relieving themselves in public places when there is no public toilet, unless the potential non-exclusionary benefits to low-income people are clear.

However, it is possible to offer a potential win–win situation in even the most intractable of situations. In a park in Melbourne, Australia, organizations representing homeless people and street prostitutes were invited to be part of a steering committee, along with middle-class homeowners who were upset at drinking, drug using and sexual acts in the park. Once there was face-to-face interaction between these two perspectives, the fact that many low-income people do not have anywhere private to engage in these activities was made clear to the homeowners, while the fact that homeowners were concerned about their own safety and the safety of their children due to broken glass and used syringes was made clear to the drinkers and drug users. Public drinking and sexual acts were voluntarily relocated to a less residential area, a syringe disposal box was placed in the park (at least one homeowner was a drug user), and several of the homeowners advocated for a new city-owned rooming house in the vicinity (Press, 2004).

If a key organization is opposed to joining a partnership, it is still possible to keep the communication lines open. If the partnership is successful, the organization may come around. While it is important to make initial alliances with partners who are supportive, rather than resistant, it is also important to create entry points to convince the unconvinced if part of the initiative's goal is transforming individuals, organizations and societies to a violence prevention standpoint.

Box 5.2 *Defining the problem and developing leadership in Toronto, Canada, 1988–1991*

Toronto is the largest city in Canada, with over 5 million people within its metropolitan area. It has seen enormous growth as a region in the past 20 years, largely driven by immigration from Asia, Africa, Latin America and the Caribbean. Over half of its citizens have a mother tongue other than English. While these economic and social changes have brought prosperity, they have also led to increasing income disparity and ethno-cultural tension. Only one third of Toronto citizens feel that all ethno-cultural groups are treated fairly by politicians and police (Shaw, 2001a, p29), and there were similar concerns from women's organizations, leading to a successful lawsuit against the police by the victim of a serial rapist who was inadequately warned about her risk (du Mont and Parnis, 1999).

In the latter half of the 20th century, there were four tiers of government operating in Toronto: the federal or national government of Canada; the provincial (state) government of Ontario; a regional government called Metro Toronto; and, within it, several local governments, including the City of Toronto. While the federal and provincial governments have ultimate responsibility for justice, taxation and employment issues, there was a growing interest during the 1970s in using the locally based mechanisms of public housing, urban planning and public health to improve neighbourhoods in the central city.

In Toronto, the well-publicized rape and murder of a young woman in a public park during the daytime led to a Task Force on Public Violence against Women and Children in 1982 at the metropolitan or regional level of government. The task force recommended the formation of an organization called METRAC (the Metro Toronto Action Committee on Public Violence against Women and Children), who worked with the police, public transportation authorities, service providers and neighbourhood-based advocacy organizations to develop mechanisms to reduce public violence and insecurity, with an emphasis on making public space safer for women, particularly in relation to sexual assault. In the first five years of its mandate, METRAC, the public transportation authority and the police reviewed over 60 subway and train stations to improve their design in terms of prevention of violence and insecurity. This led to the development of the *Women's Safety Audit Guide*, a tool for community organizations to identify unsafe places and recommend ways of improving them (METRAC, 2007). The metropolitan level of government also funded the Wife Assault Committee of Toronto (later renamed the Woman Abuse Council of Toronto), which was a multi-agency coalition of service providers (Woman Abuse Council of Toronto, 2007).

In the meantime, the City of Toronto, with 650,000 people and responsibility for planning, public health and recreation services, voted to develop its own task force on public violence against women. The immediate galvanizing event was the existence of three separate serial rapists operating in central city neighbourhoods, which led to newly formed neighbourhood women's groups demanding local action on urban design and community policing issues. Accordingly, a report with 30 recommendations was developed by several left-wing local politicians in consultation with these neighbourhood women's groups and women-serving agencies. The report was a compromise document, with an emphasis on relatively quick interventions that would become entrenched in planning policy. There was an effort by at least one of the politicians to house the initiative in the new Healthy City Office and to give it a broader health promotion mandate that would include domestic violence; but it was felt that this more ambitious approach would not be adopted by the majority of city councillors. In any case, the report was unanimously adopted, and a standing committee of the city council, the Safe City Committee, was created to monitor the implementation of these recommendations. The steering committee had 12 members, representing the police, three local politicians, the three neighbourhood women's groups, the Toronto Rape Crisis Centre, the DisAbled Women's Network, METRAC, a women's self-defence organization called Wen-Do, and Women Plan Toronto (a feminist planning advocacy association). At that time, I was a recent graduate in geography and planning and had previously worked with Women Plan Toronto; I was hired as a part-time contract staff person to this committee. The committee was co-chaired by the most active local politician on this issue, Councillor Barbara Hall, and a representative from one of the neighbourhood women's groups.

There was no particular diagnostic process involved in the production of the initial report. The police were asked, but were unable to provide, detailed information on the location of public sexual assaults and other attacks on women. The recommendations reflected the relatively limited consultation process, which was primarily concerned with crime prevention through environmental design (CPTED): introducing a by-law with minimum standards for parking garages; developing guidelines for reviewing development applications for safety concerns and a planning policy that mandated their use; training planning staff and other interested parties (police, community groups and architects) in these guidelines; and undertaking research on making parks and recreation areas safer. Other recommendations included providing free women's self-defence courses in all 30 local government-run community and recreation centres, and undertaking a women's safety audit in each of these recreation centres, as well as in other city-owned buildings. Each recommendation was assigned to a department, and an interdepartmental subcommittee was set up to support the implementation of recommendations.

One of my challenges as a coordinator, a challenge that was shared with the co-chairs, was how to approach potentially resistant partners. Resistance came from several fronts. The Toronto Rape Crisis Centre, although agreeing to join the committee, were concerned about its reformist and limited approach to violence against women. The police were exceedingly wary of this group of feminists and also did not know who to send as an appropriate representative: the coordinator of the Neighbourhood Watch programme or the coordinator of the Domestic Violence Response team. Several senior planners already felt that they reviewed plans for safety concerns and were also unsure as to whether this mechanism would add to their work or lead to poor planning decisions. While METRAC was happy to have an ally, it also saw the Safe City Committee as a junior partner and potential threat to its mandate. Finally, the three neighbourhood committees were volunteer-based and had no previous experience in interacting with the city hall. They were impatient with the bureaucratic process, and this led to tensions with administrative staff. While many department staff people were enthusiastic about the potential to provide innovative programming and policies, no one wanted to go to an evening meeting and get yelled at for not moving fast enough, even if they were getting overtime pay.

The Toronto Rape Crisis Centre was assured that once the initial recommendations were under way, a more inclusive consultation process would allow a more ambitious approach to violence against women. However, neither they nor the police were active members of the committee, partly because the recommendations did not explicitly involve them (policing being a metropolitan governance responsibility, and the separate lawsuit concerning the victim of one of the serial rapists led to some tensions between local government, women-serving agencies and the police). I decided that the training workshops with planners, police, community organizations, developers and architects would have to precede the development of guidelines, and that the expertise of these groups would have to inform the guidelines and the policy. A researcher from a local university, Gerda Wekerle, worked with me to develop the training module, the guidelines and the draft policy. This modified process led to far greater buy-in than was initially expected, especially when backed up by the threat (as the planners and architects saw it) of the police developing and utilizing their own CPTED guidelines. METRAC was given the responsibility for leading the audits of city-owned property and since it had already been involved in drafting the underground garage by-law, it was able to feel adequately respected. The neighbourhood women's groups continued to be educated in the process of local governance, and as several acted as co-chairs or spokespeople, they increased their own leadership skills. The interdepartmental subcommittee, which met during the day and without community members or politicians, became the 'safe space' for staff to be honest about timelines and barriers.

One of the most interesting processes in that first phase of the Safe City Committee was the development of a conference called Green Spaces/Safer Places in 1990, which addressed the recommendation that referred to research on park safety. This conference attracted over 200 participants, ranging from landscape architects to park maintenance staff, and from community organizations to researchers. At the conference, both staff and community activists began to hear about some truly innovative initiatives to make parks and open spaces more inclusive, as well as safer. The positive response to the conference resulted in an increased commitment from the city's parks department, who used it as a first step in developing its own guidelines, policies and programmes. Over 50 people participated in a mass safety audit the night before the conference began, one of the few significant public awareness moments for the first phase of the committee's work.

One of the most frustrating processes was the attempt to develop safety and violence indicators for Toronto's first *State of the City Report*. The Healthy City Office wanted to develop a set of indicators on urban issues, such as the local economy, the environment, transportation, community health, housing and safety, which could be updated at regular intervals. A subcommittee of the Safe City Committee gathered together police statistics and agency information in 1990 and 1991, but was unable to find a local victimization survey or obtain funding to carry one out. Furthermore, Toronto City Council decided not to act on the recommendation to carry out regular reports updating the indicators.

The first phase of the Safe City Committee's work resulted in the majority of the initial report's recommendations being consolidated into ongoing city programmes or policy by the end of 1990. Meanwhile, the Montreal massacre in December 1989 had created new momentum to tackle all forms of violence against women. The committee decided to take on a more ambitious consultation process and to produce a new report.

Stage two: Diagnostic tools and community consultation

Establishing the partnership – scoping out the individuals and organizations and coming to basic agreements, such as MOUs – should take approximately two months. The first meeting of the partnership will involve introductions, since several of the individuals and organizations are probably new to one another, and an overview of the tasks to be undertaken. It might include an expert who can provide an overview of community safety strategies that have been developed elsewhere.

It may be as early as the first meeting that sources of information on the prevalence and characteristics of violence and insecurity are discussed; but it takes approximately four months to complete this stage. The diagnostic stage includes not only a sense of needs and priorities emerging from the data, but ideally a sense of potential community resources to meet these needs. If well managed, the diagnostic stage can also contribute towards community mobilization, improved skills and interest in combating violence, as well as enhanced partnerships. It can also be a useful 'reality check'. Focus Consultants, based in British Columbia, Canada, has developed an excellent set of toolkits for developing and evaluating aboriginal justice initiatives (Focus Consultants, 1998a, 1998b, 1998c, 1998d, 1998e). They provide an example of a community who thinks it has been studied to death and just wants to 'get on with the programme'. However, they find during a community survey that the level of anger in the community around offenders is very high, and accordingly plan their restorative justice programme more carefully to work towards and publicize small successes (Focus Consultants, 1998b, p1).

The diagnostic step begins with a collation of any previous reports on crime, violence and insecurity, as well as reports that touch upon related issues, such as employment, housing conditions, education, and maternal and child health. If a place has many well-resourced organizations and there have been previous community safety initiatives, there may be a plethora of useful information. Much more commonly, there is very little helpful data on hand, particularly in low-income countries (LICs), and limited resources to gather data.

Even if there are few studies on violence and crime, some of the data for the geographic area being served may already lie in the hands of government statisticians, researchers or community organizations. For instance, basic demographic data is necessary: the population, age structure and composition of households. Socio-economic data is equally necessary, such as housing costs and affordability; rate of employment and government or charitable income dependency (welfare); and average income and proportion living below a nationally or internationally determined poverty line. Education levels, along with income and employment, help to determine social class and are good indicators of human capital. Data on access to the internet, if available, is not only an indicator of human capital but, if rates are high enough, may determine the form of surveys and public information. Health indicators, both physical and mental, and including diseases such as depression, alcohol and drug abuse, or HIV infection that may be related to violence, may be available from public health departments. Indicators of the quality of the physical and social environments, such as boarded-up buildings, housing code violations or school drop-out rates, will also be useful.

The data should be broken down by gender whenever possible, and if there is data on particular at-risk groups, such as youth, visible minorities or indigenous people, this should be collated as well. If there are longitudinal sources of data, such as a census, this will help to determine trends over time. The data should also be broken down by sub-area, if possible, and it should be compared to the average for the city or the nation. The purpose of this background data is to inform the discussion of risk and resilience factors for violence and insecurity.

Information on the prevalence of violence, as well as some of the immediate risk factors and consequences of assaults, would ideally be accessible through a triangulation of police, agency and local victimization data (Council of Europe, 2004, p12). As previously discussed, police data often records only a limited amount of crime and violence in the community. There may be categorization issues as well, such as no differentiation between public assaults and domestic assaults, or no data on the gender of victims or alleged offenders. There may be sensitive issues around releasing details of the ethno-cultural background of offenders. There may or may not be micro-locational data as to the exact location of reported crimes and details of the site and situation (e.g. behind a dumpster, in a poorly lit part of a car park or at an address where there had been 12 previous complaints of domestic assault). Time of day, week and year are important to know. The actual crime categories vary widely from nation to nation, and some-times can vary by city. Crime rates can also be affected by crackdowns on particu-lar offences, such as illegal possession of handguns; it is important to ensure that the police provide this background data. If the partnership focuses on violence, then it will pay particular attention to crimes such as murder, attempted murder, various categories of assault, rape or sexual assault, robbery and kidnapping. Thefts, break-ins and other property crimes may be of interest, as well. The data should include a sense of trends over time. Police clearance rates (i.e. the number of reported crimes where arrests take place), the amount of time it takes a case to reach the courts, and the percentage of arrests that lead to convictions are other important sources of data.

The second source of information on prevalence would be data collected by agencies, organizations and authorities other than the police. Sources would include child welfare organizations, hospitals and health clinics, services for assaulted women, legal clinics, services assisting people who have been in conflict with the law, business associations in the case of property crimes, and services for particular at-risk groups (homeless people, prostitutes, people with disabilities, sexual minorities and visible minorities, including religious minorities and new migrants). This data may not be systemically collected, and it is very unusual for most agencies dealing with victims of violence (not only physical health and victim services, but housing, legal, income support and mental health services) to have intake forms that explicitly screen for violence. Indeed, developing these protocols may be an important part of any community safety strategy. Agency and service organization data can also be used to determine the physical and mental health impacts and costs of violence, as well as to get a sense of what services are being used to escape from violent situations, and how the links between services currently work (which services refer to others). Other qualitative and anecdotal information might include particular times when violence is worst or trigger circumstances (e.g. weekends, when there is most use of alcohol or after particular sporting events), as well as locations of offences.

The third source of information on prevalence would be a local victimization survey, if there is one. Victimization surveys not only capture some of 'the base of the iceberg' (the crimes and acts of violence that are not reported to police and agencies), but are also useful in understanding perceptions of crime and justice. Victimization surveys can also be used to obtain information on offenders, keeping in mind that many people are both. Developing a victimization survey can provide a baseline measurement to compare with later surveys. It can also provide a way of informing the larger community about the initiative, train people in problem-solving and analytic skills, and allow people to think about violence issues in new ways. Moser and McIlwaine's use of visual tools to conceptualize violence with focus groups has already been discussed in Chapter 3 (Moser, 2004; Moser and McIlwaine, 2006), as has the more broad-based multi-country survey carried out by the WHO (Garcia-Moreno et al, 2004). Victimization surveys can also be used to provide micro-locational data as to where crime and violence take place, which places are particularly feared (not necessarily the same thing) and can to help prioritize areas for improvements.

Box 5.3 provides several case studies where limited resources were required to provide excellent community surveys, while Box 5.4 suggests a basic set of questions for a baseline survey. Box 5.5 looks at how safety audits have been used as diagnostic tools, leading to improvements in designing public spaces, as well as in the process of managing urban environments.

Box 5.3 *Diagnostic tools in Papua New Guinea and South Africa*

Papua New Guinea (PNG) is a small island nation of 6 million people, located between South-East Asia and Australia. It is one of the most linguistically diverse nations in the world, with 850 indigenous languages spoken. It is also one of the least urbanized nations in the world, with only 18 per cent of the population living in cities or towns, and the majority of the country still dependent upon subsistence agriculture. However, like most nations in the world, it is rapidly urbanizing: the population growth for its capital and main city, Port Moresby, has been at least 3.6 per cent per annum throughout the 1990s, more than 1 per cent higher than the population growth rate in the rest of the island. Port Moresby has the dubious distinction of having been named the worst city in which to live in the world by *The Economist* in 2002 (UN-Habitat, 2005b, p19).

Port Moresby's problems are fairly typical of low-income country (LIC) capitals, with growth in population outstripping employment opportunities and basic service provision. About 50 per cent of the population lives in informal settlements, and most of these have little access to adequate housing, clean drinking water, sewerage or other basic infrastructure. There are very high unemployment rates, particularly among young men. The problem is exacerbated in Port Moresby by there being very little economic development other than the administrative functions of the national government. There is little tourism, partly because of its terrible reputation. Since most of the population lives at a subsistence level, there is hardly any manufacturing and very little processing of the raw materials that Papua New Guinea exports, such as coffee and minerals. In fact, there are very few legal activities in Papua New Guinea. Since about 97 per cent of the land is held by traditional landowners, most housing is illegally occupied. Most small businesses and other economic activities are illegal as well, thanks to an overly restrictive legislative system that was inherited from the colonial period.

In 2002, a Parliamentary Committee on Urbanization and Social Development decided that PNG required a response to violence and insecurity in the capital city. A national commission was established, administered out of the Department of Community Development, and including the National Capital Development Commission, the police, the justice system, churches, non-governmental organizations (NGOs) and the private sector. The UN-Habitat's Safer Cities Programme, which hitherto had only operated in African cities, was brought in to administer a survey as the first stage of tackling the problem. After consulting with governments and NGOs, the Safer Cities Programme decided to use tools that could be developed and administered by local young people. Three tools were established and utilized: a survey of 1500 young people aged 15 to 30 in the city (1.5 per cent of the total population in this age group); an institutional survey of 112 agencies and organizations in the capital; and a detailed social crime mapping of one informal settlement, Burns Park, which was felt to be one of the worst problem areas.

The youth survey found that 24 per cent of respondents had committed serious violent offences, such as murder, rape or carjacking, with about 13 per cent having committed at least one serious offence in the past year. Ninety-two per cent of the crimes reported in the survey were committed by men. The main crimes were burglary, carjacking, assault, drug dealing and petty crimes. Almost half of the crimes committed by youth involved violence, while in most cities in the world, only 25 to 30 per cent of crime involves violence. Although criminal gangs have a high profile in Port Moresby, almost 60 per cent of the crimes were committed outside gangs, and only 10 per cent of respondents said they were members of gangs. Similarly, the links between drugs, alcohol and crime were not as strong as expected. About 35 per cent of the young offenders said that they used the proceeds of crime to buy alcohol, illicit drugs (mostly marijuana) or cigarettes. About 47 per cent of young people drink alcohol, 45 per cent smoke cigarettes and only 18 per cent use marijuana. Thus, substance abuse could be seen as a widespread health problem, but not necessarily a major contributor to criminal violence. The age profile of criminals tended to spike in the late teens, where the most serious crimes were concentrated, and taper off significantly after age 30. It thus appeared to make sense to focus early intervention efforts on the socialization of young men (UN-Habitat, 2005b, pp32–36).

In Port Moresby, violence rates are very high, but family and clan ties are strong, school drop-out rates are relatively low and church attendance is high. The diagnosis thus hypothesized that there might be something about these institutions that are currently contributing to violence, rather than preventing it (UN-Habitat, 2005b, p47). In terms of risk and resilience factors, there was definitely an aspect to the cultural construction of masculinity in Port Moresby that made it easier for young men to enter crime and harder for them to exit. About 44 per cent of the children in Burns Park did not regularly attend school, and while the girls tended to work in their homes, the boys were associating with peers in public space (UN-Habitat, 2005b, p44). Gang leaders have traditionally been perceived as sharing the proceeds of their crimes with their clan, attacking corrupt political leaders and foreign business owners, and fighting for the independence of the nation from an oppressive colonial regime (Papua New Guinea only attained independence from Australia in 1975). 'The government' is still viewed as a distant and corrupt institution, and there is dependence upon the 'wantok' system, solving problems and disputes within one's ethnic and linguistic group (who share 'one talk'). While there is potential to use this system to improve restorative justice, at present it acts to protect criminals and increase political and ethnic violence in urban communities. There are few male role models in most communities other than gang leaders, and virtually no female political or other leadership (UN-Habitat, 2005b, pp48–52).

There is also the lingering impact of fairly extreme gender inequalities and endemic family violence. In some parts of Papua New Guinea governed by traditional law, women's legal status is still that of property, rather than people with human rights. The legal rights of children are also a new concept. The youth and neighbourhood surveys showed that family conditions, including exposure to victimization or witnessing violence in the home, was a strong risk factor for youth violence. Twenty-two per cent of the youth surveyed had been physically abused, and 16 per cent had been sexually abused, within their families. In Burns Park, 48 per cent of households said that there was physical abuse within households, 36 per cent economic abuse (stealing money within families), 26 per cent physical abuse and 14 per cent sexual abuse. Since family violence is so much a part of life in Port Moresby, there is little recognition that it is a crime and there are few services for victims of violence, leading to a culture of silence and male victims feeling that the only way to avoid further victimization is to become perpetrators themselves. Furthermore, socio-economic pressures contribute to family violence. Only 18 per cent of adults in Burns Park were legally employed. Separation of parents for employment purposes, coupled with absence of organized childcare, weakened family ties and exacerbated violence by men in the family. On the other hand, being gainfully employed was a major encouragement for young men to exit crime (UN-Habitat, 2005b, pp48–53).

Other institutions are part of the problem in Port Moresby. There is very little weapons control in the country, leading to 23 per cent of young offenders owning and carrying a gun, and 15 per cent owning and regularly carrying a knife, sword or blade. The police, prosecutors and courts have very high arrest, conviction and imprisonment rates: over half of young offenders who are arrested enter prison. However, this vigilance is a contributor, rather than a deterrent, to crime. The largest prison in Port Moresby, Bomana, is widely known as 'the University'. Forty-four per cent of young offenders who had been incarcerated said that they had learned new criminal skills there, 49 per cent said they had improved their criminal networks and only 15 per cent said that their time in prison would deter them from committing further crimes. There are no rehabilitation or diversion programmes in Papua New Guinea prisons (UN-Habitat 2005b, p45). The institutional survey revealed that members of the criminal justice system feel incapable of handling minor delinquency, let alone organized crime such money laundering, gang violence and corruption. As for urban planners and managers, they still consider the majority of settlements in Port Moresby as illegal and are not willing to provide basic services. Housing providers also focus their efforts in the legal settlements, providing residences to middle- and upper-income groups. Burns Park, for instance, lies outside the boundaries of the city and is not formally represented in any decision-making forum. It is not served by the police or any other government services.

The diagnosis was helpful in prioritizing problems and suggesting solutions for a phase-two intervention strategy. The very high incidence of family violence led to a recommendation that churches, schools, police, hospitals and NGOs undertake coordinated campaigns on family violence prevention. The United Nations Children's Fund (UNICEF) has funded a Family Support Centre, which provides shelter, counselling and legal advice, and which has been active in developing public education campaigns on family violence (Bloeman, 2006). Rather than concentrate resources on more police or prisons, the national government received international funding to train police and judges to prioritize violence prevention issues, such as gun control. Village courts were provided with training and given further powers to provide mediation of non-violent offences, as well as land and service disputes. Urban planners and managers were directed by the national government to redraw their service boundaries and undergo legislative (by-law) reform to encourage legal housing and land tenure (UN-Habitat, 2007).

In South Africa, there have been a number of innovative audits of gender-based violence. For instance, in south-west Johannesburg, there was widespread community and institutional concern about rape and other forms of sexual violence, coupled with a lack of information on attitudes and behaviours that could inform preventive strategies. A coalition of NGOs who provide support services, the local government, police, prosecutors, health and social services, and the local university developed surveys that were then administered by 35 community-based field workers. There were three cycles of interviews undertaken over three years, involving 3700 adults and youths in 38 randomly selected areas. Four thousand women filled out questionnaires on their experiences of sexual violence, 2000 street interviews with men helped to determine their attitudes towards violence and what encouraged some men to resist the use of violence, and about 16,000 children and youth were interviewed at school in conjunction with a play about sexual violence. The surveys found that by the age of 18, 20 per cent of young women and 13 per cent of young men had experienced sexual violence. About 40 per cent of men thought it was women's duty to obey their husband, and it was acceptable to punish your wife when she did not obey. Over 60 per cent of women saw sexual violence as something they could do little about, with even higher levels among young women. The survey and resultant report was a public education and community mobilization exercise in itself. It was also a catalyst to action among youth, particularly those who had participated in the theatre performances and surveys (Shaw and Capobianco, 2004, pp37–38).

A much more intensive method was used with 39 women in Durban, South Africa, who wrote diaries for four to six weeks on their experiences of violence. They attended a focus group and were given notes to fill in details of when and where an incident occurred, who they were scared of, what happened and how they dealt with it. An example of the reporting over two days comes from 'Paula's' diary, who reported walking on campus one morning and wanting to take a shortcut behind the back of a building. Having heard that several women had been attacked and raped there, she took a long detour to the main road. The next day, she was driving when four taxis pulled out in front and behind her, keeping close to her car. She was concerned that she would be carjacked at the traffic lights, so she closed her windows, stared straight ahead and drove off quickly once the light changed. Women told many stories about managing violence and insecurity. There were several diary entries indicating the widespread use of vigilantism as a response, up to and including the death of the perceived perpetrator. The diaries provided a level of detail that cannot be attained in an interview or focus group; the women found writing about their experiences of violence and insecurity, often for the first time, empowering; and the diaries could be a useful tool in attaining an in-depth understanding of everyday violence in a community, which could then be communicated to the general public and decision-makers (Meth, 2004).

Box 5.4 *Victimization surveys in rural British Columbia, Canada and Pakistan*

Dame and Grant (2002, pp52–54) suggest a very basic victimization survey that can, depending upon the circumstances, be conducted online, via mail, on the telephone or door to door (note: this survey is not appropriate for a 'street' interview). The survey takes approximately 20 minutes to conduct per individual. The decision should be made beforehand, based on the demographics of the community, whether you will be interviewing women only, women and men, youth only, or focusing attention on a particular neighbourhood. It is best to interview only one person per household with this survey because of confidentiality issues around family violence. It is probable that home-based violence will be underestimated in this type of survey.

Begin by explaining the initiative and why you are collecting the information. Give a pamphlet with numbers to call (number for the initiative, police, and health and counselling services), and ensure that all personal information will remain confidential:

1   Are you ever concerned for your safety:
    • at home;
    • at work;
    • on the street;
    • in other public places?
    The choices are:
    • often;
    • sometimes;
    • never.
    (If one of the purposes of the campaign is to reduce insecurity, this can be a baseline for further indicators.)

2   Have you ever experienced being:
    • threatened or hit during a date;
    • threatened or hit by your spouse or partner;
    • threatened or hit by someone whom you know who wasn't a date or spouse (a friend or an acquaintance);
    • threatened or hit by a stranger;
    • forced to do something sexual against your will by a date;
    • forced to do something sexual against your will by a spouse or partner;
    • forced to do something sexual against your will by an acquaintance or stranger;

- robbed (forced to give your money or belongings to another person);
- yelled at by a date or by a spouse or partner;
- yelled at by an acquaintance or stranger?

If you have experienced one or more of these acts of violence, were they during the past year? (Mark those that have taken place during the past year.) (This question gives a sense of lifetime prevalence of violence, although it is not as thorough as most victimization surveys. The violent acts over the past year can be used as a baseline for further indicators.)

3 Please name some places in your community where you feel concerned for your safety during the day or in the evening (open ended).
- What is it about these places that make you feel unsafe (open ended)? (This question can help to identify areas that require improvement, as well as design and social factors influencing perceptions of the public sphere.)

4 Are there any places in your community where you feel particularly safe (open ended)?
- What is it about these places that make you feel safe (open ended)? (This question can help to identify potential community resources, as well as elements of the public sphere that can be strengthened.)

5 Have you ever asked for help from a family member about being threatened, hit, robbed or being forced to do something sexual against your will – for example, from:
- a friend (yes/no);
- the police (yes/no);
- a doctor or nurse (yes/no);
- a community agency or organization (yes/no)?

Did you feel the response met your needs (yes/no, place next to appropriate categories):
- why or why not (open ended)? (This can provide a sense of priority sectors in dealing with violence, as well as baseline data for further indicators on the quality of service delivery if later questions are modified to 'over the past year' instead of 'ever'.)

6 What do you think are the three most important safety issues in your community (open ended)? (This can help to determine priorities.)

7   What do you think are the three most important things your community
     can do to address these issues (open ended)? (This can help to determine
     priorities.)

8   Obtain basic demographic information (gender, age range and household
     income range). (Results can be cross-tabulated, and there may be significant
     differences between gender, age and household income in responses.)

Thank people for their information, and tell them where and when the final
report will be available.

Garrett and Ahmed (2004) describe a crime survey that was piggybacked
onto a poverty and asset survey in Bangladesh. The survey was administered
to a random sample of 610 households in a set of slum communities of 16,000
in the mid-sized city of Dinajpur (270,000 residents). Twelve enumerators
underwent one week's training to prepare them for the door-to-door survey
(see Figure 5.2).

The survey asked questions of everyone in the household, which tended
to minimize the number of family assaults reported because individuals
would not generally disclose violence if the perpetrators were listening to
the conversation. However, the survey is easy to administer and track. The
survey found that 16 per cent of households had been affected by some form
of crime in the 12 months prior to the survey. The most common forms of
crime were thefts and severe beatings, mostly committed by neighbours or
other people known to the victims (the article did not cite statistics on family
violence). There was one neighbourhood in particular that had a high level of
self-reported crime. Overall, crimes were reported to 'nobody' in 41 per cent
of cases, a community leader or ward commissioner in 40 per cent of cases,
and a police officer in only 8 per cent of cases. The police took action against
the perpetrators in only 7 per cent of cases, and the community or individuals
took vigilante action in 14 per cent of cases. The medical costs of the crimes
alone took up 64 per cent of an average household's monthly expenses.

This would have been very useful baseline information for a community
safety initiative. Unfortunately, the poverty alleviation organization that
sponsored the addition of these questions then decided that crime and
violence was not a priority for its efforts, and the local authorities also declined
to act on the survey. This experience indicates a major problem with many
of these diagnostic efforts (see also Box 5.5): if researchers or community
members undertake diagnostics that are *not* part of a coordinated community
safety initiative and do *not* undertake ameliorative actions within the year
after the survey, the effort will be counter-productive, increasing concern and
frustration in a community, rather than being part of the solution.

Figure 5.2 *Survey module on crime, violence and physical security*

In the past 12 months, has anybody in this household been a victim of any of the following crimes?

Type	Code	Did it occur in the household in the past 12 months? Yes.....1 No.....2	Who was the victim? If the person was a member but is not now, put 55. If the whole household was a victim, put 66	Who did it? (Code-1)	To whom was it reported? (Code-2)	What actions were taken against the perpetrator? (Code-3)	After it happened, did the victim receive medical treatment? Yes.....1 No.....2	Who paid for the medical treatment? (Code-4)	How much did the treatment cost? Taka	Other than medical cost, what was the cost of the loss? Taka	What measures did the household take to prevent future incidents? (Code-5)
1	2	3	4	5	6	7	8	9	10	11	12
Severe beating	01										
Acid thrown on the body	02										
Theft	03										
Mugging / robbery	04										
Rape / attempted rape	05										
Murder	06										
Attempted murder	07										
Kidnapping / abduction	08										
Arson	09										
Other 1 (specify)	10										
Other 2 (specify)	11										

Code-1: Who did it?
Household member: USE MEMBER CODE

Neighbour	21
Mastaan, same community	22
Mastaan, outside community	23
Employer	24
Police/chowkidar	25
Other (specify)	26

Code-2: Reported to whom?

Nobody	1
Police	2
Ward commissioner	3
Community leader	4
Community mastaan	5
Imam/purohit	6
Other (specify)	7

Code-3: Actions against perpetrator

No action	1
Reported to police/filed police case/GD	2
Beat perpetrator	3
Community action	4
Threatened perpetrator	5
Other (specify)	6

Code-4: Who paid?

Household member	1
Neighbour/community	2
NGO	3
Government	4
Perpetrator	5
Other (specify)	6

Code-5: Preventive measures

No measure taken	1
Informed police	2
Informed ward commissioner	3
Engaged community leader or protection	4
Engaged community mastaan for protection	5
Other (specify)	6

13. How safe do you feel in terms of your physical security (crime, violence) in this community?
Not safe at all....1 Not safe....2 Fairly safe....3 Safe.....4 Very safe....5

Source: Garrett and Ahmed (2004, p143)

Box 5.5 *The use of safety audits as diagnostic and community mobilization tools*

Since it was developed in Toronto in 1989 (see Box 5.2), the women's safety audit concept (*Women's Safety Audit Guide*) has been disseminated around the world (Andrew, 2000; CAFSU, 2002; Whitzman, 2002a; Shaw and Andrew, 2005; UN-Habitat, 2005a). According to the Women's Action Centre against Violence in Ottawa, Canada, women's safety audits are 'a process which brings individuals together to walk through a physical environment, evaluate how safe it feels to them, identify ways to make the space safer and organize to bring about these changes' (Women's Action Centre against Violence, 1995, p2). Typically, safety audits will involve a group of users of that space (experts of experience), often accompanied by professional experts such as planners or police officers, spending several hours, usually in the evening, examining the area from the point of view of their sense of safety (Andrew, 2000, p160). The questions will range from amount of litter and vandalism, to lighting, surrounding land uses, amount and speed of traffic, hidden spots along main pedestrian routes, help points, and signs. Sometimes photographs, sketches and annotated maps are used as well as or instead of written audit forms (Cavanaugh, 1998). Out of that activity will come a series of recommendations that the group will then attempt to have implemented (Andrew, 2000, p160). As we have already seen in the examples of Dar es Salaam and rural British Columbia (see Boxes 4.6 and 4.9), the recommendations can be addressed to local governments, individual residents and businesses, and may include both physical design improvements (e.g. better lighting and enforcement of by-laws) and social changes (e.g. better use of public space or employing local people to undertake improvements).

In 1995, two organizations undertook separate evaluations of how the women's safety audit tool had been used. The Women's Action Centre against Violence surveyed 250 organizations across Canada, and 69 responses gave detailed descriptions of how safety audits had been used. The Victorian Community Council against Violence organized a public meeting with over 100 participants in Melbourne, Australia, and wrote up the results of small group discussions. The two studies agreed that when safety audits 'worked' – when they led to demonstrable changes within a reasonable time period (short-term changes within a few months) – they increased individuals' and organizations' sense of ability to create change; they helped to form partnerships between neighbourhood-based organizations, professionals and governments; and they resulted not only in improvements to existing spaces, but ongoing policies and programmes that reduced opportunities for violence or harassment in public space. However, safety audits required a skilled locally based facilitator to organize both the audit itself and follow-up; leadership by practically experienced experts in local communities, rather than domination by professional experts; a wide range of participants who were adequately prepared to make feasible short-term and long-term recommendations; a strong commitment from both local authorities and community organizations to follow up on recommendations; and two-way communications mechanisms on changes that result. Safety audits must therefore been seen as only one component of a long-term community process. Their focus on women should be seen both as a leadership development tool and as a recognition that it is more socially acceptable for women to admit being afraid and uncomfortable – although this does not mean that they require being 'women only' or that they should not include other aspects of identity and marginalization such as age, status as a visible minority or disability. They should not take place without a previous commitment by local authorities to follow up on recommendations. Finally, they deal only indirectly with some of the root causes of violence hitherto identified, focusing on public space issues (Women's Action Centre against Violence, 1995; Victorian Community Council against Violence, 1995).

In Petrovadosk, Russia, the Information Centre of the Independent Women's Forum used safety audits as a tool for residents to improve public housing and form more effective residents' associations. In London, Bristol and Manchester, UK, the Women's Design Service, a planning and design consultancy, helped to organize local women, many of them visible minorities, disabled and/or elderly, to lead regeneration projects in their communities, using safety audits as an initial tool to identify upgrading priorities (Whitzman et al, 2004, pp27, 29). Children's safety audits have been developed as parts of Child-Friendly Cities projects in the Melbourne, Australia, suburb of Frankston, in many cities in New Zealand, and in Emthanjeni and Johannesburg, South Africa (Bartlett, 2006).

Diagnostic tools operate at the individual, household and community scales. Some require a face-to-face interview, such as highly structured victimization surveys, or less formally structured interviews with key decision-makers who are not a member of the steering committee, or victimization surveys. Others work with focus groups (a small number of people with something in common), while others collaborate with larger community meetings, such as youth meetings held at a school. *Focus group* meetings work best with 8 to 12 individuals who have similar experiences or roles. For instance, you could hold a focus group with men who have experienced homelessness, youth who have been in conflict with the law, or women who have undergone family mediation services, in order to hear their opinions on services and garner ideas for change. Community meetings or public forums are best with larger groups, when you want a cross-section or mixture of views, and you want to see if there is a lot of agreement in a community. Even within community meetings, it might be beneficial to separate out discussions into tables of 6 to 12 people and have a 'chair' of each table instructed to ask everyone for their opinion. Two hours is a good time period for any meeting, and providing refreshments is essential. Focus Consultants suggest a set of questions that you might want to ask a community meeting around alternative sentencing: should the programme serve youth, adults or both; what offences (give a list) should be dealt with and not dealt with; what ways can the victims be involved and supported; what is the best way to involve the community in the process; and how should the results be publicized (Focus Consultants, 1998b, p16)? If you were talking to direct service providers, you might want to ask about what they think works well at present; what does not work well; how service coordination might be improved; and training and other needs that would facilitate coordinated service delivery. In the case of any of these methods, keep questions short, open ended and limited to a maximum of four or five. Once again, it is important to end meetings with thanks, a sense of the next steps, and where and how people can find out about the results of consultations.

In all of the case studies described above, community members were trained as surveyors and group facilitators, increasing leadership capacity. Interviewing people, organizing and facilitating focus groups, and analysing information from secondary sources all require good communication skills, the ability to see the larger picture (explaining terms and the purpose of questions), and a certain amount of thoughtfulness and consideration (particularly when people disclose violent incidents). There is no reason not to include young people as leaders in this exercise or other people without formal research training who exhibit the potential for these skills (Focus Consultants, 1998b, p4). The surveyors must always be trained to refer people to services if requested or needed, and to give a sense of where the survey fits into the initiative – for instance, when and how results will be available. Results should be well publicized, and if it is not possible to provide individuals with a copy of the survey report, it should be made available through local organizations, community centres and libraries.

Focus Consultants also warn about the tendency to use community responses as 'ammunition' in a diagnostic survey. If the steering committee has already chosen to focus on a particular form of violence, then that should be stated at the onset of a survey or meeting. If there are real choices to be made through a consultation process, they should also be made clear. Any form of jargon should be explained, and people should be asked questions that relate to their experience. Finally, leading question such as 'Do you think that mediation is a good idea?' should be avoided in favour of questions that might elicit more useful information, such as which offences are appropriate for mediation (Focus Consultants, 1998b, p13).

It is important in any diagnostic, but especially ones in communities that are associated with high levels of crime and violence and low levels of social and human capital, to identify *potential resources*, as well as needs and problems. John Kretzmann and John McKnight, two US community development experts, have written about how viewing communities as a nearly endless list of problems and needs leads directly to the fragmentation of efforts; directs funding not to residents but to service providers, such as health and social workers; and works against potential community leaders who are forced to denigrate their own communities to obtain needs-based funding. In contrast, focusing on developing the assets of individuals, organizations and places in communities can build local capacities and leadership, as we have seen in the examples of Buenos Aires and Raising Voices (see Chapter 4) (Kretzmann and McKnight, 1993).

Kretzmann and McKnight (1993) suggest developing resource inventories at the individual, associational and institutional level. Individual resources at the neighbourhood scale might include experiences and abilities in caring for the physically and mentally ill, people with disabilities, children or the elderly; office and administrative skills; construction, repair, equipment operation and maintenance skills; hairdressing and jewellery making; cooking and tailoring skills; access to transportation; sales experience and abilities; supervision experience; and music, art or dance capacities or interest. These individuals can further develop such skills into enterprises, use them in furthering a community development initiative (e.g. building a community centre) and teach them to others. Young people, in particular, often have time, ideas and creativity, and enthusiasm and energy, which can be tapped, while older people have experience, knowledge of the community and time as well. People with intellectual or physical disabilities are often overlooked as potential assets; but they, too, can often have valuable skills, experience and time, and can offer inspiration to others. Local lawyers, accountants, police officers, librarians, school teachers and nurses can all assist in particular tasks or events.

Similarly, a map of organizations at any scale will usually discover artistic, business, religious, seniors, ethnic or linguistically based, health, media, women's, men's, youth, neighbourhood, self-help, political, school-based, veterans, environmental and sports/recreation groups who are either doing work related to violence prevention, or whose assets could potentially be utilized. In high-income countries (HICs), directories, newspapers, and libraries can be good places to find out about groups. In both HICs and LICs, a 'snowball' survey – asking one well-connected person of groups whom they know, and then asking each group what groups they know of – can provide a workable inventory.

Although Kretzmann and McKnight (1993) talk about institutions, I would rephrase this as specific place-based assets. Schools, parks, businesses, local banks or credit institutions, hospitals, community colleges or universities, libraries, and unused buildings or land can all be mobilized as assets. We have already seen in the example of Dar es Salaam that houses turning on exterior lights improved night-time visibility in a settlement without street lighting. Two examples of place-based asset building, one using a park and another tapping local artistic abilities, will be described in Chapter 6. Even waste can be utilized as a resource: food waste can be composted for community gardens, and recycling or waste collection in informal communities without formal collection services can become a lucrative business.

The resources of the partnership itself require another inventory. Each organization should be willing to disclose financial, human and equipment resources, as well as be honest about its needs. Another aspect of developing a resource inventory is scoping potential funding sources for the initiative itself and for specific potential programmes. Governments, charities, the private sector and individuals are all potential sources of money and in-kind donations (e.g. a dedicated project officer or a community space). Although available grant streams may fit into priorities as they are emerging, initiatives should be cautious about completely changing their priorities for the sake of a pot of money.

A simple survey at the city scale, used by the Toronto Safe City Committee in 1990, asked a large variety of organizations what they were currently doing to prevent violence, what they would like to do and what kind of resources they would need to accomplish these activities. This exercise led to a new grants programme, which was able to fund innovative violence prevention programmes for small amounts of money (see Box 5.7). A third aspect of developing a resource inventory is an ongoing search for what has worked in similar communities. This book attempts to provide a sense of the range of potential interventions; but, fortunately, the number and scope of community safety initiatives have been constantly expanding, as have the excellent sources of information. National, regional and international crime prevention websites and conferences are good sources of current information, as are any networking opportunities with similar initiatives. Finding out and learning from success stories are good tasks for steering committee members to take on at this stage.

The diagnostic stage will usually result in a report, which includes a description of the area; the prevalence, manifestations and consequences of violence and crime, compared, if possible, with a national average or some other comparative data; some sense of who the victims and offenders are; trends over time; a sense of particular locations where violence is most prevalent (this could include people's homes); particular times of the day/week/month/year when violence occurs; immediate trigger circumstances; and longer-term root causes that have been identified. Aside from needs identified in the report, there should also be a sense of resources. The report should also include existing community safety activities and their effectiveness, and some potential sources of new energy and ideas. The report should end by describing the next steps for the partnership, and including contact information and ways to get involved in the initiative. The report is an opportunity to highlight need among policy-makers and the general public. It should be written in an accessible style and launched by 'champions' as part of a media campaign (Butchart et al, 2004, p28).

Stage three: Developing work plans based on a logic framework

The next stage can be the most challenging, but also the most creative, aspect of a community safety partnership. It involves prioritizing the problems and needs identified; developing a draft plan with goals, objectives, strategies, responsibilities and benchmarks; eliciting constructive criticisms from the broader community and revising the draft plan; and getting the plan adopted by some level of governance. There are many tensions at this stage, including the delicate balance between consensual consultation and keeping the momentum of the initiative. At any scale, it will usually take at least two to three more months to accomplish this stage. Any less time, and you probably have not received feedback from the right people. Any more time, and you may further frustrate people who, quite legitimately, want immediate action.

The work plan will be guided by certain parameters. The organization providing funding will often determine the timeline. For instance, if it is a local government plan, it may make sense to adopt a plan that will cover the political cycle of a council (often three years). If the initiative is being funded by senior government or a charity, the amount of time may vary and may also come in two stages: the diagnostic stage and the implementation stage. Although secured funding may only be available annually, it makes sense to plan for at least two years of action and to indicate possible longer-term initiatives that might secure funding from another source. It is rare for a community safety initiative to be funded for more than three years. There will also be some sense of a budget allocation, although the initial scoping may have identified other sources of potential resources and budgets can change before the implementation phase begins.

The partnership should now have worked together to accomplish the concrete task of a diagnostic. As Rosenbaum (2002, p204–205) points out, partnership dynamics need to be cohesive, consensual and committed for a community safety strategy to succeed; so it may be time to evaluate what is happening at and between meetings. There will have already been conflicts; how they are resolved, or left unresolved, is important. To what extent have the organizations involved been able to work out conflicts with one another in and around meetings? Are they being honest about their strengths and weaknesses? If not, is there anything the leader can do at a meeting or by discussing issues with individuals to improve consensus decision-making? Does the partnership meeting occur often enough and is it effective enough to make decisions? Is the right person chairing the meetings? If not, is there another person who can set agendas or chair? Is attendance beginning to decrease? Does everyone appear to know what is going on, or is there a frequent need for bringing individuals up to speed during meetings, which is a waste of time? If the latter, can the minutes and other methods of communication be improved upon?

Consensus is a misunderstood concept. It does not mean complete agreement on all issues: that would be impossible, as well as undesirable, in a diverse and democratic process. It does mean that the perspectives of all participants in a discussion are heard and incorporated within the final decision. It also means that there is a code of conduct in meetings that works to create an environment where all representatives feel comfortable in sharing ideas and opinions without fear of ridicule. Consensus always requires debate and compromise. One of the tasks of a meeting chairperson is to ensure that it is not always the same representatives who are compromising, and that a few individuals do not dominate discussion. A common technique in a steering committee is to have an initial two minute go-around when a contentious topic comes up. Everyone has a chance to state an initial opinion, with no interruptions and cross-talk. Then the meeting chairperson starts with areas of agreement, and disagreements are discussed until a compromise is reached (WICI, 2007a, p18). If it looks as if agreement will not be reached within the time limit of an agenda item or a meeting, the chairperson can convene a small subgroup to work out details, which usually involves the strongest dissenting voices. Alternatively, the item can be put to a vote.

Developing priority issues usually depends upon a risk management framework, which involves ranking risks by seriousness, frequency and how likely it is that prevention will succeed (Northern Territory Office of Crime Prevention, 2003, p28). I have already argued that the initiative will usually begin by defining its problems, but that partnership dynamics and funding sources may have an influence on the identification of problems. Another influence on the definition of priority issues are the data and opinions that come from the community as you accomplish your diagnostic. In other words, looking at the data, there may be particular types of violence that frequently occur and involve serious harm to individuals and communities. They may include the expected (youth violence around particular clubs or drinking establishments, or intimate partner violence) and the unexpected (a hitherto hidden aspect of violence, such as a very high rate of abuse against people with disabilities). As for the question of whether prevention will work, it is important to reiterate that a combination of short-term measures that can control violence and perhaps demonstrate immediate and visible reductions in acts, along with long-term measures to address the root causes of the problems identified, are best. For instance, if a quick and demonstrable change can be accomplished through a programme to reduce violence in and around licensed premises, and the applicable partners (such as owners of licensed premises and law enforcement) are ready to collaborate, it may make sense to include this as a priority issue, particularly if this form of violence is prevalent and harmful in a community.

Confirming priorities also depends upon the existing resources that are identified in the diagnostic or scoping stage. There may be programmes or policies operating in the community that have good evaluations or otherwise are acknowledged as working well to prevent priority problems. These policies or programmes can be supported, integrated within other services and possibly expanded, particularly if they fit into existing or emerging priority problems. For instance, there may be a young offenders' diversion scheme that has worked with a small group, but can be expanded either geographically, in terms of additional offences, or with another population group such as adults. This will be particularly important if youth violence, or reduction of numbers of people imprisoned in a community, is a priority. Or a public education campaign operating out of an ethno-specific agency can be translated for use by other ethno-specific and mainstream organizations if the marginalization of particular communities, or violence within a particular community, is identified as a priority. A third example might be an excellent programme or policy that has worked in another place, and which an organization is able to immediately adopt. For instance, it may be possible for a hospital to fairly quickly adopt an intake form that scans for violence, and has already been tested in a nearby hospital, if inadequate identification of, and response to, child abuse or elder abuse has been identified as a priority. For a community safety plan that spans the next one to three years, three or four violence prevention priority issues should be an appropriate number.

It is important that the partnership develops a *vision* of a safer community, or a *mission statement*, during this phase. This may sound like a 'touchy-feely' exercise to some, and, in fact, is not really appropriate as a first step for a partnership when members have not previously worked together. But assuming that the diagnostic stage has taken a couple of months and regular meetings, there may be enough trust in the group to explore the ultimate purpose of a community safety strategy. A logic-based model would suggest that the group agree on some ultimate *goals*, or overall purposes and directions. For instance, the ultimate goals might include violence being a rare occurrence in X community, and justice (help to victims and censure to offenders) being timely when violence transpires. This sort of goal involves influencing people. Who would need to be influenced to start developing this goal locally? How might they best be influenced? What specific actions would move you closer to influencing people? How would you know that positive change can begin to happen?

The group might then begin to develop *objectives or recommendations*, specific actions that would work towards these goals. The objectives must be specific, measurable, attainable, realistic and timely (SMART), given the timeframe. Objectives might include developing a protocol for gathering information in hospitals, clinics and health centres on the incidence of violence within the next year. This would comprise an *output* objective and might require a preliminary *input* objective: holding four training sessions with frontline medical staff within the next year to acquaint them on how to ask questions and how to refer victims of violence. There would be an anticipated *outcome objective* to this measure: that the amount of victims of violence correctly identified and assisted by the participating health organizations double within a year of implementing the protocol.

There is no magic number of recommendations or priority programmes for a draft community safety strategy report, nor is there a magic timeline. Aside from the aspect of timing (combining short-term, medium-term and longer-term measures), the question of budgets (both immediate and longer-term amounts) will help guide the number and type of recommendations. It is possible to say that additional funding for a particular programme will be sought in a draft report, and then a funder is found before the final report is adopted. Short-term recommendations can generally be funded and accomplished in the current fiscal year. Medium-term recommendations require an allocation in subsequent budgets for one or two years. Longer-term recommendations will require funding for at least three to five years, and it will probably not be possible to show immediate impacts.

Each recommendation must have a benchmark, an indicator of success and a lead government department or organization that is responsible for its implementation. The SMART principle applies to these recommendations. The problems of violence can often seem overwhelming, particularly in the wake of diagnostic research. It is important to take an 'incrementalist' approach, even towards a problem as immediate and devastating as violence. The roots of violence in individuals, families, communities and societies take a long time to develop, and they will not be dug out overnight. On the other hand, specific and seemingly small-scale successes, as we have already seen, can quickly spill over into much more significant changes at all scales. Thus, recommendations should provide a balance between relatively low-cost, easy-to-accomplish ideas, and those which are more risky, developmental and longer term.

While it is important to learn from past successes and what works in other communities, each place is unique and innovation has to start somewhere. Initiatives should not be afraid to modify tools and strategies that have been used elsewhere. The safety audits described thus far are perfect examples: a tool that starts in one place and then is constantly modified to meet the needs of different user groups. Initiatives should not be afraid to take a creative approach, particularly when there are interesting resources on tap. A newly formed community centre in Toronto decided to promote Capoeiera, a Brazilian form of self-defence that incorporates aerobic and dance elements, because there was a recently arrived migrant instructor willing to give free demonstrations. Six months later, the weekly classes had brought together dozens of young and old people of both genders and all backgrounds. The classes became a cross-cultural and intergenerational meeting place for the neighbourhood, particularly when they went on to provide very popular demonstrations at the local park on summer Sundays.

The draft action plan will include a very brief summary of the diagnostic or at least a sense of the main problem to be addressed, with one or two illustrative statistics; a vision of a safer community (e.g. what you want your community to be like in three years, and in the next generation); a sense of specific and measurable goals over the time period of the initiative; the strategies, programmes and policies that will be undertaken to achieve these goals (some of which will be new and some of which may already exist and be 're-branded' as part of a community safety strategy); links to other ongoing initiatives; outcome targets or indicators that will be used to measure progress towards the goals; timeframes; and resources. It will also include mechanisms for community comment, such as telephone numbers, a website or email address, and times and locations of public meetings. The draft plan should be kept short, perhaps ten pages at most, and as little as three pages, in order to ensure that as many people as possible will read it. It might be summarized in a poster or a single page on a website. There should be at least three weeks, and preferably at least one public meeting, before the draft plan is amended. A more typical review period is six weeks to two months.

The draft plan should be sent to the people you want to influence and potentially work with, including the general public. This could include politicians in senior and junior governments, community organizations, charities and businesses, and the target groups with whom you will work. For instance, if one of your priorities is violence against women, try to get out to as many relevant women's organizations as possible, including those who were initially resistant. It is also important to think of ways of reaching women who are not involved in formal organizations through targeting particular media outlets (e.g. women's magazines). The same principle applies to youth violence, child abuse, elder abuse and hate crimes. This is the time when your champions should reach out to the media. In many LICs, radio is a much better mechanism to reach a broad variety of citizens than television or print media. Posters and copies of the report in shopping centres, libraries, parks, schools and other public places can increase recognition of the draft plan and potentially increase its political approach.

Every agency or organization named as a lead on a particular recommendation must sign off on their agreement before the plan goes on to be adopted. The steering committee may have the authority to sign off on a final work plan. It is much more common for the work plan to be approved by a local or senior level of government, particularly when it provides funding. This is where groundwork with politicians pays off.

Try to keep track of requests for information through tracking hits on a website, telephone log books and attendance records at public meetings. In addition, keep track of every bit of media coverage. This is important not only for evaluation, but in order to facilitate further information dissemination. For instance, if you do another report at a later date, remember which reporters are most interested in the topic and which community members most want to be involved. It is not unusual, when a draft plan is in its final stages, for the media to run an 'exposé' on one particular controversial recommendation – for instance, an injection site for intravenous drug users or a youth restorative justice campaign. It is important that champions are prepared to counter negative publicity with a set of clear messages on the effectiveness of a harm reduction or non-prison based correctional approach. Fact sheets or briefing notes on the main strategies will help.

The final product of this stage is a work plan that has been adopted and is ready for implementation. Box 5.6 provides an example of a logic-based work plan from Wales. Box 5.7 focuses further on the question of how 'community' and 'consensus' are defined, and the potential negative impacts that simplistic assumptions about consensus can have on marginalized communities.

Box 5.6 *A logic-based work plan in Cardiff, Wales*

Cardiff is the largest city in Wales, with a population of a little over 300,000. The Cardiff Violence Prevention Group was formed in 1996, led by police and health promotion agencies. The initial impetus for its formation was concern expressed by health professionals that only a small proportion of violent offences in and around licensed premises that required medical treatment were being reported to police, and that 30 per cent of these victims who were treated developed severe psychological problems as a result of their experiences (Butchart et al, 2004, p42). The programme received funding for an initial study in 1998, based on a detailed database from police and hospital sources. It found that alcohol-related incidents heavily concentrated on Friday and Saturday nights. Only 25 per cent of incidents were reported to police, which means that 75 per cent did not receive any formal victim support. Over half of the violent incidents occurred within or just outside licensed premises. Most of those involved as victims or offenders were young white males, 42 per cent with previous arrests for violent or public order offences. Door staff were involved in 16 per cent of offences as victims or offenders. The most common form of assault was hitting or kicking; but 10 per cent of incidents involved broken glass, with the use of knives and other weapons being rare.

While many hospital cases were quickly dealt with, 15 per cent of victims suffered broken bones and 12 per cent had severe cuts requiring stitches. There was also considerable loss of teeth.

A coalition was formed during the diagnostic stage consisting of police, accident and emergency consultants at the hospital, magistrates in charge of licensing premises, the local government and consultant psychologists associated with Victim Services. This was a high-level team, and the police were willing to include the initiative in their priorities. Many bar owners saw the potential for a win–win situation in terms of renewing licences and promoting the night-time economy.

In 2000, a one-year action plan was implemented. This included a range of programme and policy changes. A licensees' forum with police led to regular sharing of incident reports, the development of training modules for drinks servers (Servewise) and better selection of door staff. Many bars also changed the glasses they served drinks in to tougher glass or plastic. The hospital implemented a new and simple incident reporting form that asked the victim when and where the assault occurred, who had committed the assault (including how many people, what gender and whether the offender(s) were known or not to the victim), whether the assault had been reported to the police, and whether the victim would like to report the incident to the police. A Victim Support team was located at the hospital on weekends, which led to better and more immediate psychological services for victims. There was a publicity campaign, involving local media and posters, on the nature of violent crime in licensed premises, with a simple message: 'Silence hurts too. Tell someone if you have suffered a violent attack. That way we can help.' A degree of 'shaming and blaming' of clubs that did not take action on violence occurred through the media, which included targeted policing in hot spots and the threat of removing licences. A cognitive behavioural programme for repeat offenders was introduced.

The outcome was a 4 per cent decrease in hospital-reported assaults in a year, although there had been a 10 per cent increase in licensed premises capacity in Cardiff. Data analysis, based on trend analysis since 1996, predicted that without intervention the expected level of violent incidents would have increased by 8 per cent. About 100 assaults were estimated to have been prevented over the first year of the initiative, and if even one of them had involved a serious wounding, it would have cost the National Health Service more than the entire cost of the project. A comparison of hospital rates and police rates suggested that reporting of violent incidents had doubled to about 50 per cent. The initiative then spread to tackle hate crimes and violence against women, using some of the same reporting, publicity and service delivery mechanisms that had been developed over the previous years (Maguire and Nettleton, 2003).

Reasons for success included a long well-researched lead up to the action plan, which involved building trust and cooperation with key players as well as the development of a very useful database. Both bar owners and the media promoted the initiative widely. Police and politicians were prepared for an increase in reported violent crime and did not panic when that occurred.

Box 5.7 *Questioning appeals to 'community'*

Over the past 20 years, there have been many excellent and thought-provoking critiques of mainstream crime prevention initiatives, often on the basis of the exclusionary nature of these initiatives. As discussed previously, criminological theory has tended to focus on so-called deviant behaviour, and assumes that crime is committed by a small group of easily recognizable 'anti-social' individuals, concentrated in 'problem' communities. These problem communities have traditionally been associated with the central city, although now the locus for concern is often suburban, particularly in Europe. Elizabeth Wilson (1991) has tracked the emergence of this discourse in the 19th century, where women and children needed to be protected from the 'evils of the city'. Don Mitchell (2003, p200) has described the current discriminatory consequences of the quest to attain perfect 'order' and 'control' in cities – the tendency to criminalize classes of people such as 'the rowdy teenaged boy, the ill-smelling drunk man and the importuning beggar'. Iris Marion Young (1990, p227) contends that 'the ideal of community denies and represses social difference, the fact that the polity cannot be thought of as a unity in which all participants share a common experience and common values'. Specific case studies, such as focus groups with five 'identity groups' in Newcastle upon Tyne, England, show conflicting attitudes to measures taken to improve community safety in the city centre, such as closed-circuit television (CCTV) and Anti-Social Behaviour Orders (ASBOs) (Pain and Townshend, 2002).

Adam Crawford (1999, p515) has described the 'ideology of unity' behind much criminological theory and practice that takes a moral consensus as given, rather than constantly negotiated. We have already seen how much violence has remained hidden in the crime prevention discourse until recently, and we cannot assume that the boundaries of what are considered acceptable and unacceptable behaviour will ever become static. The particular problem of crime prevention, which to some extent is shared by the 'softer' notion of community safety and the more focused notion of violence prevention, is that it tends to rest on the notion of 'defensive exclusivity', protecting one set of people (or places) from 'others' or 'outsiders'. This can be seen most extremely in crime prevention through environmental design (CPTED) notions of 'defensible space' and criminal justice notions of 'zero tolerance', but is also implicit in strategies such as the use of CCTV, neighbourhood watch, private patrols and regulated entry systems. These strategies assume that offenders are found outside the home and the community, and deny that they might be our families, our familiars or ourselves. Strategies that locate the problem with 'others' tend to feed insecurity and reinforce stereotypes and thus are an extremely inappropriate focus for community-building (Crawford, 1999, p516).

What, then, are the strategies that can knit communities together in the urban fabric, that can develop (in the current jargon) bridging social capital, and can recognize difference while developing a social consensus? As Crawford (1999, p517) points out, trying to coerce civility through the threat of criminal sanctions, as occurs with ASBOs in the UK, makes little sense. Civility, like non-violence, may be influenced like coercive social controls, just as cigarette smokers found it successively more difficult to smoke in public places. But the ultimate impetus for being a better family member, neighbour and citizen must come from an individual understanding of the benefits of this behaviour. There may be an irreducible tension between 'feeling secure' and 'being social'. For instance, if I'm told to stay indoors because I'm a threat in public, why would I not turn my frustration onto my family? If I live alone and never go out, I may minimize my risk of assault, but at what cost to myself and to my community? If children are never allowed to explore their neighbourhoods independently, if people avoid places and situations where they might feel unsafe or uncomfortable, we will have all retreated to voluntary prisons of our own design to the greater detriment of our families, our communities and our societies.

As many feminist theorists have pointed out, the right to the city not only entails the right to full and complete use of open space, but also the right to participate in decision-making, including redefining what is public and private, and fighting for the right for comfort and belonging in both the public and private spheres (Fenster, 2005, pp219–220). Many writers, such as the African-American feminist bell hooks (1984), have spoken about how black women experience home space as safe and public space as threatening because of racist, as well as sexist violence. Others, such as the migrant domestic workers in Singapore interviewed by Belinda Yeoh and Shirlena Huang (1998), or the homeless and socially excluded youth interviewed by Rachel Pain and her colleagues (2002), find public space safer and more conducive to privacy and autonomy than where they live. The problem is when one person's comfort and belonging interferes with another person's freedoms. This is true whether it refers to a man hassling a woman on the street or a woman insisting that a man simply asking her for money constitutes harassment; when a man insists on his children being quiet and dinner being ready when he returns home from work; or when your neighbour's teenage daughter has her friends over for loud parties once too often.

We live in a global society where protection of the rights of the family appears to extend to tolerance of abuse within families, and protection of the rights of individuals only appears to apply to individuals who need the least protection (Eisler, 1997). The right of communities and societies to feel safe also needs to be challenged, particularly when it leads to exclusionary practices such as the labelling of one age or identity group as 'the problem'.

What does that mean in terms of community safety plans? Simply that the intended or unintended impacts of strategies aimed at making one group safer and that result in making another group less safe need to be continuously monitored, and ameliorative counter-strategies need to be adopted if the injustices continue. I have written about how a campaign to catch a man who exposed his genitals to girls and women for three years in Toronto's largest central city park was used as an excuse to crack down on consensual homosexual activity by the police, which was certainly not the intent of the women who complained to city staff (Whitzman, 2002b).

Community safety policies also need to address bridging social capital strategies. Measures that support intergenerational or intercultural cooperation should be supported, as should measures that link, as well as strengthen, neighbourhoods within cities. Measures that seek to resolve conflicts at the most local scale possible, such as community mediation centres, should be encouraged. In all aspects of violence prevention, an approach that promotes autonomy, the right to make one's own choices so long as they do not harm others, must be preferred to an approach that promotes dependence on 'authorities' to keep individuals, families and communities safe.

Source: Crawford (1999)

Stage four: Implementation and monitoring

The end of a plan's development and the start of a plan's implementation often mark a break in the community safety process. The first six months to a year, where partnerships developed, a diagnostic analysis takes place and a plan is developed is one of excitement and challenge. The steering committee may be meeting once every three weeks to manage the information flows and make decisions. The outputs are concrete: a diagnostic and an action plan. There is often a lot of media attention towards this new issue.

The next one to three years involve the slow development of actual programmes and policies. This process can be very frustrating. The pace slows, with the steering committee usually needing to meet only every month or two. The action plan may have to be adjusted in terms of the actual funding available. Members of the steering committee may become dissatisfied with the slow pace or move on to new positions that necessitate the orientation of a new representative. Occasionally there is the painful process of adjusting the membership of the steering committee to reflect new priorities or new sources of energy and ideas. It is important to keep attendance at meetings high: keep meetings tightly structured and have every agenda item attached to an action unless it is for information only (such as a progress report on a recommendation). It is also important to ensure that all steering committee members feel that their work counts, and that it is not only up to the leader and the coordinator. Involving them in training activities, the development of protocols and the creation of an awards programme (see below) can be one method of keeping these people involved. Good communications structures, such as the use of email to disseminate information about new funding opportunities and progress on strategies, can be another way of encouraging steering committee members to feel part of the project.

An important aspect of the implementation phase is maintaining a research agenda on violence beyond the original diagnostic. The World Health Organization, discussing the national scale, suggests developing a research agenda on interpersonal violence, supporting a research centre based at a university or research institute, developing dissemination methods for research findings, including media plans and policy workshops, and integrating violence prevention within undergraduate and postgraduate research in many disciplines through scholarships and research funding (Butchart et al, 2004, pp28–29). This rather ambitious strategy would need to be scaled down at the local or neighbourhood level; but keeping research partnerships going is vital for both evaluation and documentation of initiatives.

Celebrating successes is a key to sustaining energies for the long haul (WICI, 2007b, p27). When working on a sometimes overwhelming problem such as violence, it is important to recognize smaller short-term successes: a 4 per cent decrease in violence around licensed premises, as was described in Cardiff, or a better-lit residential area, as was the case in Dar es Salaam. Establishing annual awards for exemplary individual, community organization, private-sector and public-sector accomplishments is an excellent way of celebrating small victories. The recognition of these accomplishments is also very helpful to further information on what works to prevent violence. Asking the award recipients to write up their lessons or present to their peers can also be a useful method of learning from success. It is also important to provide joint capacity-building activities for a steering committee or a group of people working on strategies. One of the best activities we ever devised at the Toronto Safe City Committee was a training session with a corporate media coach for members of the committee and recent grant recipients. There we were taught how to focus on delivering our key messages, no matter what questions were asked of us.

This skill became very useful almost immediately, when a negative media campaign, engineered by a politician who did not like the committee, asked what we were doing in reaction to an extremely well-publicized shooting incident. The nature of a proactive and long-term initiative on violence prevention is always challenged when a particular incident appears to require a strong immediate reaction. There may be times, during the implementation phase, when 'a series of unfortunate events' requires human or monetary resources to be spent on short-term reactions to escalating incidents. But it is also important to constantly return to the 'dollars and sense' of longer-term prevention, to point out that an initiative is dealing with the root causes of violence, and to use mechanisms that are based on those that have been proven to work. It is also important to be able to point to successful short-term recommendations that have already led to small changes.

Annual monitoring reports help to maintain the momentum of a project, provide useful media opportunities and, last but certainly not least, keep implementation on track. These monitoring reports might include progress on recommended actions; other aspects of progress (the results of community safety awards, new partnerships and related action from government, community organizations and the private sector); some measures of participation in programmes, enquiries or the distribution of public information materials; annual indicators that measure the impacts of actions; media reports on the strategy and its components; and any changes that have occurred in the strategy. The London Domestic Violence Strategy has produced particularly good annual reports, usually released in conjunction with an annual conference/training session, and attracting considerable media interest.

Stage five: Evaluation – the hardest part

Evaluation is a thorough and objective process that assesses the relevance, effectiveness and impact of a work plan and the policies and programmes within it. It seeks to determine whether goals and objectives have been met, whether strategies are working as intended and whether activities are implemented as planned. Evaluation is thus a continuous process from the problem definition and partnerships stage onwards as goals and outcomes will influence indicators and other measures of success and impact (WICI, 2007b, p28). It proves successes and analyses failures, it informs modification of strategies and it allows others to learn from your initiative. About 10 per cent of your total budget should be set aside for evaluation, and the evaluation process will take at least two months.

Some of the reasons why evaluations of community safety policies are so problematic have already been discussed. The quasi-experimental criteria discussed in *Preventing Crime: What Works, What Doesn't, What Is Promising*, otherwise known as the Sherman report (Sherman et al, 1997), are virtually impossible to replicate when dealing with a diffuse set of interventions at the community, city or nation scale. There can be no random sampling of individuals that will undergo the 'treatment', and the selection of a comparison control site where no intervention takes place is also virtually impossible since no two communities are alike. Saying that the murder rate declined faster in Bogotá than in Cali and Medellín, two other Colombian cities, may have less to do with the impacts of the integrated strategy itself than the fact that the two latter cities are located closer to the drug trade-related 20-year Colombian civil war. Proving causative relationships, as opposed to correlation between initiatives and impacts, is also virtually impossible. The well-publicized decline in police-reported crime rates in New York City during the period of 1993 to 1996 was associated by promoters of zero tolerance, including the police chief and the mayor, as an outcome of these policies. But reported crime rates went down in 17 of the 25 largest US cities during that same period, and many cities without zero tolerance policies showed larger decreases (Young, 1998, p64). Research findings are often mixed and contradictory. For instance, one of the most heavily evaluated strategies in the US – mandatory arrests on incidents of domestic violence as a means of preventing repeat violence – found three cities where there was an increase in incidents and three cities were there was a decrease (Tilley and Laycock, 2000, p216). If an evaluation does not show the intended impacts, it is often difficult to tell whether the intervention did not set in motion the causal processes/activities identified in the logic model (programme failure) or the activities went 'by the book' but did not result in the expected effects (theory failure) (Rosenbaum, 2002, p209). It is for this reason that many criminologists reject the notion of quasi-experimentation in evaluating community safety initiatives and instead take a more ethnographic or 'realist' approach to the context, mechanisms and outcomes in a particular community (National Community Crime Prevention Programme Australia, 1999, p94–95).

Evaluations are highly political. Any form of research takes time and money, and these factors make them problematic in terms of policy-making schedules and budgets. Annual victimization surveys take time and money, and demographic data may only be available during census years. Once there is a policy commitment, research findings that are equivocal, or that suggest the intervention did not work, are highly unwelcome (Tilley and Laycock, 2000, p215). The very governments and organizations which support community safety initiatives are afraid of bad news. To give another example from Toronto, attempts to evaluate interventions in making Toronto's subway system and largest central park safer were repeatedly blocked because politicians and bureaucrats were concerned that findings that the public was still insecure would be seized upon by the media as evidence that the local and metropolitan governments were wasting money with 'soft' community safety efforts instead of more policing.

Focusing on evidence-based policy can also lead to the phenomenon of 'evaluation-led priority setting', the process by which governments fund initiatives that can provide quick and demonstrable wins and neglect the harder long-term issues. For instance, the UK had a national target of reducing residential burglaries by 25 per cent between 1999 and 2005 as part of its Crime Reduction Strategy. Because this was considered a fairly straightforward issue, with a relatively strong research evidence base on which to build policy, it became a lead initiative. Areas with significantly higher than the national rate of home burglaries were targeted, and university researchers were contracted to provide process, outcome and cost-effectiveness evaluations. The initial funding was UK£50 million over three years (one fifth of the total available budget for all crime prevention initiatives). But even this straightforward initiative soon foundered in delays, and an independent evaluation in 2000 found that almost half the round-one budget went to projects with 'very serious' or 'significant' implementation problems (Homel et al, 2004, pp32–37). Despite these problems, and the stated commitment to evidence-based programmes, a second round of funding almost immediately commenced.

A contradictory attitude was found in relation to the Violence against Women (VAW) initiative. This initiative started later, in 2000, and received only UK£10 million in funding over three years. According to the same UK Home Office evaluation report:

> ... *the VAW initiative aimed to develop and implement local strategies at reducing two types of violence experienced by women: domestic violence and rape, and sexual assault by known perpetrators. Significantly, the VAW initiative is working in an area in which there is an acknowledged poor evidence base about effective programmes.*
> (Homel et al, 2004, p39)

The VAW initiative therefore focused on an initial collection of good practice literature, followed by the awarding of UK£6.3 million in total to 34 closely evaluated pilot projects (Hester and Westmarland, 2005). Unlike the burglary reduction programme, the national government did not set targets for the reduction of violent crime or 'racial incidents', which may be related to the fact that this violence prevention initiative received only one fifth of the funding of the burglary reduction initiative. While some emphasis on quick wins is important, the fear of evaluation should not be used as an excuse to neglect deep-rooted violence issues and long-term interventions. Concern about evaluations can also detract from the flexibility of initiatives. If programmes are modified in response to new ideas or priorities set by the client population, this can sometimes be resisted by those concerned about straying from the logic model that originally informed the programme (Rosenbaum, 2002, p210).

There are many different types of evaluation. *Programme* evaluation measures the 'what' of strategies: whether they proceeded according to plan. It includes elements such as whether the initiative carried out recommendations as stated in the plan; whether policies and protocols were incorporated within appropriate legislation or organizational structures; and whether programmes did what they said they would do and were able to secure ongoing funding. *Process* evaluation measures the 'how' of strategies and initiatives. It includes how many people commented on the draft of a plan and whether they included the people whom the strategies were aimed at reaching; increased public awareness of the intervention; and how satisfied people on a steering committee, other key organizations or the general public were with the deliberations and the results of a community safety strategy. *Outcome* or *impact* evaluations measure the 'why' of strategies by identifying changes in the behaviour and outcomes of targeted populations. Ideally, it is preferable to measure not only outcomes (the measures of changes), but *effects* (the outcomes minus other things that might have happened without the intervention); however, this is almost impossible without an identical comparison group (Rosenbaum, 2002, p208). Outcome evaluations also depend upon timeframes. A short-term outcome might include increased public awareness of an issue as a result of a public education campaign, such as the number of people attending or being aware of Bogotá's Women's Night Out. A medium-term outcome might be changed attitudes or behaviour, such as decreases in violence around licensed establishments in Cardiff over the course of a very well-planned year. A long-term outcome might be reductions in adolescent and adult criminality in a group of children who received pre-school education, such as the evaluation of the Perry Pre-school programme 22 years after the intervention. All varieties of evaluation require both 'objective' and perceptual data, and both quantitative and qualitative data.

Evaluation can also look at changes to places, people and processes (White and Coventry, 2000, p22). Changes to places include not only specific adjustments to the built environment, but also additional services in places and transformations in the way that people feel about and use places. Changes to people include changes in the number of victims and offenders, as well as modifications to the way in which people perceive, and behave towards, one another and particular institutions. Changes to processes include organizational capacity-building and training, and increased inter-organizational linkage.

The importance of gender analysis has been an underlying theme of this chapter in terms of problem setting, partnership building, diagnosis, and plan development and implementation. A breakdown by gender of evaluation results can result in significant differences, and the Canadian National Crime Prevention Strategy requires a gender analysis in evaluations of its large-scale funded projects. For instance, a project on Promoting Peaceful Conduct in Quebec, a school-based project on conflict resolution and peer mediation involving over 3000 children aged 7 to 12, found that female participants gained improvement in emotional control, which led to decreased anti-social behaviour. Male participants were found to have increased their conflict resolution skills; but there were actually heightened levels of problem behaviour after the intervention. Gwinch'in Outdoor Classroom, a project for 112 aboriginal youth aged 6 to 12, combining traditional learning from elders, life skills and communication skills, led to much higher social skills for males and 20 per cent higher school attendance. Female participants did not show statistically significant improvements in either school attendance or social skills (Leonard et al, 2005). Finding that impacts are greater for one gender does not mean that the programme should be abandoned or even provided to only one gender. It simply means that a range of strategies should be used in all settings.

Most evaluation processes involve a combination of self-evaluation and external evaluation. The advantages of self-evaluation are that they help to build staff and steering committee expertise, and force the partnership to start thinking about evaluation from the first. The great disadvantage, of course, is that the evaluation will rightfully be seen as less credible, involving as it does a conflict of interest between doing the work and judging the work, and it will also take a great deal of time and internal expertise to handle all tasks. The advantage of hiring an external evaluation is that you can get an 'expert' who will hopefully provide an objective perspective. The disadvantage of an external evaluation, aside from cost, is that the evaluation expert may know little about the field of community safety and violence prevention, the history of the initiative, and is usually hired only for a short period of time (Focus Consultants, 1998a, p3). A combination approach can mean that much of the work (a logic model that matches goals and objectives with strategies and indicators) is done beforehand as part of the community safety process (possibly with a little start-up help from an evaluation expert), minimizing cost and also maximizing the potential that evaluation will reflect the needs of the organization.

Evaluation of community safety initiatives often includes changes in reported police crime rates, but rarely do they include a greater confluence between rates of victimization as reported in surveys and agency statistics, and reported police statistics. I would certainly suggest that this as an important evaluation measure. The amount and type of media coverage, not only of the initiative but of the idea of community safety and violence prevention itself, might be a good measure, as might awareness of the initiative and its programmes. The number of people involved in particular programmes and events might be a measure of success, particularly if community mobilization is a goal, as might the number of people requesting information on the initiative. The extent to which activities involved their target populations might be a measure of success in initiatives directed at a specific group, as might increases in the target population's awareness of, and satisfaction with, violence prevention services. Increases in the number of people using public spaces and services might be a criterion, as might decreases in a gender differential around both use and insecurity, especially during evening hours. Specific improvements to public spaces and services might be a criterion as well, particularly if they were in reaction to tools such as safety audits. The establishment of particular protocols and policies would be an important measure in any initiative, as would the number of organizations involved.

Keep in mind that a well-organized community safety process will have established baseline measures dealing with at least some of these items at the start of the process. Police and agency statistics, victimization surveys, interviews with key informants, focus groups, inventories of community resources and initial indicators can all be replicated after one to three years to see where change has taken place. Goals and objectives may have been modified over time; but the initial goals can be compared to this progress. Monitoring and documenting activities and programmes, a well-kept set of meeting minutes, maintaining informal feedback databases such as phone and email records, website hits, and comments left on websites or at public displays will be useful sources of both qualitative and quantitative information for evaluation (Focus Consultants, 1998a, p7).

It is important not to over-rely on either quantitative measures such as indicators and other statistics, or qualitative measures such as pre- and post-interviews with partners. Numbers, such as indicators, can send the clearest message about success or failure of a programme or initiative. Every programme should have a realistic target for prevention and be held to that target. But sometimes an anecdote, such as the one related in Chapter 4 about Julio's sneakers getting returned, can add interest to an evaluation report, as well as explain what happened in a much more comprehensible way than any statistic. Here is another example of anecdotal information from the excellent series of booklets produced by the Aboriginal Justice Directorate in Canada on the specific issue of evaluation of diversion programmes:

> *We've developed a two-page summary of key justice statistics in our community for the three years since we've started the diversion programme. It's for the Aboriginal Justice Directorate and the Province; but I think we'll give several copies to our school. The teacher in the education committee has been saying she has no information about our community that she can give our students.* (Focus Consultants, 1998a, p13)

This anecdote relates that there are baseline statistics that can be compared, but that the partnership products are being used creatively in the community, and that partners are listening and responding to one another (an aspect of process evaluation).

The anecdote also reinforces the point that a good community safety process is accountable not only to its funders and government sponsors, but also to the organizations on its steering committee, to the general population and to the high-risk populations whom it serves. As many people as possible should be informed of, and involved in, the evaluation process, from the funders or government bodies themselves, to clients of particular services, to staff of organizations involved in initiatives, to the general public. This ensures multiple sources of information that will provide a much more rounded form of evaluation.

It is important not to be mechanistic about evaluations. Replications of the Duluth education programme for intimate violence offenders did not work as well to prevent repeat violence in some other US sites (Jackson et al, 2003). This was seized upon by some detractors as 'evidence' that the model did not work, full stop. What the results probably meant was that the context of the programme was different in different places, with varying levels of inter-agency coordination, public awareness around violence, and other supports to victims and offenders. The conclusion might be that it is important to learn from strategies that have worked elsewhere; but it is also vital to modify strategies in order to reflect the needs and strengths of a particular place, conduct evaluations of how the strategy works in a particular community and find contextual reasons why the results may vary. It is worth repeating that there is no one 'magic bullet' strategy to prevent violence.

Evaluation is an ethical process, with explicit and implicit values underlying what measures are used and how evaluation takes place (White and Coventry, 2000, p18). For instance, if a participatory process is a goal, then measures of participation, particularly of target groups such as youth or women, should be included. If administrative change in organizations such as the police and local government was an implicit goal, then changes in the way decisions are made, or public satisfaction with these organizations, should be measured. If conflicts took place, it is important to record these conflicts and how they were resolved. There are also formal aspects of ethics – for instance, if a research institution is involved, it may have to undergo an ethics review process to ensure that confidential information is not disclosed or that psychological harm is not caused by the research.

If possible, the evaluation should include not only intended impacts, but any unintended effects, which may be positive or negative. For instance, two organizations on a steering committee might have developed an initiative on another issue, which is an unintended positive impact. An example of an unintended negative impact was given earlier in this chapter, when I received a call from the head of a police division saying that we had asked them to stop one man from showing his genitals in a non-consensual manner to women in a park, but the police had been able to stop eight men from showing their genitals in a consensual manner to one another in the park that week! I hasten to add that the head of the police division genuinely appeared to see this as an eightfold multiple of success, rather than an illustration of his inability to distinguish between consensual and non-consensual sexual activity.

Evaluation should thus not be thought of as a distinct activity at the end of a community safety process, but a continual aspect of the process. The products should include annual reports, as well as a more lengthy report at the end of the mandate or funding cycle of a community safety initiative. All reports should strive to include what worked, what did not work and should be changed, and what is promising in terms of future actions. The report should be explicit as to the linkages between goals, objectives, inputs, outputs and outcomes. It should explain the sources of data and the methodologies used to answer the question of whether the goals and objectives were met. It may also summarize evaluations of particular components of community safety initiatives, such as those that are discussed in Chapter 6. It should end with recommendations for further action based on the findings of the evaluation. Appendices may include the actual survey or interview tools used, which is very useful to other initiatives that may incorporate the evaluation (Focus Consultants, 1998e, p9).

Stage six: Modification, maintenance and mainstreaming

Community safety initiatives may be successful if they last only a year or two, leaving behind a legacy of improved community capacity, innovative programmes, entrenched protocols and policies, and a sense of hope. In most cases, however, it takes several iterations or cycles of community safety processes to get it right. Box 5.8 returns to the example of the Toronto Safe City Committee to demonstrate community safety planning over the long run.

Box 5.8 *Successive community safety processes: The example of the Toronto Safe City Committee, 1990–2007*

During the first three years of its mandate, the Toronto Safe City Committee focused on urban planning and design issues, creating guidelines that were eventually developed into a book (Wekerle and Whitzman, 1995), and became the basis of safe design guidelines in other areas, including the European Union safer design guidelines developed in 2003 (prevention of crime through environmental planning and design standard ENV-14383-2). But, as mentioned earlier, by 1990, members of the Safe City Committee felt that the initial 30 recommendations were well under way and there was the need to look at a more ambitious mandate. Accordingly, over 120 neighbourhood and city-wide organizations were consulted on what they were currently doing to prevent violence against women and other vulnerable groups, what they would like to be doing, and how local government could help them to achieve these aims. The outcomes of this second round of consultation included a recommendation for a new grants programme called Breaking the Cycle of Violence, which would assist small organizations such as ethno-specific groups or neighbourhood houses to carry out violence prevention projects.

A key feature of the second report was a public education campaign that

---

included posters and pamphlets on violence prevention in ten languages, highlighting available services for women and men, along with a guide to preventing violence against women at the community level. The Toronto Labour Council worked with the city to develop and implement a workplace education programme on wife assault, delivered to approximately 5000 employees in 50 organizations or businesses. The Safe City Committee now included representatives of men's anti-violence organizations, an advocacy group for women with disabilities, ethno-specific organizations and neighbourhood houses, as well as women-serving agencies and community groups. The grants programme not only funded hundreds of excellent community initiatives, but influenced both provincial and national crime prevention funding priorities, as well as private charities such as the United Way.

As the Safe City Committee moved to a broader community development approach, the small staff complement (I had by now been promoted to full-time coordinator and provided with a part-time administrative assistant) moved from the planning department to the Healthy City Office, which brought together a range of related equity-building and health-promoting initiatives, including committees on homelessness, drug abuse prevention, ageing, disabilities, racism and homophobia. The health promotion approach also involved the establishment of baseline indicators of community health, including indicators of violence, which were intended to be regularly updated. Unfortunately, both the indicators reporting and attempts at evaluating specific safety initiatives foundered in the face of political opposition. When the City of Toronto was amalgamated with five other municipalities in 1997/1998, the new councillors were far more conservative. A community safety strategy that attempted to meet the needs of the new City of Toronto's 2.5 million inhabitants, and which involved consultation with over 700 organizations, was adopted by the local government (City of Toronto, 1999); but the citizen task force was disbanded soon after, leading to the author leaving the city's employment. The Safe City Committee's legacy of the grants programme (renamed the Community Safety Investment programme) and safer design guidelines remained, while a new phase of work began in Toronto, focusing on youth violence in low-income neighbourhoods.

One lesson from the Safe City Committee comes from its leadership, particularly the dynamic balance between its political and community-based leadership. On the one hand, the city councillors who participated (especially Barbara Hall, who later became mayor of Toronto and then chair of Canada's National Crime Prevention Council) provided political guidance on what was feasible and were also able to apply pressure on recalcitrant arms of the bureaucracy. The proactive support of senior-level bureaucrats, particularly in the departments of parks and recreation and public health, was also critical to the success of the committee. But it was the advocacy of representatives of community organizations, meeting monthly and also providing guidance between meetings, which shaped the mandate of the committee and ensured the success of its recommendations. For instance, the report that recommended the Breaking the Cycle of Violence grants was initially opposed by a majority of councillors. Every member of the Safe City Committee targeted one councillor and met with him or her to try to convince them of the benefits of preventing violence. At the next city council meeting, not only was the report unanimously adopted, but several councillors who had previously been opposed to the grants, spoke movingly of their own past experiences with violence.

Another lesson from the Safe City Committee is the ongoing tension of an initiative that was specifically focused on one gender: women. Many councillors felt that the Safe City Committee was a women's committee, rather than an initiative dealing with violence prevention, crime prevention or community safety, and attempted on several occasions to set up a parallel Crime Prevention Committee. At the same time, several women's service organizations were concerned about the committee's initial emphasis on public violence and that its emphasis on prevention would somehow undermine service delivery organizations. The grants programme's focus on vulnerable groups included funding for several organizations working primarily with men, particularly young men, and also addressed issues other than gender-based violence. Unfortunately, the notion of gender mainstreaming at the local governance level, which is gaining ground in Europe, Latin America and Africa, has not really taken hold in Canadian cities, and the gender analysis of the violence prevention work faded away after the departure of the author and several political and grassroots allies during the late 1990s.

In the case of Toronto's Safe City Committee, there were four community safety strategies, each associated with the three-year timeframe between local elections. It took almost a year to develop each strategy; so the final year of each cycle was devoted to developing the next plan. Each strategy was also associated with a broadening of the mandate, with the final strategy reflecting an attempt to introduce a gender analysis to all aspects of violence. Most importantly, each strategy was associated with the institutionalization of a major policy or programme, such as reviewing development proposals for community safety and inclusiveness concerns, or the ongoing grants programme on Breaking the Cycle of Violence.

Finding durable solutions is a primary objective of any community safety work (Henderson and Associates, 2002, p13). Some techniques have already been described that sustain energy for long-term initiatives. In the case of Papua

New Guinea and Cardiff, a strong evidence base on the problem, deriving from a diagnostic that involved many stakeholders in the analysis, helped to develop enthusiasm. In the latter case of Cardiff, some demonstrable wins, and the fact that this success was well publicized, helped to maintain the enthusiasm. In Bogotá, the public awareness campaigns within the violence prevention initiative helped to ensure that there was high-level political support, even when the mayor changed. A sense by the organizations involved that their voices are being heard and that the needs of 'their' communities are met can maintain commitment. Building capacities of organizations, individuals and the initiative itself is important as the mandate grows and evolves. Having a solid structure to the initiative, a history of good meetings and minute-taking, good communications channels and trust that is built up over the long term are all essential to long-term sustainability.

While more extensive forms of evaluation are important to the sustainability of an initiative, the most essential form of evaluation is learning what works, what does not and what is promising within the unique circumstances of any place. Annual reports, or at least a regular overview of the progress of recommendations, are important chances to build on strategies that are working, and examine why some strategies are stalling. We have seen how New Zealand accomplished a national 'stop and assess' process that changed the way in which the nation's community safety strategy operated.

Sustainability of initiatives involves learning – from one another, from what has worked and what has not; but it also involves 'unlearning'. Traditional approaches based in oppositional and competitive relations between organizations and governments, top-down hierarchies and needs-based thinking are all approaches that stand in the way of creative solutions (Landry, 2000). More than time and more than money, the process of community safety requires a commitment to openness: to including new organizations, new ideas and new ways of thinking to solve the entrenched problems of violence and insecurity.

6

The Components of Community Safety

As discussed in Chapter 3, there is no one simple cause for violence. There are, however, risk and resilience factors that operate at different scales. These include a culture of fear and tolerance of violence, as opposed to a culture of mutual respect and alternatives to violence; isolation from, or access to, resources that assist in building less violent lives; and powerlessness or power to change one's circumstances. Thus, there is no single intervention that will work to prevent any or all forms of violence. Instead, components of successful community safety include *policies, programmes and practices*. A policy is a plan of action, usually developed by a government, to tackle a problem that has been defined as a political priority. Examples of policies discussed in Chapter 5 include reviewing all development applications for community safety concerns in Toronto or legalizing land tenure in Papua New Guinea. A programme is a particular time-limited action undertaken by government, non-profit organizations or the private sector that often derives from a policy. Examples of programmes in Chapter 5 include training police and judges in Papua New Guinea to prioritize some of the determinants of severe violence in that country, such as gun control, or undertaking a series of women's safety audits in London, Bristol and Manchester as part of regeneration processes occurring in those cities. A practice is a customary way of operation or behaviour, and can be undertaken at any scale, from the individual to the global. For instance, counting to ten when you are very angry would be an individual practice, and police in Cardiff regularly sharing information on reported violent incidents with licensed drinking establishments is an institutional practice.

Most of the programmes, policies and practices that are addressed in this chapter deal with at least one of these causal aspects at the individual, family, community or societal levels. Programmes work to provide better options to parents who might physically harm their children. Programmes and policies provide the message that bullying is not okay and that there are non-violent

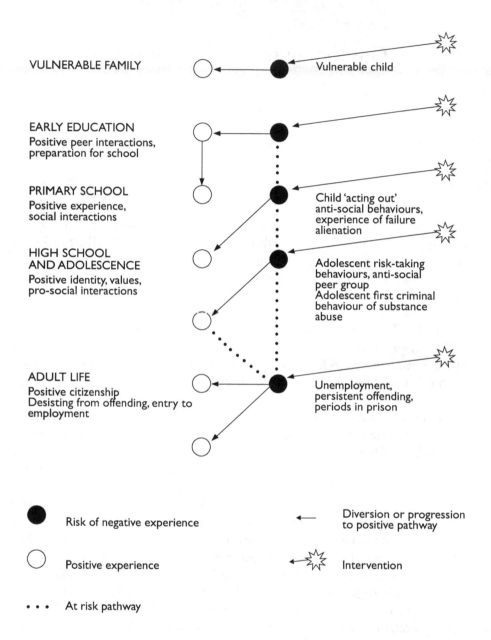

VULNERABLE FAMILY ○ ← ● Vulnerable child

EARLY EDUCATION
Positive peer interactions,
preparation for school

PRIMARY SCHOOL
Positive experience,
social interactions

Child 'acting out'
anti-social behaviours,
experience of failure
alienation

**HIGH SCHOOL
AND ADOLESCENCE**
Positive identity, values,
pro-social interactions

Adolescent risk-taking
behaviours, anti-social
peer group
Adolescent first criminal
behaviour of substance
abuse

ADULT LIFE
Positive citizenship
Desisting from offending, entry to
employment

Unemployment,
persistent offending,
periods in prison

● Risk of negative experience ← Diversion or progression to positive pathway

○ Positive experience ⟵✲ Intervention

• • • At risk pathway

Figure 6.1 *Possible intervention points in a life cycle*

Source: National Community Crime Prevention Programme Australia (1999, p11)

alternatives to hitting a bully back, as well as instilling a culture c
people's human rights at an early stage. Policies and everyday practice
economic and social power and options to at-risk individuals and c
Programmes can provide messages to the general public or particula
violence is a violation of human rights and is not acceptable and that
available from authorities. They can provide skills and services that
to overcome the everyday violence in their lives and to provide publ
public forums that bring people together across difference. Policies
can change the practices of public guardians such as the police, and l
from a punitive justice system that does not work to prevent rec:
restorative model that promotes individual responsibility for the h
been caused and often works to prevent recidivism.

This chapter is not intended to provide a comprehensive overv
possible programme, policy or practice that works to prevent violenc
this chapter, we return to the life-cycle approach taken in Chapter :
of possible intervention strategies found at the end of Chapter 3. ,
the Australian government report *Pathways to Prevention,* the life-cy
assumes that life is a series of phases, each with transition points,
are opportunities to intervene to create better life chances for both
offenders (National Community Crime Prevention Programme Au:
p8) (see Figure 6.1). The intervention strategies recognize that there
fix' approach to the complex issues of violence prevention and that
not a 'one-off' event, but a set of possible life lines that can be foun(
of services and settings.

The chapter thus focuses on the key types of intervention, across
and in many settings, which might create safer communities.

Early childhood strategies

The first transition point is the parental decision (if, indeed, it *is* a
not forced on the mother or father) to have a child. As we have see:
2, a life-cycle approach to violence prevention starts with tackl
against pregnant women, and the promotion of less violent familie
holds during the early years of an infant. The pre-natal and peri-na
essential to the physical and neurological development of an infa:
substance abuse, inadequate pre-natal care leading to pre-maturity
injury, inadequate health of the mother leading to malnutrition of
utero, and inadequate peri-natal care leading to birth injury or the
mother are all risks for later violence, as well as tragic health con
their own right. The infancy and early childhood stages are essent:
developing a sense of affect, or attachment to others, as well as a :
worth. Neglect and abuse of the child or his or her parents, pa
mother, can have a harmful impact upon these essential attributes

setting more important than the family in the early years of a person's life, and no equally effective substitute for loving parents (National Community Crime Prevention Programme Australia, 1999, p134).

Farrington and Welsh (2002) investigated six different types of early childhood intervention: home visitation by public health nurses; parent education plus childcare or pre-school; clinic-based parent training plus child training; school-based training plus parent training; home–community parent training; and multi-systemic therapy. While some of these techniques will be dealt with in the next section on interventions with school-aged children, it should be immediately noted that almost all of these approaches are both therapeutic and selective: they are based on the early identification of 'at-risk' families and communities, rather than taking a more universal approach. The interventions studied by Farrington and Welsh (2002, p22) also focused on 'family risk factors such as poor child-rearing, poor supervision, or inconsistent and harsh discipline', ignoring risk factors such as intimate partner violence. With that caution in mind, home visitations of 'at-risk' women by public health nurses or social workers during pregnancy and immediately after birth, with an emphasis on increasing family and friend support structures for the mother, and referral to appropriate health and social services, have been shown in several settings to be effective in reducing child abuse (National Community Crime Prevention Programme Australia, 1999, p147–150; Farrington and Welsh, 2002, p26–30; Leonard et al, 2005, p238). The famous Perry Pre-school programme, which combined pre-school education to children aged three to five, along with weekly home visits, in a low-income community resulted in significantly increased educational, employment and crime prevention outcomes after 22 years (Farrington and Welsh, 2002, pp30–31). More recently, the Pathways to Prevention Project in Queensland, Australia, has worked with low-income pre-school children aged three to five to improve young boys' readiness for school and classroom behaviour, although the same improvements were not statistically significant for girls. The programme has also worked to integrate service networks for families in low-income communities, providing individual support and counselling for adults and children; formal and informal behaviour management programmes for parents; increasing the number and quality of play groups and other programmes for children and youth; and supporting literacy and language skills in early school years. Particular emphasis was placed on providing more culturally appropriate services for families with indigenous, Vietnamese or Pacific Islander backgrounds. Early outcomes from this project, evaluated in 2005 after four years of operation, found that some of the most vulnerable and difficult-to-reach families were using the services, and had rated themselves and their children as having increased self-esteem and confidence, increased ability to help others to value themselves, improved ability to form and maintain relationships with the other parent, and increased sense of efficacy (knowing you can do something, and having the knowledge, resources, skills and support to do it) (Homel et al, 2006).

The 'missing people' in most of these programmes is the father as an improvable parent, or as a source of positive protection to children (National Community Crime Prevention Programme Australia, 1999, p79). Box 6.1 examines some programmes that have aimed at improving men's parenting abilities, while Box 6.2 discusses mothers' centres as community-building organizations.

The initiatives described in Boxes 6.1 and 6.2, whether focused on at-risk individuals or communities, or taking a more universal approach, share a commitment to increasing knowledge, skills, resources and support to mothers and fathers facing the early years of their child's development. The most successful elements appear to have been starting early, especially in the case of those programmes that provided pre-natal support to both fathers and mothers; increasing links with a range of potential supports, including neighbourhood services such as parks and libraries, health centres, social services and early childhood education; duration

---

Box 6.1 *Men working with men to become better fathers in Mexico and South Africa*

In 90 per cent of domestic violence cases in Mexico, the aggressor is the father or husband. During the 1990s, there was a 50 per cent increase in reported child abuse. There is often limited participation by fathers in family life, particularly in the 25 per cent of Mexican households with children that are headed by women (Shaw and Capobianco, 2004, p30).

In response to these problems, CORIAC (Colectivo de Hombres por Relaciones Igualitarias, which translates as Men's Collective for Equal Relations) was founded by psychologist Francisco Cervantes in 1993. Its Men Socially Renouncing Violence programme aims to transform 'macho' Latin American culture, develop more flexible attitudes to gendered roles at home and work, and strengthen equal participation of men in family life. The collective has developed workshops with accompanying guides, videos and other public awareness material such as posters to address four significant periods in fatherhood: men about to become fathers for the first time, those with young children up to 12, those with children becoming adolescents, and those men about to become grandfathers. Workshops are given at child development centres, schools and other institutions to groups of professional educators such as social workers, who are trained to promote and replicate the project. CORIAC has also worked with specific groups such as police officers, adolescent boys in schools, indigenous groups and men who have been in prison (Society for International Development, 2002, p20).

In South Africa, the Men as Partners programme has been funded by Planned Parenthood since 1998. The five aims of this programme are to improve men's awareness and support of their partner's reproductive health choices; increase awareness and responsibility for sexually transmitted diseases such as AIDS; increase understanding of the benefits of gender equity and healthy relationships; increase awareness of, and strive to prevent, domestic and sexual violence; and improve men's access to reproductive health information and awareness. The emphasis has been on men working with men to discuss developing healthy relationships with women (Michau and Naker, 2004, pp40–41). The assumptions behind the programme are that men have as much capacity to be good and rational as women, that it is important to hold men accountable for their own violence, and that recognition of women's and children's needs are essential to healthy relationships (Michau and Naker, 2004, p46).

There are no published evaluations of either of these initiatives.

Box 6.2 *The international growth of mothers' centres in Eastern Europe*

Mothers' centres are self-managed publicly owned community centres that offer a wide range of services for mothers of small children. They began in West Germany in the 1980s as a way of combating the social isolation of 'stay-at-home mothers', and have grown to an international movement of over 750 centres in 22 countries. The growth of mothers' centres in the Eastern European countries of the Czech Republic, Slovakia and Slovenia has been particularly strong. Depending upon the abilities and funding of the particular centre, a mothers' centre can include children's activities; childcare and/ or eldercare; communal hot meals and laundry machines; appliance repair; courses on parenting, languages and computer literacy; more formal job training or leadership training in skills such as public speaking and fundraising; holistic health; and advocacy and research on women's and children's issues. Underlying these services is a philosophy that sees mothers' centres as a 'safe and caring space, where mothers of all ages can be supported and learn from other moms, a place of easy access, a home outside of home, a place to find support, a place of recognition and backing for parenting' (MINE, 2006).

An evaluation of mothers' centres in 2006 found that 70 per cent of participants learned tolerance skills with regard to their children and to other parents; 56 per cent said they had increased their public participation; 55 per cent said that they had improved their skills in 'learning to say no'; 52 per cent said that they had learned to state what they needed and to accept help; and 46 per cent said that they became more involved in local government issues (UN-Habitat, 2006c, p19). Advocacy has increased on issues such as social isolation, community crime and substance abuse issues, family violence, and sexual abuse of children (MINE, 2006).

of at least two years; and support for parents, particularly mothers, to fulfil aspirations (National Community Crime Prevention Programme Australia, 1999, pp150–151).

School-based interventions

The transition to primary school can be easy or traumatic for both child and parents. Developing peer relationships, adjusting to school schedules and rules, and learning from successes and failures are all critical social tasks for children to learn in the early school years. As children move on to secondary school (if, indeed, they do so), a sense of autonomous values and independence grows, and teenagers begin to establish intimate relationships. These years, from 5 or 6 to 16 are where troubles in the home – violence, neglect or merely inconsistent parenting – can become apparent in schools, with bad behaviour such as bullying or poor academic performance. As the child's horizons expand, so too do the range of potential influences for good or ill. Not only are parents and other family members important; but peers, teachers and other older role models begin to take a more prominent role (National Community Crime Prevention Programme Australia, 1999, p134). In Chapter 2, we discussed how some schools can be unsafe places, not only because of violent fights and bullying, sometimes exacerbated by weapons in schools, but because of institutional violence, such as physical and sexual abuse by teachers. School-based interventions tend to focus on creating a safe space for all students, and to provide social skills for children that will help them resist violent and unhealthy pathways and stay in school.

School-based interventions, like those aimed at younger children, can be universal or targeted. An example of a targeted programme is the Montreal Prevention Project, aimed at boys who had displayed disruptive behaviour in pre-school and kindergarten. Their parents received training in using effective discipline and encouraging pro-social attributes, such as daily 'star' charts to monitor behaviour. Evaluations at the end of primary school indicated that these boys were achieving significantly more highly at school and getting involved in less fights than a control group. An example of a universal programme was the Seattle Social Development Project, which provided a teacher training programme for better supervision of disruptive children, child training in non-violent problem-solving and parent training for effective management. The project was aimed at children beginning school. An evaluation of the intervention group near the end of primary school indicated that significantly fewer children were exhibiting delinquent behaviour or experimenting with alcohol use, and parents demonstrated better child management skills and greater involvement in their children's education (National Community Crime

Prevention Programme Australia, 1999, pp154–155). Another example of a universal and cross-sectoral approach is the national Peace Builders Programme in Norway beginning during the late 1980s, which provided a 'whole-school approach' with key messages that included 'praise people', 'avoid put-downs' and 'seek wise people as advisers and friends'. This included better information to children, teachers and parents; working with schools to create positive climates with clear rules of behaviour; applying appropriate and non-hostile sanctions for unacceptable behaviour; and providing support and protection for victims of bullying. Evaluations have demonstrated reductions in bullying of up to 60 per cent; better attitudes towards schools; and lower rates of theft, vandalism and truancy (National Community Crime Prevention Programme Australia, 1999, pp154–155; Shaw, 2001b, p13; Gottfredson et al, 2002, p82).

In The Netherlands, a national programme on the prevention of bullying and delinquency requires two teachers in each school to undergo training on developing a school action plan, based on analysis of each school's problems and strengths. A national three-year curriculum has been instituted to instil positive values of respect for peers and teachers; acceptance of rules; solving problems non-violently; and active listening to one another. The evaluation of the pilot project during the early 1990s was promising; but there are no nation-wide results (Shaw, 2002, p11). A feature of the Dutch model is the link between their safer schools programmes and a national planning policy to situate community services in schools or their immediate vicinity, aimed at addressing area-based disadvantage. The Community School Programme grew from concerns expressed during the 1970s that local services to children and families at risk for abuse or delinquency were fragmented, and that the gaps in educational achievement between high social status and low social status, and between Dutch-born and new migrant families, were increasing. From the early 1990s onwards, senior government funding for new social and recreational services were targeted at creating a network of spaces and services around primary and secondary schools. For instance, the following services were encouraged to locate near existing primary schools: public health facilities such as well-baby clinics; childcare centres and parent–child drop-ins; libraries, including toy libraries; community centres, swimming pools and recreation centres; legal clinics; cafés; and adult education, language and job skills training. By January 2003, 500 primary school-based community schools and 90 secondary school-based community schools were in operation, with 264 municipalities working towards the development of community schools (NIZW, 2003, p3). The programme also trains parents to act as 'neighbourhood mothers' who encourage other parents to become more involved in their children's education. Specific parents' rooms or meeting spaces are set aside in most schools, and there are trainee placement programmes within schools for unemployed parents. Although there may be specific pockets of funding for specific target groups, such as visible minority new migrants, the intent of community schools is to provide universal free services in all neighbourhoods.

Unfortunately, there appear to be no evaluations of the impact of this national programme upon spatial disparities, student outcomes or community safety. However, the programme was inspired by a successful initiative in Stockholm, the Ringeby School (see Box 6.3).

Particularly in Europe, school safety initiatives have gone the route of promoting strong parental involvement (often facilitated through encouraging the location of services in schools), as well as involvement from local businesses, community organizations, youth services, and sports and cultural clubs (Council of Europe, 2003, p29). As discussed earlier, coordination has an organization and case management aspect, ensuring that every child and family has access to the right services working together, as well as a co-location aspect, ensuring that services are readily accessible to the families most in need.

As children approach secondary school, initiatives often begin to move beyond an emphasis on making interpersonal relationships with peers more mutually respectful, and to address the same aspects in intimate relationships. Unfortunately, these latter programmes have generally not been adopted as 'whole school' approaches, with training of teachers and integration within the curriculum. Instead, they have been under-funded as one-off, 'one-dose' events. For instance, the Bridgend Domestic Abuse Forum in the UK developed a drama production called *Breaking the Silence, Breaking the Chain*. A before and after survey on attitudes among the approximately 450 grade 11 students who viewed the production showed small positive improvements in awareness around domestic violence issues. However, the need for a more comprehensive approach was suggested by teachers (Hester and Westmarland, 2005, pp18–19). A slightly more comprehensive approach was taken in Thurrock, England, where a curriculum package for both primary and secondary schools, including the use of a short interactive play, was developed along with a mass media and public awareness campaign, training teachers to develop the curriculum and supporting a young person's counselling service to cater for possible increased demand. The primary school intervention focused on communication, the right to be heard and the responsibility to listen, and respect, like the Dutch campaign described earlier. The gender focus was introduced with a session on challenging stereotypes of 'being a boy, being a girl'. The evaluation of these sessions showed that there were limited positive impacts nine months after the sessions, particularly among the girls; but that teachers felt that for maximum impact, the programmes should be incorporated within the curriculum (Hester and Westmarland, 2005, pp19–21).

A more comprehensive approach was demonstrated in a rural British Columbia, Canada, setting (once again) with the Respectful Relationships Project (R+R) (see Box 6.4).

Aside from integrating violence prevention within the school curriculum and promoting schools as community hubs, a third emphasis, particularly in low-income countries (LICs), has been to keep children in school. The Kenya

Box 6.3 *Community building around schools in Stockholm, Sweden*

The Ringeby School is an elementary school of approximately 400 students, within a suburb of Stockholm built during the 1970s. Eighty per cent of the new school's residents were of foreign origin, with over 100 nationalities represented. There were issues of high unemployment and welfare dependency in the suburb itself, and the school soon had a poor reputation for academic achievement, as well as a high incidence of racism and other bullying behaviour, and extensive graffiti and vandalism. Half of the board of management had resigned.

In 1989, a comprehensive plan to revitalize the school began by convening a coordination task force of local government services: leisure, culture and social welfare. A local music school was relocated to the site, and a culture and dance school was established on the property in which two-thirds of the students are now active. The social welfare contribution to the school was a day-care centre with two specialized teachers, recreational staff and two social workers to respond to the children with the most serious behavioural problems. The offices of the social welfare fieldwork staff were relocated to the school, reducing costs and improving contact with young people and their parents. Several municipal youth clubs, including a café run by and for young girls and a boxing club, were moved nearer to the school and are now open 365 days a year from 4.00 pm to midnight. There is an after-school homework club. Unemployed youth aged 18 to 24 have access to the school gym after hours. There was an effort to rebuild a more inclusive home–school association and management board, as well as a pupil's council. Students were given responsibility for maintaining the school. A comprehensive action plan against bullying, school violence and racism was introduced, with clear rules, student agreements, follow-up on incidents and better parent contact. A civics programme on cultural differences was developed.

By 1998, when the school was nominated for a European Crime Prevention Award, there was a radical reduction in school violence, property damage and insecurity, and 84 per cent of parents and pupils said that they were 'satisfied' or 'very satisfied' with the school. There was an increase in the number of pupils involved in school activities, and considerable cost-savings from the coordination of services (Shaw, 2001b, pp34–35). As for actual decreases in school violence, the Swedish government tends to treat reported school crime rates with caution. There was a threefold increase in the number of reported school assaults throughout Sweden from 1993 to 2001; but a study of the actual reports revealed that this consisted of minor assaults that had previously gone under-reported, not serious violence (Shaw, 2002, p4).

Box 6.4 *A comprehensive violence prevention curriculum in rural British Columbia, Canada*

The Respectful Relationships Project was a five-year national demonstration project, funded by the Canadian National Crime Prevention Strategy and based on a partnership between the district school board, the police and Saltspring Women Opposed to Violence and Abuse (SWOVA). The programme was precipitated by the death of a local woman at the hands of her husband in this small island community of 9000. SWOVA contended that most violence against women and girls occurs within intimate relationships, is a behaviour learned early and can best be dealt with by violence prevention supported by the entire community (SWOVA, 2007).

An integrated school curriculum was developed in 1998. From kindergarten to grade 6, ten workshops focus on respectful relationships and preventing bullying. Grades 7 and 8 have a more intensive curriculum of 12 one-hour in-class workshops, focusing on healthy relationships. One of the features of this programme is training for teen leaders, as well as teachers and parents, although the workshops are generally led by two adult leaders, one female and one male. The teen leaders help with the primary school training and take a major role in organizing a half-day workshop on social justice that is incorporated within the year 7 to 8 curriculum. In years 9 to 12, there is an opportunity to train as a teen leader, and there is also an annual Freedom from Fear day that involves students, staff, parents and the general community, and includes theatre performances, discussions and workshops.

A survey of over 500 school-aged participants from grades 7 to 12 in 1999 found that 77 per cent of girls and 52 per cent of boys said they had already experienced a 'bad or unhealthy relationship'. A comparison of pre-test and post-test responses found that girls were more likely to say they would 'get out of' an unhealthy relationship, while boys were more likely to say they would 'work on problems' in a relationship, rather than 'just dump her'. The programme rated highly as 'enjoyable' and 'a learning experience' for grade 7 students, especially for girls. Intriguingly, the findings were reversed for grade 9 students, with more boys than girls rating the programme highly for enjoyment and learning. Teachers also rated the programme favourably. A comparison in 2001 between the Saltspring schools and a similar school district without the intervention found that recipients of the programme scored significantly better in attitude and knowledge scores about violence (RESOLVE Alberta, 2005). Based on the generally positive evaluation, SWOVA produced materials for dissemination to other school boards, including an activity book for elementary students, parents and educators; a how-to guide for teen and adult leaders; and a 20-minute video on how the programme worked in Saltspring.

Alliance for the Advocacy of Children's Rights focuses on encouraging girls to complete primary and secondary schooling, and advocates the prevention of forms of violence against girls (such as early marriage and sexual abuse) that act as barriers to education. They have established child rights clubs in primary schools, which educate children on their rights through creative writing, poems, songs, drama and debates. SINAGA, the Woman and Child Labour Centre, also based in Kenya, works with girls employed in domestic labour, providing basic schooling during periods of the day that are negotiated with employers, and also offers counselling in cases of abuse (Pickup, 2001, pp25–26). In South Africa, where rapes and other violent assaults are common even in primary schools, a project in the state of Gauteng (where Johannesburg is located) works to provide teacher training and support, including trauma management support groups; student support for peer counselling, mentoring and life skills; and training student leaders for community safety projects. It also works with local businesses, police, women's service organizations and sports organizations to provide a range of life skills courses (Shaw, 2001b, p29). In Durham region, an industrial area outside Toronto, Canada, as part of the Together We Light the Way programme, each classroom in their elementary and middle schools were 'adopted' by a local business, who provided mentoring and some job readiness skills. This successful programme has been exported to other parts of Canada and to Trinidad (Dean 2000; Shaw, 2007b, p30). A number of interventions aimed at providing alternatives to school suspension and exclusion are being developed, particularly in the US and UK, where these 'zero tolerance' techniques have been overused in the past (Shaw, 2001b, p21). For instance, the Cities in Schools programme has developed 75 projects across England and Wales, working with suspended and excluded students aged 8 to 19. Each local project has its own board of management, made up of educators, police, social services, job training and local business leaders. They have been able to reintegrate 75 per cent of the students with whom they work into further education or job placements, demonstrating a cost-effective as well as humane approach (Shaw, 2001b, p33).

Features of successful school-based interventions include a comprehensive approach that integrates violence prevention within the curriculum; treating schools as 'community hubs' and gathering government services, community organizations and local businesses to provide programmes in and out of school hours; and student, parent and staff leadership development and capacity-building on violence prevention attitudes and skills.

Community economic development approaches

Chapter 2 discussed the importance of legal employment and independent sources of income and capital as a lifeline to people trying to escape violent relationships, as well as a possible pathway out of violence for offenders. Community economic development has been a feature of many successful safety initiatives in three forms. First, there are the people directly employed as a result of community safety strategies: the young people hired as surveyors for community safety diagnoses in Port Moresby, the women hired as waste collectors as the result of a safety audit in Dar es Salaam, and the traffic warden mimes in Bogotá. Second, there are the indirect impacts of increased social infrastructure in neighbourhoods and localities: recreation workers attached to schools in The Netherlands, social workers in estates in Denmark, childcare workers in San Jorge. Third, there are explicit skill development and employment creation projects attached to many of the community safety initiatives that have been discussed.

The opportunities for direct employment as community safety workers have been explored in a recent report from the International Centre for the Prevention of Crime (Gray, 2006). Community safety workers are not private security guards, but fill a perceived void between citizens and institutions, such as the police and court systems. They also provide a more humane, and quite possibly more effective, mechanism to reduce crime and insecurity than technological approaches. For instance, a comparison of 'concierges' or door staff, and entry phones or video security in housing estates in England 20 years ago found that after allowing for installation and maintenance costs, hiring people to secure the front entrances to buildings instead of relying on technology was both cost-effective and resulted in much higher satisfaction levels among tenants (Safe Neighbourhoods Unit, 1985).

The first country to employ this approach as part of a national programme was The Netherlands, which funded a pilot City Guard programme in Dordrecht in 1989, and after a positive evaluation, rolled out 20,000 such jobs in 150 communities during the 1990s (Gauthier et al, 1999, p21). The City Guards, despite the somewhat militaristic name, simply provide formal surveillance of downtown streets, parking lots and commercial establishments, and provide directions and advice to citizens and visitors. Since 1999, neighbourhood and street wardens employed as part of the Crime Reduction Programme in England and Wales have patrolled public and private spaces, reporting litter, vandalism and graffiti for clean up; informally referred people to appropriate services; and sometimes acted as advocates for neighbourhoods in administrative situations. They do not have the ability to arrest people; but they are able to issue tickets for minor disorders, direct traffic and ask for the names and addresses of people behaving in an anti-social fashion. An evaluation after three years of the programme found that wardens have a positive impact upon resident satisfaction and have reduced insecurity, particularly among the elderly. There was a 28 per cent reduction in victimization levels compared with increases in control areas, as well as increased local employment. However, another evaluation after six years of the programme found that there was little decrease in reported crime in sites with wardens, probably because of the low level of many of the offences prevented (Gray, 2006, pp13–18).

In France, social mediation agents have been employed as part of national–local government contracts since 1997, and police auxiliaries have been hired as part of a youth employment scheme. By 2000, there were nearly 20,000 such jobs created, although the youth employment scheme was cut back in 2003. These mediation and prevention agents patrol in public areas, particularly after dark, dealing with neighbourhood disputes and misuses of public space; provide information in public transport vehicles or stations; and facilitate relations between neighbours, while referring cultural and linguistic minority people to appropriate social and health services. The first two functions tend to be filled by younger men; the last function, that of social and cultural mediator, is usually filled by new migrant women. Most local and national evaluations of this programme focus on process rather than impact, with greater resident satisfaction, increased attendance at sporting and cultural events, and decreased relocations from public housing in response to complaints (Gray, 2006, pp19–24). In Colombia, there has also been heavy investment in social mediators to resolve neighbourhood disputes, with some form of conciliation in 83 per cent of cases and full agreement in 46 per cent of cases (Shaw, 2006, pp10–11). Previous case studies of Tanzania and Papua New Guinea have also seen the recommendation for neighbourhood-level dispute resolution, partly to deal with huge backlogs in court cases.

In Australia, over 50 aboriginal communities have been provided with national or state funding for night patrols, particularly after enquiries into the deaths of aboriginal people in police custody. They prevent the escalation of aggressive behaviour in violent situations, many of them alcohol-fuelled; provide young people and women with referrals to support organizations; and provide transport to those in need. There is no national evaluation of the programme; but local evaluations have shown reductions in the numbers of reported crimes and lock-ups in the order of 30 per cent, a welcome finding in a country where aboriginal people represent 2 per cent of the total population and 20 per cent of prisoners. There is anecdotal and agency evidence that both community and family violence has been reduced in many communities. Despite this evidence of success, there are problems in providing sustained funding for these patrols, and most participants are volunteers (Gray, 2006, pp30–34).

More indirect employment creation programmes are common components of violence prevention initiatives in LICs. The Chattisgarh Women's Organization and Jan Jagriti Kendra, two organizations in the state of Madhya Pradesh, India, have helped over 5000 female bonded labourers to free themselves and, in some cases, win financial compensation for their slavery. The organizations provide new skills and trades for women, such as farming and weaving co-operatives, in order to avoid a return to bonded labour (Pickup, 2001, p179). Fifty-five 'knitting corners' were set up in Bosnian refugee camps during the

1990s, where women could gather together to take part in a traditional home-based activity that was no longer feasible when home was a tent. It provided a safe social space to support one another; but the products also provided some income to participants (Pickup, 2001, pp188–189). Also in Bosnia, Medica Zencia provided direct social and health services to survivors of genocide and torture, along with four-month training courses in sewing, hairstyling, furniture upholstering, weaving, computers and language, to women who were often the sole breadwinners in the family (Pickup, 2001, pp180, 191). In Kenya, where there are 14 million unemployed of a total population of 31 million, and people aged under 30 comprise 75 per cent of the population, a one-stop youth shop was established in 2003 in a former railway headquarters in downtown Nairobi. It provides services for unemployed out-of-school youth aged 15 to 24, many of whom are HIV positive and/or have drug and alcohol addictions. The centre provides training in business skills (e.g. resumé writing and job interview skills), and its self-management structure provides opportunities for leadership and organizational skills, such as fundraising and management. While funding mostly comes from international sources, there is a strong connection to the Nairobi Safer Cities initiative within local governance, as well as many community organizations and businesses (UN-Habitat, 2006c, p24).

A comprehensive example of regenerating an unsafe area through community economic development is provided in Box 6.5.

Common features of successful community economic development approaches include building on existing resources and capacities, strengthening local leadership and developing transferable skills.

Box 6.5 *Generating employment and safety in Durban, South Africa*

Durban, or as it is known in Zulu, eThekwini, is the second largest city in South Africa, with a little over 3 million people. The central business district has traditionally been zoned for 'formal' businesses only, which in the apartheid era largely excluded blacks. Warwick Junction is the main downtown public transport hub, as well as the site of the largest number of taxi ranks, and is accessed by 300,000 commuters per day, mostly from townships and informal settlements (Dobson, 2007). By the end of the apartheid era in 1994, it had become the centre of downtown Durban's informal economy as well. The businesses located in Warwick Junction provided very different goods and services to those found in middle-class commercial areas. Traditional African herb sellers and healers are found there, as is the traditional delicacy of bovine head and the cheap and filling 'mealie' (seed corn on the cob). Informal waste collection, particularly cardboard salvaging, had also become established in Warwick Junction.

Unsurprisingly, the official attitude towards the informal economy and informal settlements under apartheid had created a literal and administrative mess by the mid 1990s. With 'white flight' to the suburbs, dozens of downtown office buildings had been abandoned and transformed into residential squats, with no clear sense of ownership and no maintenance or infrastructure provided by the local government. There were also the more traditional shack dwellings of informal settlements, as well as a considerable number of adults and children living on the street. There were few basic services in the Warwick Junction area, such as waste collection or water and sewage provision, and *shebeens* (illegal premises where alcohol and, often, drugs and guns are sold) and houses of prostitution were found in large numbers. At the same time, both the national and local governments were investing heavily in downtown tourist promotion through the construction of an international conference centre, casino and high-end residential and commercial developments. As is often the case in downtowns all over the world, the two extremes of rich and poor uneasily sat side by side, with few connections or benefits from these mega-developments trickling down to poor people (Hemson, 2003, p3). City intervention was limited to single-issue blitzes, such as tearing down all posters, which only revealed the sad state of the utility poles.

In 1997, the local government established a Warwick Junction Urban Renewal Project, which eventually expanded to become iTRUMP (inner Thekwini Renewal and Urban Management Programme). The project team's leader was Richard Dobson, from the architecture and urban design section; but the health, waste management and licensing departments were involved as well. The aim of the project was:

> ... holistic and integrated redevelopment of the area in order to improve the overall quality of the urban environment in terms of safety, security, cleanliness, functionality, efficient public transportation usage, and facilitation of economic and housing opportunities. (Hemson, 2003, p8)

The project was also intended to redress the previous lack of participatory governance and spatial equity under apartheid land-use planning. The notion was to build on community resources, such as the vibrant informal economic activities, the cultural diversity of the area and the potential for citizenship already apparent in some informal management processes (Dobson, 2006).

At that point, Warwick Junction was unappealing to any of the senses. The area was very congested, with pedestrian and vehicle traffic competing for limited space with street vendors. Unfinished flyovers and *ad hoc* bridges joined the train station with bus and taxi ranks in an uncoordinated and unsafe fashion. Music sellers and *shebeens* blasted out the latest hits, combined with car horns, the calls of street sellers, the cries of roosters and the roar of accelerating buses to create a constant din, day and night. *Mealies* were being cooked in 200-litre recycled metal drums over huge wood fires located on the sidewalk, with ambient temperatures rising to over 120 degrees Celsius on summer days. Most of the cooking waste from bovine heads was dumped into curb-side sewers, which, in turn, discharged into the city's recreational water. Herbs such as 'mpempo' added their pungent aroma to the mix of food, refuse, and human and animal waste smells (Hemson, 2003, p6; Dobson, 2006).

The first step was to renovate a derelict warehouse, which doubled as an office for iTRUMP staff and an informal community centre. The project worked on formal sectoral agreements, where the provision of physical infrastructure was tied to increased self-management and some formalization of licensing. To give one example, a new collection area for cardboard salvaging was accompanied by curb-side collection bins in car parks. This allowed some informal surveillance of car parks, as well as a reduction in litter (Dobson, 2006). The city also hired several female cardboard collectors as parking lot wardens. Bead-makers, whose market operated only one day a week, came to a time-sharing agreement with other sellers, which allowed them to have a prominent collective display area. A designated *mealie*-cooking facility was created that cooks approximately 28 tonnes of product a day at the height of the growing season, at a street value of approximately US$200,000 a week. There was another communal cooking facility for the bovine heads, attached to an expanded food court (Dobson, 2006). Encouragement of other businesses, such as private security, taxi-washing, hairdressing, driving schools and the formalization of some *shebeens* led to a total increase in micro-enterprises in Warwick Junction from 7500 in 1996 to 12,000 in 2001 (Hemson, 2003, p3). Many of the enterprises were owned and managed by women, especially cardboard collection, bovine head cooking and serving (an activity traditionally confined to men), and bead selling (Hemson, 2003, pp13–14; Dobson, 2006, 2007). The association of women traders also developed a childcare facility and advocated for better access to local schools (Hemson, 2003, p18).

As the project expanded and city revenues increased, more funds became available, from the European Union as well as local government, with an annual budget of about US$2 million by 2003/2004 (Hemson, 2003, p8). Five other districts besides Warwick Junction became part of iTRUMP, and the principles behind this project informed the redevelopment of much of central Durban (Dobson, 2007). The provision of essential infrastructure, such as clean water and public toilets, was accompanied by new artwork, such as a street mural of an open-handed 'Big Mama' that has become an icon of central Durban. The iTRUMP centre is now used for weekly meetings of the Informal Traders Management Board, the national organization for traditional healers, regular workshops for fruit and vegetable traders run by the health department, and a handicraft training institute managed by the women street traders association.

The process was crucial to the project's success, and involved five essential components: area-based management embedded in the community; repeatedly acting on priorities revealed during consultations, which slowly built trust within previously excluded groups; a multifaceted approach that was based on a gendered analysis of needs and opportunities; paying equal attention to design improvements and social development; and building on the distinct strengths of the district (Dobson, 2007, pp101–103). Street traders developed internal leadership and also began to see the benefits of working with local government. As the head of the Informal Traders Management Board observed in 2003:

> iTRUMP is the vehicle for development and building, and will give people what they want in this area. This is their parliament. (Hemson, 2003, p11)

Apartheid planning had no provision for informal selling. As it was slowly legalized, traders needed to see benefits, and build relationships with police and licensing officials, before trusting local government with revenues or rules.

In 1997, there were about 50 violent deaths in the Warwick Junction vicinity, mostly related to economic tensions over space. In 2002, there were only six homicides in the same area, a decline attributed to improved economic conditions by Richard Dobson, the coordinator of the programme. Crimes reported to the police decreased throughout central Durban during the period of 1996–2001, including a 35 per cent decrease in homicides, which sharply contrasted with the general trend in South Africa. An organization called Traders against Crime took the lead in negotiating with the police for a more visible presence, and also attempted to mediate between local tensions. However, in April 2003, one of the leaders was shot dead during an intervention, leading to increased conflict with police over the amount of formal surveillance (Hemson, 2003, pp19–20).

There continue to be unresolved issues. Several adjacent residents' associations, dominated by 'coloured' and 'Indian' households as opposed to the predominantly 'black' traders, feel left out of the process and betrayed by the continued presence of the market. Sellers want better lighting, water, toilets, electricity and shelters for their businesses; more police presence;

better banking facilities; and more affordable housing in central Durban. They argue that the economic potential could be increased if the area was made 'safer' for tourists. There continue to be high rates of sexually transmitted diseases and tuberculosis in the area, although the existing public health facilities were improved as part of the renewal project (Hemson, 2003, pp13–18). But despite these problems, the iTRUMP project stands as a stellar example of a democratic, resource-based and creative approach to deep-seated structural inequities and violence.

Public awareness approaches

Public awareness, or 'communication for social change' as the current jargon would have it (Capobianco, 2006), is hardly a new idea. As long as there has been crime prevention, there have been public service messages to individuals and communities on what they can do to avoid becoming victims. Unfortunately, many of these messages – ranging from women holding their car keys spread between their fingers in car parks to parents holding the hand of any child younger than 12 as they cross a road – have been both fear inducing and largely ineffective in dealing with the root causes of violence and insecurity. The programmes described in this section take a different approach. Raising Voices talks about how change at the individual level can happen through repeated exposure to new ideas. It gives the example of an individual man who might hear a sermon about family unity in a church, see a mural questioning domestic violence on his walk to work, hear a radio programme about human rights, and be invited by a neighbour to join a men's group to discuss parenting skills, all over the course of one week (Michau and Naker, 2004, p7). The rationale behind this new generation of public awareness approaches is changing the everyday messages reaching people from ones that condone violence and limit autonomy, to ones that promote respect and responsibility for one another.

Public awareness approaches develop pamphlets, comic books, workbooks, posters, games, radio programmes, theatre, public meeting 'speak-outs', videos, websites and other materials that expose the realities of violence and provide positive alternatives. The materials need to be age, culture and language appropriate. For instance, the Violence Is Preventable (VIP) project, based in Dundee, Scotland, has rolled out its extensive range of anti-violence products across the UK and around the world. The *Wee VIP* pack is suitable for pre-school children at nursery schools or playgroups. It consists of a video, story book, song, game, colouring sheet and badge (along with a parent or staff pack and trainer's note), all with the simple message of teaching children to 'Say no! Go! Tell!' if they are upset or hurt. The *Tweenee VIP* pack, for children in primary schools or youth groups, promotes the same message through an interactive story about 'Jonny Cool', a group game called 'Truth Dare Scare', and a video. The *Teen VIP* pack is made of up six hour-long sessions with worksheets and exercises, along with a video made by and starring teens. There is also a *Senior VIP* pack with quizzes, games and songs for people over the age of 60. The emphasis changes with the age of the pack, from prevention of child abuse, through bullying and personal safety (feeling safe in public spaces), dating and intimate partner violence, and preventing elder abuse and insecurity. The VIP website also has a child-friendly '18 and under' website. The VIP project has directly worked with over 20,000 children and adults. A recent external evaluation of the Tweenee VIP programme found that there was a higher awareness of safety issues after the intervention, and that there was a disclosure rate of one third of the children on incidents of domestic abuse, bullying, sexual abuse, rape or abduction (Whitzman et al, 2004, p24; Violence is Preventable Project, 2007).

In Canada, Project Respect works with young people aged 14 to 19 to stop sexual violence, particularly 'date rape', also addressing related problems such as homophobia, racism and abuse of alcohol and drugs. The programmes, which are developed and delivered by youth trainers (Respect'rs), include an interactive set of workshops, a *Respect Revolution* video with a teaching guide, posters, stickers and various community events, such as a sponsored walk, Walk a Mile in Her Shoes, where men walk a mile in high-heeled shoes to raise money for violence prevention. Its website includes young people's stories of rage and resistance, along with a 'chat room', and the poster slogans, which have been developed in workshops, include: 'She asked for it ... respect' and 'He only wants one thing ... respect.' Its main message is 'Only yes means yes' (Whitzman et al, 2004, p13; Project Respect, 2007).

The Soul City Institute in South Africa has developed full-colour comic books on gender-based violence, 1 million copies of which have been distributed. As well, they have developed 13 prime time television shows, including a 45-part radio drama in nine languages. A toll-free helpline allows readers or audiences to disclose their own abuse. In South Africa, television audiences are mainly middle class; but poor people listen to radio; messages have thus been slightly modified for each medium (Michau and Naker, 2004, pp33–34). In Delhi, India, where going to the movies is such an integral part of everyday life, a short film produced by the women's organization Jagori has taken aim at sexual harassment in a humorous manner and has been widely shown before the features (video downloadable from Jagori, 2007). Five thousand auto-rickshaw (taxi) drivers have also agreed to place stickers in the back of their taxis saying: 'Eve teasing is not a joke but a crime/make Delhi safe for women' as of April 2007. Raising Voices has also developed a wide variety of visually appealing learning materials, such as posters, flyers, comic books, card games, videos, community assessment surveys, mural designs and travelling exhibits. It provides training for organizational development across East and Southern Africa, including specific training sessions for journalists and editors, community volunteers, local leaders and educators. In 2006, it launched a new set of materials on preventing child abuse (Michau and Naker, 2003; Raising Voices, 2007). For instance, the card game 'Who Do You Want To Be?', pictured in Figure 6.2, is based on Old Maid; the only card left at the end is the Alone Abuser.

Collective public awareness campaigns against violence have already been discussed, particularly in the context of Bogotá. The use of theatre as a public education tool has been especially well developed in sub-Saharan Africa and Latin America. For instance, the Stepping Stones programme, created in South Africa in 1995, uses an interactive play as part of a training package on gender, HIV, communication and relationship skills. The play can be stopped at any time by a suggestion from the audience. For instance, if a man hits a woman in the play, the group can decide where, what time of day, can position neighbours or family members, and then tell each actor what to do next. The original manual, now translated into seven languages, is used by over 1500 organizations in 45 countries. Numerous evaluations of local projects have found that participants report declines in domestic violence, improved attitudes and increased condom use by men (Pickup, 2001, pp208–209; Stepping Stones, 2007).

The Women's Circus in Melbourne, Australia, is a unique combination of training and job creation, therapy and public education. Since 1991, it has trained hundreds of women survivors of sexual abuse to trust their bodies again by providing circus and physical theatre skills training. It also provides 'techie training' in sound, lighting, stage management, and health and safety. Aside from regular performances, it provides outreach workshops for women, men and children to develop skills and discuss violence issues (Women's Circus, 2007).

In many countries, national, state and local governments have used public awareness campaigns as part of their coordinated strategies. In Tasmania, Australia, a poster campaign to highlight changes in legislation stressed that The Rules Have Changed to mandatory arresting, and in the UK, the Zero Tolerance campaign, which began as an Edinburgh City Council project and soon spread, had a similar message. In the US, the My Strength is Not for Hurting campaign invited men to redefine masculinity as involving non-violence and respect for others, and in New South Wales, Australia, the Violence against Women – It's against All the Rules campaign focused on similar messages from high-profile male sports figures. Similarly, a number of campaigns have had similar messages to Project Respect, encouraging young men and women to notice and respond to the warning signs of an abusive relationship. A number of campaigns supporting increased reporting to police or social services have

Figure 6.2 *Card game developed by Raising Voices*

Source: Michau and Naker (2003, p135)

been accompanied by toll-free telephone numbers, often with a message similar to the one used in Swansea: 'Break the silence, make the call'. Other campaigns, such as the Victoria Australia Family and Friends campaign, have encouraged friends and family members of someone using or experiencing violence to phone a helpline for advice or talk with the person in helpful ways (Donovan and Vlais, 2005).

Many gender-based violence campaigns are centred on the 16 Days of Activism to End Violence against Women, which were endorsed by the United Nations after a Women's Global Leadership conference in 1991. The 16 days begin on 25 November, the International Day against Violence against Women, and end on 10 December, the International Human Rights Day. The notion is that a set of linked international campaigns will attract more media coverage than an isolated campaign. Even before the campaign was launched, in 1989, SOS Femmes in Mauritius covered the island nation in posters for the International Day against Violence against Women, and has followed up each year with a national event (Michau and Naker, 2004, pp28–29). Since 2003, the international cosmetics chain The Body Shop has supported public awareness campaigns on violence against women through its 2000 stores during the 16 days, and its foundation has also raised over US$4 million for violence prevention in 45 countries. Most recently, it has collaborated with the United Nations Children's Fund (UNICEF) to focus its attention on domestic violence against children (Body Shop, 2006).

The Body Shop is only one example of using businesses – both big and small – to raise public awareness on violence and insecurity. The CEO Challenge idea has been used in both the US and in Queensland, Australia, to raise awareness among business champions of the need to speak out against violence and to fundraise in their organizations for the family violence sector. Unions can also provide workplace training on violence, as was the case in Toronto. A number of cities, such as Charlottetown in Canada, have adopted public awareness campaigns that include training for all municipal staff on how to respond to family violence as well as public violence (Victorian Community Council against Violence, 2003; Whitzman et al, 2004, p11). In Montreal, a group called Conscience Urbaine (both Urban Conscience and Urban Consciousness) used black-and-white posters of unsafe places at night, placed at the sites themselves, to encourage residents to advocate with local government and landowners to improve those spaces. Three thousand postcards were also left with participating businesses in the areas. The project led to a number of safety audits and further improvements (Whitzman et al, 2004, p17). In Toronto, a project by the Working Women Community Centre developed flyers in six languages, which were distributed by 80 volunteers in 'community access points' for new migrants, including hairdressers, ethnic groceries, laundromats and bowling alleys. The evaluation showed increased awareness, not only among the people who picked up the flyers, but among the business people who distributed the information (Whitzman et al, 2004, p7).

Aside from government, non-governmental organization (NGO) and private organization public-awareness campaigns, storylines in mainstream media may have a powerful impact upon public perceptions of violence. For instance, in the UK, a storyline in the popular soap opera *East Enders* about a character experiencing domestic violence may have led to more women seeking help from the police (Hester and Westmarland, 2005, p45).

Public awareness campaigns are one of the components of community safety that are least likely to have independent evaluations. This is partly because tracking community attitudes, especially in broad-based campaigns, is so difficult. Campaigns need to be pre-tested with primary target audiences, as well as others who would be exposed to the materials, in order to ensure that messages do not inadvertently reinforce some of the attitudes and beliefs that perpetuate the problem – for instance, that women and children are somehow responsible for violence committed against them. Campaigns should never be undertaken without adequate services in place to handle the response or victims will be put further at risk (Donovan and Vlais, 2005). In Victoria, Australia, the Victorian Health Promotion Foundation (VicHealth) has been tracking changing social attitudes towards violence against women using data sets from 1985, 1995 and 2005 to determine whether and how public awareness and other approaches are most and least effective (VicHealth, 2006).

Most of the examples in this section focus on the prevention of family violence, particularly against women and children. This is because community awareness is a powerful mechanism for making hitherto 'private issues' safe for discussion in the public realm. All of the initiatives described focused on positive and empowering messages, not ones that promoted fear or dependence upon authorities for simple solutions. Like all of the examples given thus far, they use creative, inclusive and participatory approaches to challenge traditional ways of thinking and action.

Capacity-building and the question of self-defence

Capacity-building strategies support individual and collective ability to prevent violence and support social inclusion and citizenship. Some develop job-related skills, although they are not, strictly speaking, community economic development projects. For instance, the MY Circle project run by the Multicultural Youth Service in Vancouver, Canada, provides peer support for newcomers aged 14 to 24. There are weekly meetings that focus on facilitation skills (with members expected to take turns facilitating), develop and implement projects, and discuss issues ranging from racist violence and discrimination to mental health issues. There are also weekly soccer games with settlement service workers, and a 'buddy' or peer mentorship programme between newcomers and more established youth. One hundred and forty youth leaders have been trained in an 80-hour leadership programme and can then work with service agencies, and there are over 500 young people involved in this programme in various ways (UN-Habitat, 2006c, p25). The same agency provides a ten-week Cross-Cultural Peer Support Programme for Immigrant and Refugee Women to become leaders, which includes information on legal and human rights, as well as family violence issues. The women can then become volunteers or paid workers within their own linguistic or cultural communities (Immigrant Services Society of British Columbia, 2007)

Both informal peer-based youth development programmes and adult–child mentoring have been identified as promising primary prevention practices (Butchart et al, 2004, p38). Long-established high-income country (HIC) programmes such as Big Brothers/Big Sisters and Boy Scouts/Girl Scouts/Girl Guides have had positive impact evaluations upon violence and substance abuse, although the programmes that are universal rather than targeted, such as the Boy Scouts versus Big Brothers, tend not to involve the most at-risk visible minority youth (Quinn, 1999; Benard and Marshall, 2001). Other education and recreation programmes for youth have been posited as preventing violence, from providing public libraries where young people feel comfortable, to providing facilities (such as swimming pools, museums and cultural centres, and skateboard parks) and programmes (such as sports or drama, dance and other cultural expression).

Increasingly, the emphasis is on promoting youth leadership development and enhancing positive decision-making and mediation life skills, rather than simply 'keeping young men and women busy and safe' (Quinn, 1999, p98).

A number of projects in both HICs and LICs focus on developing a greater representation of women in both formal politics and public advocacy. The Kadjebi district initiative in Ghana has already been mentioned (see Box 4.6), as well as the development of neighbourhood-level political structures involving the training of both male and female political leaders in Buenos Aires and Dar es Salaam. Successful safety audits have been a way of developing women's urban advocacy and leadership skills in the UK, Russia, Tanzania and Canada. The Education Centre for Women in Democracy in Kenya was created in 1993 by women who participated in Kenya's first multiparty general elections the previous year. It provides training on women's rights, including training for 227 women who volunteer as paralegal educators (Michau and Naker, 2004, pp20–21). The Ekta Women's Resource Centre, based in the South Indian city of Madurai, provides leadership training for both rural and urban poor women to provide health, education and vocational skills information in their communities. It has enabled women to document inequalities and violence at the local scale, and then advocate for policy initiatives with both the local and state governments. Following the Boxing Day tsunami in 2004, Ekta focused on ensuring that the livelihood needs of women from the *dalit* (so-called 'untouchable' caste) and tribal communities were not made subservient to men's livelihood needs in international aid contributions (Whitzman et al, 2004, p22; Womenkind Worldwide, 2007).

One problem in increasing women's leadership and economic self-sufficiency has been a backlash from men in several sites. For instance, the interim evaluation of a small-scale loan programme in Bangladesh by Oxfam found that up to one third of loans to women had been appropriated by male partners, often accompanied by increased violence. Responses to this finding involved publicizing the issue, funding group discussions of violence in small communities, trained staff providing separate discussion sessions with couples, and working with local violence against women organizations to support a network of women receiving loans (Pickup, 2001, pp38–41).

A more controversial capacity-building strategy has been the provision of self-defence courses for women, children and older people. Some people have seen self-defence as putting too much of the onus for protecting oneself on the individual or 'blaming the victim'. Others see it as an essential empowerment tool. Certainly, some programmes discussed in this chapter, such as the 'Say no! Go! Tell!' message of the VIP project in Scotland, use the same analysis as most successful self-defence programmes.

The Child Assault Prevention (CAP) programme started in Columbus, US, in 1978, as a project of the local agency Women against Rape. The organization responded to the rape of a second-grade student in a school by providing all children in the school with simple and effective tools to deal with uncomfortable and unsafe experiences. It recognized that the vast majority (90 per cent, according to their website) of physical and sexual assaults against children are by people whom they know and trust, including parents and other family members. CAP worked with children on saying 'no' or yelling in as loud a voice as possible, then removing themselves from the situation and seeking help. Today, there are trained CAP facilitators in 19 countries (International Centre for Assault Prevention, 2007).

The CAP approach was adapted by a large number of organizations providing women's and children's self-defence. For instance, the Action Programme provided by the Montreal (Canada) Assault Prevention Centre provides women and children with a variety of strategies to deal with aggressive situations so that they feel they are equipped to handle even the most extreme scenarios. Like other strategies discussed in this chapter, it encourages people to make positive choices, while providing them with the means to facilitate them (Heilig, 2002). Aside from numerous anecdotal examples of both women and children graduates using skills to successfully defend themselves, a 20-year-old US foundational study of resistance strategies found that 81 per cent of women who ran, 68 per cent of women who used physical force in self-defence, and 63 per cent of women who yelled or screamed successfully avoided sexual assault, while begging or pleading increased the likelihood that a sexual assault would continue. Even in cases where resistance was unsuccessful, mental health impacts were reduced among women who used resistance strategies during a sexual assault (Bart and O'Brien, 1985). The most recent meta-evaluation of rape avoidance techniques also found that knowing and using a variety of resistance strategies are highly correlated with avoiding sexual assault from family members, acquaintances or strangers, without increasing risk of physical injury. The one exception is when the offender has a gun or knife, and even this question is inadequately researched, rather than disproved. There have been very few evaluations of self-defence using the rigorous methodology supported by the Sherman report, but one reported by Ullman (2007) indicated that self-defence programmes increase women's confidence, assertiveness, control over one's life, self-efficacy and mastery of specific physical skills. These skills are particularly important to women with a previous history of childhood or adult sexual or physical abuse (Ullman, 2007).

The use of women's self-defence as one of a suite of strategies to prevent gender-based violence is especially well developed in the US and Canada, particularly in tertiary education settings. As mentioned earlier, the City of Toronto supported free women's self-defence courses in 30 community centres from 1989 to 1997, developing many purpose-built courses with the delivery partner, Wen-Do Women's Self-Defence, such as courses for teenaged girls, older women, lesbians, aboriginal women, women with disabilities, and women who required translation into sign language or another language other than English. Most of the tertiary education institutions in Toronto have also organized free women's self-defence courses (Whitzman, 1992). The Empowerment Project in Canada provided train-the-trainer toolkits to sexual assault centres, women's shelters and organizations working with female ex-offenders across Canada (Whitzman et al, 2004, p10).

There are many charlatans associated with self-defence and a surprising absence of international policy-related literature on the impact of self-defence programmes as part of a comprehensive strategy to prevent violence. However, self-defence and other capacity-building programmes have their place in community safety.

Service provision: Better coordinated and more responsive services

Strengthening and integrating support services for both victims and offenders has been a theme of almost every community safety initiative described. While the majority of the components described in this chapter deal with primary prevention of violence, the provision of good support systems has been widely recognized as a crucial element in minimizing harm and preventing re-victimization (Butchart et al, 2004, pp62–63).

For instance, the best chance of preventing death and disability after a severely violent incident is for the victim to receive emergency medical services within the first hour of an injury. A comparative study of emergency services in Kumasi (Ghana), Monterrey (Mexico) and Seattle (US) found that 51 per cent of severely injured died 'in the field' in Ghana, versus 40 per cent in Monterrey and 21 per cent in Seattle. Emergency health workers can also provide immediate information and referral to victims if they are conscious, and with the victim's consent can begin evidence gathering. The last is particularly important to rape victims; usually forensic evidence needs to be gathered in the first 72 hours for it to be admissible in court (Butchart et al, 2004, pp62–67).

We have seen in the Cardiff example how co-locating emergency mental health support staff near a hospital emergency room can increase the likelihood of the victim receiving immediate and appropriate services. Similarly, locating emergency support services in or near police stations can increase immediate support for victims. This strategy will be discussed in the section on policing. The importance of case management with both individuals and families, and enhanced coordination between support services, police and justice systems, has already been discussed in the Duluth and London domestic violence initiatives. Case management and coordinated approaches rely on consistent messages being developed across service organizations, such as creating welcoming environments for victims, where they are believed, given options and supported in their decisions (Pickup, 2001, p158). Service organization coalitions have developed joint training, protocols and monitoring mechanisms (including client surveys) to ensure that victims receive consistent messages as they move between services.

Another mechanism developed by service coalitions has already been described in the Cardiff example. This is screening, or routine enquiry for experiences of violence, of all people seeking emergency healthcare. Screening by hospital emergency room staff, doctor's offices and public health clinics, and home visit staff (e.g. maternal health nurses, midwives and homecare for the elderly) are the most common forms of screening, particularly with women who are pregnant or who have young children since they are most at risk of unreported intimate partner violence (Butchart et al, 2004, pp63–64; Hester and Westmarland, 2005, p27). Screening by child protection officers, emergency housing and welfare services staff for intimate partner violence has also occurred in some areas. This is a highly controversial issue. On the one hand, because of the high rates and hidden aspect of child mistreatment, intimate partner violence, sexual violence and elder abuse, screening can allow increased detection, recording, reporting and response to violence. On the other hand, there is concern that routine enquiry combined with mandatory reporting could put victims at additional risk (mandatory reporting of child abuse is common because of the potential severity of the consequences and the question of ascertaining informed consent; mandatory reporting of sexual or physical violence against other people is much more rare). Service professionals often complain that they have no training, time or skills to do this kind of sensitive enquiry, and might put themselves at professional or personal risk if they do so (Butchart et al, 2004, p63; Hester and Westmarland, 2005, p28). An evaluation of screening programmes in the UK suggested that both patients and health professionals found screening acceptable only when it was conducted in a safe environment with adequate support systems in place. Another evaluation of routine screening for intimate partner violence in cases of child protection found that level of disclosure of domestic violence increased by between one third and two-thirds, and that routine asking gives the message that it is acceptable to disclose domestic violence and that no one is being specifically targeted for enquiry, which could have safety implications (Hester and Westmarland, 2005, pp28–29).

In addition to better provision of emergency services, coordination of health services and making services more effective by routine enquiry, providing new services, or services that are more inclusive of newly identified clients, is another common service provision strategy. The Woman Abuse Committee of Toronto has been a leader in promoting better access for visible minority women, women whose first language is not English, and women with disabilities in all services that are part of this coalition (Woman Abuse Council of Toronto, 2007). Houses of refuge for women over 50, who may be victims of elder abuse by children or grandchildren or intimate partner violence, have recently been set up in the west and north of Canada (Whitzman et al, 2004, p12).

All of these strategies assume that there are existing violence prevention and support services to coordinate and improve upon. An example of where to begin where they are no existing services is found in Box 6.6.

Box 6.6 *Developing services in Bacolod, the Philippines*

The partnership between Bacolod, a city of 340,000 in central Philippines, and Kamloops, a city of 76,000 in British Columbia, Canada, began in 1995, facilitated by the International Centre for Municipal Development, Federation of Canadian Municipalities (2002). While the first phase focused on recreation, urban planning, solid waste management and computerization, the second phase, from 1999 to 2001, included improving services for women among the priorities. There was a small drop-in centre for women and children victims of abuse in Bacolod, which had begun operation in 1995; but the weight of domestic violence, unwanted pregnancy and sexually transmitted diseases was too much for this largely volunteer-run centre. After a diagnostic workshop, 40 local women's organizations agreed that there were two priorities: a community-based Quick Response Team that would be staffed by volunteers trained to deal with domestic violence; and a health facility that would be staffed by health professionals and trained volunteers, and could provide information and referral services to single females on pregnancy and sexually transmitted diseases in a non-judgemental fashion. Eight delegates from Bacolod came to Kamloops for train-the-trainer sessions, and then transmitted their learning in 'echo training' sessions with 45 health workers, para-legal police known as peace officers, elected officials, court officers and representatives of seniors' organizations. The purpose of the first set of workshops was to sensitize various key partners in issues of domestic violence and to build links between them.

During the spring of 2000, training shifted towards the development of response mechanisms in the central city neighbourhood of Baraguay. Drawing from the pool of those who had received echo training sessions, participants were selected to receive Quick Response training from the Kamloops team in Bacolod. The team was established with a clear mandate, a schedule of operations and specific roles for each member; a protocol for responding to incidents was developed; and monthly planning meetings were instituted. The new health centre, funded by both Philippine and Canadian sources, offered classes on contraception, baby visits and immunization for infants, as well as information on family violence. By 2001, the health centre had over 1200 users and over 100 women and children had benefited from the Quick Response Team. The Women's Issues Programme also led to an increase in local government budgeting for social and gender development, and the community-based approach which led to a health centre in Baraguay is now being replicated in the rest of the city. Canadian participants also reported greater knowledge of international violence against women prevention issues as a result of their volunteer work, and the programme was felt to be a good model for locally based high-income country–low-income country cooperation (International Centre for Municipal Development, 2002).

Safer spaces: Spatial planning

As previously discussed, planning-related strategies have often been assumed to be limited to crime prevention through environmental design (CPTED). First-generation CPTED tended to operate in isolation of, and often in competition with, social development approaches. It took a simplistic and mechanistic approach that emphasized environmental determinism over any root cause factors that might lead to violence, and only attempted to prevent violence and insecurity in public space. Even 'second-generation CPTED', which takes a more social development-oriented approach, still tends to reinforce a 'fortress mentality' (Kitchen and Schneider, 2002) and cannot see any role for planning beyond that of a mechanism for providing safe public space (Whitzman, 2007).

In contrast, both the urban planning and management approach to violence prevention championed by UN-Habitat and the poverty reduction approach to violence prevention supported by the World Bank assume a much more comprehensive role for spatial planning. According to material prepared for the Third World Urban Forum in Vancouver in 2006, urban planning can resolve conflicts over space at the local scale through supporting democratic approaches to urban governance; they can promote social inclusion through upgrading existing slums and providing better infrastructure and land management to prevent slums; and they can respond quickly to post-disaster and post-conflict situations, where violence is rife, to rebuild communities and institutional capacity for planning (UN-Habitat, 2006b). We have seen in the example of Durban's iTRUMP project how local conflict management can be part of neighbourhood planning; we have seen in San Fernando and Dar es Salaam how upgrading slums can contribute to the prevention of violence and insecurity; and we have seen how providing 'spaces of safety' for women to congregate in Bosnian refugee camps can contribute to emotional healing and economic self-sufficiency. Planning can thus contribute in at least three ways to violence prevention in both public and private space: providing 'safer public spaces' through improved design combined with community development and a participatory process in specific sites; providing 'spaces of safety', such as health and social services that screen for domestic violence, and neighbourhood centres where peer support, leadership development, and life and economic skills can be provided, and ensuring 'discursive safe space' where the process of preventing both public and private violence, including discussing and resolving disputes over 'fair shares' of public goods, services and spaces, can be supported (Whitzman, 2007).

In Mumbai, the Gender and Space Project of Partners for Urban Knowledge, Action and Research (PUKAR) has been researching on all three aspects of planning to prevent violence. It has provided detailed site maps of four sites in Mumbai that provide both land uses and amenities, and people's use over the course of the day, including both stationary and moving individuals. It has found that while men and boys linger in a large number of places, including shops, playgrounds and areas with large numbers of street vendors, women and girls tend to follow a 'tyranny of purpose', moving to pick up groceries or children, quickly get lunch and return to work, or travel to and from public transportation. The one exception was a low wall near a school, where mothers, coming to pick up their children, appear to 'take over the edge' for about an hour before and immediately after the end of school. Another exercise has asked participants – architecture students, clients at a legal clinic and attendees at an international conference – to map out where women and men would probably be found in a drawing of a neighbourhood on a weekday evening, and to map out paths along a mixed-use urban street. The findings of this research have been used in advocacy for more inclusive urban spaces, more attention to gendered use of space in planning for new communities and evaluation of existing spaces, and can also be used in the development of specific places where women can congregate (Ranade, 2007). A similar project in Göteborg, Sweden, tracked women's 'time–space maps' in terms of specific routes that they took throughout the day to develop recommendations aimed at establishing safer, more accessible and more inclusive public spaces (Listerborn, 2002b). Both of these projects can be seen as variants of the women's safety audit projects described earlier. Both projects aim to extend the number of people credited as having safer design professional expertise, such as architects, urban planners and police, to people with expertise of experience, such as both male and female users of a place.

Institutionalizing or mainstreaming these practices through the development of guidelines, interdisciplinary training sessions and ongoing programmes such as regular safety audits has already been discussed in the examples of Toronto and New Zealand. Another example of good practice comes from the Australian state of New South Wales, where a bottom-up advocacy project, led by the Liverpool Women's Resource Centre as part of the Healthy Cities Project during 1991 to 1994, influenced the development of guidelines across the state. The Plan It Safe project began with a series of safety audits; then the project developed a video, a guide to organizing for safer public space and a series of good practice examples. For instance, one local council encouraged cafés and outdoor restaurants as a way of encouraging a greater variety of people on main streets in the evening. In a laneway where the violent rape and assault of a lesbian had taken place, a property was converted into Mary's Place, Sydney's first space dedicated to eliminating hate-related violence, and the laneway itself was lit, landscaped and painted with vibrant street art as a way of symbolically 'reclaiming' it as safe public space (Liverpool Safe Women Project, 1998).

A conference on cultural and religious diversity in Sarajevo in 2003 discussed research on why cities became centres of conflict, while others became 'peace enclaves', in the chaotic aftermath of the dissolution of Yugoslavia during the early 1990s. The 'peace enclaves' appeared to have genuinely shared public spaces, civic networks that crossed cultural and religious boundaries to work on common urban goals, education systems that promoted integration, and cultural activities and museums that broke down stereotypes. One of the conclusions was that local leaders needed to promote poly-cultural and multi-use spaces, as opposed to the kinds of mono-cultural spaces that can result from gated communities and 'defensible space' (Council of Europe, 2004).

Unfortunately, external evaluations of inclusive spatial planning strategies are rare. A large-scale project to develop Vancouver's Downtown East Side in British Columbia, Canada – a neighbourhood notorious for substance abuse – included design improvements, the provision of new social infrastructure and community engagement. In 2002, six years after the project commenced, drug overdose deaths had fallen by 68 per cent, homicides had decreased by a similar amount and robberies had decreased by 38 per cent. There were 1300 new affordable housing units in the neighbourhood, four new health facilities, including a safe injection site, and new businesses and social enterprises (Shaw, 2006, pp13–14). However, in smaller and safer sites than Vancouver's Downtown East Side or Durban's Warwick Junction, there may not be a critical mass of police-reported violent incidents to provide a valid before-and-after comparison. In that case, the number and variety of people using the space at various times of the day and evening, and user satisfaction with the space, may be the best indicators of good practice. This could be provided through both before-and-after surveys and comparisons with similar spaces where an intervention has not taken place. It would be important to break down this data by gender, age and other grounds of difference.

Two examples of planning for inclusive public spaces are provided in Box 6.7.

Box 6.7 *Planning for safety and inclusion in Toronto, Canada, and Melbourne, Australia*

Dufferin Grove Park is a mid-sized park in west-central Toronto, Canada. Approximately three-blocks long by one-block across, it is bounded on one side by a major road, with a shopping centre across the street. There are eight elementary or secondary schools within a ten-minute walk of the park, leading to a large number of young people in the vicinity. The neighbourhood is a mixture of relatively well-established first-generation Eastern and Southern European migrants, and relative newcomers from South-East Asia and Latin America.

During the late 1980s, Dufferin Grove Park and the adjacent Dufferin Mall were both suffering from poor reputations. The mall had a number of vacancies, and there had been both thefts and robberies, including one stabbing of a shop owner as he was making a bank deposit after hours. The park was dominated by young men who were believed to be members of gangs and was reputed to be a haven for drug dealing and prostitution. In 1991, the mall brought in a new manager, David Hall, who decided to form a committee consisting of city staff, business owners, community associations and religious institutions. The committee also formed a youth advisory board to suggest positive alternatives to a repressive approach towards young people in the mall. A new security company was hired to work with the youth advisory board on better policies to deal with disruptive youth. With the help of Toronto's recreation department, they hired a youth worker for the mall and donated space to a local high school to create a satellite campus for students at risk. The students participated in classes in the morning and worked in the mall for the afternoon. An inter-agency network also operated a storefront youth centre, which provided counselling, advocacy and referral. It found that the mall provided anonymity to youth using services. The religious institutions formed a God Squad to explore cross-cultural youth projects. Aside from providing 'licit' activities and spaces for the inevitably large number of young people in the mall, mall management worked on 'leavening the mix' by attracting other users. Another abandoned storefront was converted into a mother and child centre, including a secluded breastfeeding area. A portion of the food court seating was set aside for older men to play cards, a popular activity for migrants from Southern Europe (Catallo, 1994, pp35–36).

The mall also offered Cdn$25,000 for park improvements, recognizing that park safety influenced the reputation of the shopping centre (Friends of Dufferin Grove Park, 2007). The city's parks department had held a public meeting to discuss the allocation of the funds; but it was poorly attended and failed to generate any concrete ideas. At this point, Jutta Mason, a local activist known by David Hall, was approached by him to organize a two-day telephone poll of local residents. Aside from a basketball court, the residents decided that they wanted some sort of installation that would build on resources in the neighbourhood, including cooking abilities and cultural skills.

By 1993, the Big Backyard Programme applied for a permit to hold regular campfires, which led to the construction of a fire pit as a summer youth employment project and food being cooked on the campfire for Breakfasts in the Park and cultural activities. This, in turn, led to the construction of a communal bread oven, used by local schools for park-based activities and by some Latin American migrant women for catering. The existing playground, largely abandoned, was transformed with a large mural and numerous arts-based and ecological activities that now take place there, especially during the summer (Catallo, 1994, pp21–22). A large sandpit provides poles, ropes, shovels and photographs of early cabins to stimulate children's imaginative play. In the summer, a used treadle machine sits near the wading pool so that South-East Asian mothers can sew and watch their children at the same time. There have been open-air theatre events, children's puppet shows and food festivals (Project for Public Spaces, 1998).

The main winter activity in Dufferin Grove was a skating rink; but during the early 1990s, the adjacent rink house was unheated and the rink itself was dominated by tough young boys playing pick-up hockey. The Friends of Dufferin Grove, as the informal residents group was now calling itself, worked with the city's parks department for a major renovation in 1996. The blank walls of the rink house were punched out with eye-level windows so people could see out and in. The small office was converted into a kitchen, which was used for baking cookies and making hot chocolate, and a wood stove was installed in the change room. This made the interior much more inviting for parents of young children, and Jutta Mason also noted that putting after-school snacks in the mouths of young people calmed them down considerably (I should come clean at this point and state that it was Jutta who provided the Julio's sneakers story I referred to in Chapter 3; she is a master of anecdotal evaluation). Female rink guards assisted in offsetting the male dominance of the hockey players, and the rink was divided into two halves, one for shinny hockey and one for family skating. The rink house was also used on a regular basis: Tuesday mornings it provided a parent and child drop-in, with a small collection of toys, and on Wednesday afternoons it hosted an older men's card club.

There was considerable debate about whether a new community garden, which was assumed to appeal largely to older people, would be located close to or far away from the basketball court. The decision was made to co-locate the two attractions and also offer some checker tables and seats between the two. There have certainly been incidents when the young people's bad language offends people in the community gardens; but the Friends of Dufferin Grove have worked on conflict resolution mechanisms so that most of the incidents can be dealt with immediately.

The park's constantly updated website provides incident reports of criminal activity, and of how the police and courts have followed up on incidents. Unfortunately, there has been no formal evaluation of Dufferin Park's transformation over the past 15 years; but the skating rink has become one of the most popular in the city, local businesses have contributed enthusiastically to the activities in the park, and the park's transformation has won numerous international awards. The annual income of Cdn$30,000 from park food sales has all gone back to park services. Elements of success include building on local resources (e.g. 'comfort' smells and activities such as campfires and food preparation), purposely co-locating activities to support intergenerational and cross-cultural interaction, and constantly breaking local government 'rules' (e.g. food preparation guidelines, as a way of challenging a high-income country regulation focus!).

In Melbourne, Australia, a similarly inclusive process worked to transform a smaller park. Talbot Reserve is bounded by a major road, the National Theatre School, high-density apartments and lower-density residential housing. It is in a part of Melbourne with quite a few licensed establishments and hostels for low-budget tourists, as well as increasing gentrification of older residences once used as rooming houses. With a somewhat tired playground structure, it was employed by residents with families and dogs, members of the National Theatre, as well as by homeless people, street sex workers and their minders, intravenous drug users and problem drinkers, and people living with psychological and physical disabilities, all of whom are also residents.

The default response in this situation would be to install more lighting, increase the police presence and arrest more people, and remove seating. Instead of this 'zero tolerance' approach, the goal of the Design In process was to promote a more inclusive and cohesive community, focusing as much on building relationships between neighbours as redesigning the reserve. The first step in this process was to approach a range of people: council planners, community development staff, local police, neighbouring residents, prostitutes' rights groups, social service agencies for homeless people, people with psychiatric illnesses and drug users (not necessarily the same people), and the 'trouble-makers' themselves. The majority of the 36 participants were residents whose initial agenda was to keep people with problem behaviours out of the reserve. There was a smaller group of advocates, people who had either experienced substance abuse personally in the past or who worked at agencies that supported marginalized groups. Each participant was provided with a disposable camera and asked to photograph the positives and negatives of the reserve over a week. This was followed by an introductory evening workshop where the participants were given a role card and asked to 'be someone else' as they expressed their views on the park. They then collectively visited the park in the evening, interviewing other people using the reserve. A second workshop divided the participants into small mixed groups who spent a weekend afternoon preparing plans for a redesigned space, followed by a ranking of the top three priorities. An action plan was developed at the meeting, including a community event in the park to display the plans prior to adoption. When the park was redesigned in 2003, there was a certain amount of dispersal of problematic activities out of the park. More importantly, residents began to recognize one another, say hello and negotiate over the shared space directly, rather than avoid the park or call the police. The process has been adopted in other public spaces owned by the local government (Press, 2004).

Policing approaches

Police help in identifying and analysing problems; they are vital actors in most strategies; and police statistics can help in evaluating the success of initiatives. The participation of police is thus necessary for any 'place-based' or 'whole-of-government' approach to the prevention of violence and insecurity.

Increasing the size of the police force and the numbers of those incarcerated in prisons tends to be the default position for political decision-making that is uninformed about what works to prevent crime and violence. But in recent years, there has been a growing understanding of the fact that most violence is unreported to, and thus unaddressed by, the police and justice systems. Research has confirmed that it is not the quantity of policing, but its quality that matters. Policing has thus moved in many jurisdictions from a bureaucratic and hierarchical institution with a centralized structure and reactive response system – evaluated by rapid response, number of arrests and successful prosecutions – to a more strategic, flexible and decentralized organization with a professional rather than a quasi-militaristic culture and an ability to work with other prevention-oriented organizations, evaluated by public satisfaction and the quality of police services. A confluence of reports have agreed on 'what works' in policing: deploying police officers strategically; working on specific problems in partnership with others; improving data collection and then sharing that data with researchers and other organizations; focusing on reducing repeat victimization; empowering victims to feel safe in disclosure; and working on mediation of minor anti-social incidents rather than arrest (Butchart et al, 2004, p7; see also Rosenbaum, 2002).

Sherman and Eck (2002), in their meta-evaluation of crime prevention, add that directed patrols in hot spots, proactive arrests of serious repeat offenders, including employed suspects of domestic assault, and proactive drunk-driving arrests work to prevent repeat offending. With few exceptions, Neighbourhood Watch police–community campaigns do not work to prevent crime, violence or insecurity. The one exception is a form of situational crime prevention that reinforces locks and engraves possessions, along with a tightly focused Neighbourhood Watch campaign. This approach, pioneered in the Kirkholt UK public housing project in 1985, has been shown to reduce repeat burglaries, although its effectiveness in preventing violence or insecurity would be moot (Chalom et al, 2001, p25). Arresting juveniles for minor offences does not decrease the likelihood of repeat offences, and simply hiring more police officers does not prevent crime, violence or insecurity (Sherman and Eck, 2002, p321).

A number of policing models have been advanced within community safety partnerships. *Problem-oriented policing* uses the same process of problem identification, diagnosis, analysis and assessment that was described in Chapter 5. It can thus be seen as a component of the process of community safety planning, as in the case of violence around licensed establishments in Swansea. *Community policing* seeks to improve relationships between groups who have tended to distrust the police and the policing service through community participation, accountability and transparency (Gray, 2006, p10). Keeping track of the anti-social incidents at Dufferin Grove Park, as well as of how the incidents progressed through the justice system, is an example of community policing.

This section focuses on three aspects of the policing component of community safety: improving coordination between police and other support services for victims of crime; developing better policies on response to violent incidents; and working together with community organizations on problem-solving.

Examples from London (England), Duluth (US) and Bacolod (the Philippines) have already been provided of how police, the health sector and services for assaulted women can work together to offer better assessment, intervention, information and referral. This requires an ongoing partnership that diagnoses and addresses service gaps, provides training, and develops protocols and ongoing evaluation mechanisms. One component of coordinated strategies is co-location, providing services within or adjacent to police stations, or police officers who are located near existing social services. The Survivors of Rape Trauma Room was established within a busy police station in Cape Town, South Africa, in 1999.

A counselling service located in this room provided immediate emergency coun-selling to survivors of rape, as well as simple written information on the next stages of the criminal justice process and the possible symptoms of post-traumatic stress disorder, and there is an accompanying packet of information for children who are victims or accompanying their mother. An outreach service to the emergency room of the local hospital now provides the same service (Whitzman et al, 2004, p23). In two projects in the UK – one of which placed women's service workers in a police station and the other placed police officers in a women's service – the result was the same: a greater level of reporting to the police and referrals from the police (Hester and Westmarland, 2005, p46).

Mandatory arrest policies in cases of domestic violence fall in the category of controversial ideas. The UK meta-evaluation of effective domestic violence prevention strategies indicates that projects that seek to increase the number of police calls ending in arrests must put in place adequate legal, emotional and financial support for victims in order to be effective and not increase the danger to victims (Hester and Westmarland, 2005, p49). An evaluation of 1980s manda-tory arrest policy in London, Canada, which was accompanied by police training and inter-agency partnerships, appeared to meet with considerable satisfaction from victims, a decline in repeat calls to the same address (a somewhat equivocal finding) and, perhaps most significantly, a marked decrease in youth delinquency from the children involved in domestic violence over time (Chalom et al, 2001, p22).

Another fairly controversial policy has been the establishment of women's police stations. Women's police stations employ female officers, generally accom-panied by volunteer para-legal workers. The City of São Paulo first established women's police stations during the early 1980s, and the number of domestic violence cases reported there increased from 2000 in 1985 to over 7000 in 1989. With the support of police authorities, the programme had 70 women's police stations throughout Brazil by the mid 1990s (Chalom et al, 2001, p22). Although women's police stations have undoubtedly increased reporting and provided better services to victims than before, it still takes years to bring perpetrators to justice, and women are still at risk of retaliation from their partners (Pickup, 2001, p284). Once again, the research indicates that women's police stations are only effective if provided as part of a larger project of transforming legal and social services to support female victims of family violence.

Two Canadian projects have worked with a particularly vulnerable group: street sex workers. In Winnipeg, the West End Women's Safety Project was initi-ated by Sage House, a drop-in centre for homeless and low-income women, many of whom are aboriginal. It worked to build bridges with police, local busi-nesses, residents who were involved in the sex trade, and residents who were not. Two part-time outreach workers provided street sex workers with condoms, 'bad trick' sheets and referrals to community organizations. One innovation was distributing the 'bad trick' sheets to local schools and resident associations, which resulted in the capture and conviction of a serial rapist (Whitzman et al, 2004, p9). In Vancouver, the police department worked with an organization called Prostitution Alternatives, Counselling and Education (PACE) in the Downtown East Side neighbourhood previously described as a centre for substance abuse and street prostitution. Training for police officers by PACE in 2002 and 2003 led to a two-day 'train-the-trainer' programme run by PACE and the police for leaders in the street sex trade, teaching them to prevent, defuse, disengage and defend themselves against potential assailants, and have them pass on this training to other street sex workers (Whitzman et al, 2004, p18). Like the Melbourne park example in this chapter (see Box 6.7), the initiative took an approach that assumed that all residents have an equal right to live without violence, which resulted in positive outcomes for the entire community.

An effort to improve community policing in Mumbai slums is described in Box 6.8. Like examples previously provided from Dar es Salaam, Durban and aboriginal Australia, Mumbai's programme combines improved public guardianship and conflict resolution with better police community relations. This is particularly important in LICs, where social cleansing of street youth and prostitutes by police, and their participation as agents of undemocratic regimes, has led to lingering distrust of formal police and justice systems (Moser and McIlwaine, 2006, p94). However, unlike the European schemes outlined in the community economic development sections, these schemes rely on volunteers to provide basic social infrastructure and can be seen as somewhat exploitative for that reason.

Legal and correctional approaches

Two seemingly contradictory, but actually complementary, approaches to violence have already been discussed throughout the book. On the one hand, making the abuse of women, children and parents within families a crime, and developing specialized court systems to deal with these cases are attempts to increase the efficacy of the formal justice system in responding to serious and recurrent violence. On the other hand, developing community-based mediation and conflict resolution programmes is an attempt to divert more minor offences from ever reaching an already overburdened criminal justice system.

If we return to the overview of what works and what does not in Chapter 3, shock deterrence, boot camps and other mechanisms to increase the severity of sanctions against young offenders do not work. Rehabilitation-based programmes in and out of prison that emphasize changing behaviours, located within programmes that also work to increase academic, employment and social skills, do tend to work, but are rare within most prison systems in the world (Mackenzie, 2002). In other words, prisons do work to keep violent people out of the general population if and only if court systems work effectively to put the

Box 6.8 *Community police stations in Mumbai, India*

About half of Mumbai's 15 million inhabitants live in slums, which like other informal settlements that have been described, lack basic services and infrastructure. In India, police have a particularly bad reputation. During 2001/2002, there were 165 deaths in police custody, 113 deaths in police 'encounter killings', 80 further cases involving disappearance of suspects, and over 5000 cases related to other alleged police excesses. Organizations working with homeless people in Delhi state that over 50,000 pavement dwellers have said their foremost problem is the behaviour of police officers (Commonwealth Human Right Initiative, 2004, p4).

In Mumbai, India, a partnership between the new police commissioner and a grassroots organization called Slum Dwellers International has led to community police stations being established in 65 slum neighbourhoods since June 2004 (Roy et al, 2004). Each '*panchayat*' is made up of ten representatives from the slum (seven women and three men) and a local police officer, and is located in a building within the slum. All community representatives, who like their São Paulo counterparts, are volunteers, receive a photo-badge authorized by the police commissioner and undergo training by the police. But they are appointed by the residents' organization, not the police. The preponderance of women in these community police stations recognizes the fact that women are disproportionately the victims of crime. This also facilitates victim support in cases of domestic violence. In addition, there are strong savings and credit groups formed by women slum and pavement dwellers, and *panchayat* workers are often drawn from these groups. The community representatives help to patrol the settlement and seek to resolve neighbourhood and family disputes before they escalate into violence. Slum inhabitants can bring disputes to the *panchayat* at a set time of day, where under the auspices of the police, disputes can be resolved. This mechanism is much quicker and more likely to result in a positive result than going through the formal court system. An example of a dispute concerned a woman who worked as a domestic servant. She came to the *panchayat* after her employer had not paid her for six months. When the employer heard of this, he lodged a formal complaint against her for unruly behaviour. After discussion with both parties, the formal charge was dismissed and the police made sure she received her back pay. Similarly to Dar es Salaam, the organization of women slum dwellers also works with people who brew illegal alcohol, to support them in new livelihoods (Roy et al, 2004).

Work is under way to see how the *panchayats* might also provide a location for doctors' consultations, as well as provide a basis for more constructive relationships with local utilities. The coverage is also expanding rapidly in Mumbai, apparently informed by reviews of the experiences to date, which thus far unfortunately remain unpublished.

most violent and recurrent offenders behind bars. But they are remarkably ineffective at rehabilitating people into useful members of society, particularly given their cost.

Because of the sheer number of violent crimes in many LICs and within particular communities of HICs, there has been a growing interest in *restorative justice* programmes, particularly in relation to young offenders. These programmes originated in Canadian aboriginal communities during the late 1980s (Laprairie, 1998) and soon spread to New Zealand, where three pilot schemes from 1990 to 1993 led to wide-scale implementation throughout the country, and to Australia, where youth diversion through restorative justice has been implemented in most states (Daly, 2001). Similar victim–offender mediation schemes have been introduced during the 1990s in the US, Europe and many LICs. The purpose of these programmes is to return 'ownership' of crime and violence problems and solutions to those individuals and groups who are most affected by the behaviours at hand, and who have the most stake in finding a satisfactory solution (Laprairie, 1998, p61). This would include, in most cases, the victim(s), the offender(s), their families and their immediate communities.

Restorative justice programmes are often used as an alternative, or *diversion*, from court prosecution. Although there are a number of formats, the most common is called *a community conference* or, as it is called within certain aboriginal communities, *a healing circle*. An offender (who has admitted to the offence), his or her supporter (often, a parent or guardian), the victim, his or her supporters, other affected members of the community (sometimes including community elders, particularly within aboriginal communities), a police officer and a justice of the peace come together to discuss the offence and its impact. The offender is given an opportunity to talk about the circumstances of their offence and why they became involved in it, and the victim and others have an opportunity to talk about how the offence has affected them. The police officer may provide other details of the offence. The meeting then moves on to a discussion of the agreement or undertaking that the offender will complete. The reparations that are part of the agreement include verbal and written apologies to the victim, paying some form of monetary compensation or other compensatory work for the victim, doing other community work and attending counselling sessions, among others. Various jurisdictions have different criteria as to the minimum number of people who must agree to the settlement; but it always includes the offender and court official, and usually the victim. The outcome is a legally binding document (Daly, 2001).

Many evaluations of restorative justice programmes have been positive. In Nova Scotia, Canada, a restorative justice programme dealt with 6000 young people, aged 12 to 17 over five years, who had committed both minor and serious offences. After 26 months, 78 per cent had not re-offended, as opposed to 49 per cent of those youth who had gone through the traditional justice system (Leonard et al, 2005, p239). An evaluation of 351 young offenders, victims and parents in

Queensland, Australia, found that over 97 per cent were satisfied with the process and the outcomes. There were similar findings from studies in other Australian states, including statistically significant findings from a study that compared randomized cases assigned to restorative justice and traditional court programmes. A much more equivocal finding emerged from the first pilot projects in New Zealand during the early 1990s, where over 80 per cent of offenders were happy with the outcome of their conference, but only half of victims were satisfied, and a quarter said that they felt worse as a result of attending the conference. This led to modifications in the programme, ensuring that victims attended the conference and that outcomes were agreed upon by victims (Daly, 2001).

While the majority of restorative justice initiatives deal with young offenders and relatively minor violent and non-violent offences, there has been some implementation of adult healing circles, particularly in aboriginal communities in Canada, Australia and New Zealand. In Manitoba's Hollow Water Reserve in Canada, male offenders of intimate partner violence who admit their guilt publicly are offered support over two to five years, as are their victims. The contract usually involves community work, as well as restitution to the victim. When the contract is fulfilled, a cleansing ceremony takes place to symbolize the return of balance. While these approaches may work in small communities, they may not be appropriate for more mobile urban societies where community-based supervision is more difficult (Pickup, 2001, pp214–215). The evaluation of the Hollow Water Holistic Healing Circle also found that while 78 per cent of offenders experienced the sentencing circle as positive, only 28 of victims felt the same way (Laprairie, 1998, p72). There is a concern that reconciliation-based approaches – not only restorative justice but also family-based mediation – tend to assume that the violence is caused by conflict, and are insufficiently cognizant of power differentials and the need of victims to feel adequately supported and safe in the process (Pickup, 2001, p156).

In terms of domestic violence, there is no doubt that a coordinated approach that combines criminal justice sanctions with social services to both victims and offenders works to prevent recidivism. In a large research project in Calgary, Canada, with 4500 participants, a 24-month follow-up found that only 12 per cent of those accused had committed new offences, versus 34 per cent of the control group (Leonard et al, 2005, p239). A study in Bradford, UK, found that issuing immediate protective orders that kept the man away from the family home, along with 'target hardening', such as improved locks, the provision of mobile phones and monitored alarms, had a large impact upon the immediate safety of women pressing charges against their intimate partners, and thus their willingness to carry through with prosecution instead of withdrawing their statement. The Bradford Staying Put programme also provided women with social service workers to accompany them to court. In half of the cases where the woman was accompanied to court to give evidence as witnesses, a guilty plea was recorded, as opposed to only one fifth of the cases where the woman was unaccompanied

(Hester and Westmarland, 2005, pp58–59, 77–79). Training of court officials in the Hammersmith and Fulham borough of London, UK, led to an increase in convictions from 10 per cent in 1996, before the intervention, to 27 per cent in 2000, after two years of the training (Hester and Westmarland, 2005, p61). In the Croydon borough of London, black and other visible minority women were provided a support worker throughout the criminal justice process, using principles adopted from the Duluth Domestic Abuse Intervention Project. Repeat victimization rates decreased three times more for project users compared to a non-intervention sample (Hester and Westmarland, 2005, pp71–72).

Successful policing and justice approaches must therefore proceed cautiously in applying mediation and restorative justice approaches to many minor offences, while ensuring that serious and recurrent domestic violence does not fall into the 'minor offence' basket. Even in the case of extreme communal violence, a restorative justice approach is possible, as in the case of South Africa's Truth and Reconciliation Commission (Boraine, 2000). However, alternative sentencing approaches must recognize the severity of violent offences, as well as the need of victims to achieve a measure of safety and restitution, if alternatives to the criminal justice system are to be sought for adult violent offenders.

Conclusion: A wide menu of community safety strategies

This chapter has provided a remarkable range of health promotion, poverty reduction and spatial planning community-safety strategies that can work to prevent violence and insecurity. The strategies work with individuals, families, communities and societies at every stage of governance, and in both the public spaces of business and shopping districts, schools, community centres, parks and residential neighbourhoods, and the private spaces of people's homes. As diverse as these components are, they share certain principles (Shaw, 2002, piv). One is seeking to intervene as early as possible: before children grow up in violent families, before the warning signs of abusive relationships turn into violence, before small-scale tensions escalate. A second is making creative connections: between problems, resources and organizations. A third is the principle of adaptation: building on what works and changing what does not. Together, these examples show how much people and places can learn from one another if we are willing to work together to prevent violence.

7

The Future of Community Safety and Violence Prevention

The renowned writer on urban creativity, Charles Landry, recently wrote:

> *Misery is exactly where the greater focus of creativity should be. Forget for the moment the more attractive glamour of new media industries or the latest icon building in a city centre. Finding imaginative solutions to day-to-day needs, human distress, thwarted ambition and crime and violence is a far more creative act.* (Landry, 2006, p93)

This book has been dedicated to the proposition that violence and insecurity are complex and interrelated problems, but that creative solutions are being developed around the world, and it is possible to adapt ideas and inspiration from these creative projects to develop safer communities.

There have been considerable expansion and evolution in international efforts on community safety since the 1980s, moving beyond a relatively narrow policing function to one that involves a much broader set of approaches and actors (Shaw, 2007a, p9). This transformation has been informed by global movements in health promotion, urban planning and governance, and poverty reduction. However, there have been very few books or academic articles that have attempted to make the links between these three movements, between the prevention of violence in public and private spheres, and between 'violence' and 'violence against women'. Exceptions include the work of Caroline Moser and her colleagues, funded by the World Bank; the World Health Organization and its Global Campaign on Violence Prevention; Margaret Shaw and her colleagues at the International Centre for the Prevention of Crime; the team at UN-Habitat's Safer Cities Programme; work on 'everyday violence' funded by the European Forum on Urban Security, the Council of Europe and the national governments of Canada, Australia and New Zealand; and a number of sterling local governance-based initiatives. Most of this truly innovative work dates from the last decade. If critical mass has been reached, it is still reflected, for the most part, in work on the ground and in organizational reports, rather than in the academic and theoretical discourse or mainstream policy analysis. Gender mainstreaming within crime and violence prevention is still a rarity, rather than a norm (see Box 7.1).

Box 7.1 *Gender mainstreaming: A concluding note*

According to the United Nations Economic and Social Council, gender mainstreaming is:

> ... the process of assessing the implications for women and men of any planned action, including legislation, policies or programmes, in any area and at all levels. It is a strategy for making women's as well as men's concerns and experiences an integral dimension in the design, implementation, monitoring and evaluation of policies and programmes in all political, economic and societal spheres so that women and men benefit equally and inequality is not perpetuated. The ultimate goal is to achieve gender equality. (Butchart et al, 2004, p51–52)

Gender mainstreaming in relation to this book means making connections between different types of violence, particularly violence in public space, which is associated with male offenders and male victims, and violence in the private space of the home, which is associated with male offenders and female victims. It means getting beyond the 'silo mentality' that has, until recently, split health promotion approaches from urban planning and management approaches, poverty reduction from situational crime prevention, 'crime' from 'fear of crime', and both from 'violence against women'. In most crime prevention theory, violence against women has been treated as an 'add-on' to a laundry list of problems when it is not simply ignored (Shaw and Capobianco, 2004, p3). Over the past 40 years, the feminist movement to end violence against women has broadened its perspective beyond an initial focus on intimate partner violence, sexual harassment and sexual assault to include dating violence; stalking; workplace harassment and violence; peer violence; forced prostitution and trafficking of women; female genital mutilation; forced marriages; the impact of armed conflict and rape as an instrument of war; 'crimes of honour'; dowry-related violence and crimes against widows; and violence based on racism and homophobia (Shaw and Capobianco, 2004, pp5, 15; Johnson, 2007). But at the same time, violence against women has been put in a set of increasingly smaller boxes by government responses, simplifying violence against women to 'family violence', family violence to 'wife assault', and the prevention of 'wife assault' to, at best, mandatory arrest policies and a women's shelter in every community, perhaps with a service coordination committee and a public awareness campaign to keep everyone busy and feeling noble.

In the meantime, the majority of crime prevention money has gone into policing and incarcerating young men, or programmes to prevent young men from offending. The majority of crime prevention research has focused on the 'problems' of young men in the public sphere, with an occasional nod in the direction of family violence, mostly to state that these programmes are notoriously difficult to evaluate. This imbalance of financial and human resources not only does a disservice to female victims of crime, but also to children, older people, female offenders, people victimized by racism, homophobia and able-ism, and others who do not fit the stereotype of 'gangs, guns and drugs' that has been grafted onto a complex and interrelated problem. It is unfair to women, treating them as victims to be protected from the dangerous 'other', instead of autonomous beings with the right to choose better lives and the right to resources that enable those healthy choices. It is also desperately unfair to men and boys, assuming that violence is somehow natural to them, a necessary phase in their maturation, or a fair and transparent selection process that separates out 'evil' men in order to protect society, placing them in prison for so-called offences such as possession of marijuana that will one day appear as absurd and unjust as executing someone for stealing a chicken.

Gender mainstreaming in relation to crime and violence prevention goes beyond making the links between facets of violence. It means creating new partnerships that reflect the potential contribution of services dealing with violence in the home, as well as violence on the street and in workplaces. It means a greater inclusion of women in decision-making around violence prevention, including the use of tools such as safety audits and leadership development. It means a commitment to gender and social equity in politics, economics and social life as a precondition for a safer community and a safer world. It means disaggregating statistics by gender in the diagnosis of the prevalence of victimization and offending. It means examining all possible strategies, from employment creation to public awareness, for differential impacts on women and men. It means analysing for differential gender impacts in the evaluation of violence prevention strategies and initiatives.

Gender mainstreaming is sometimes opposed by feminist services, who are concerned that this approach will threaten their autonomy. But gender mainstreaming does not mean that all components of a community safety strategy need to be equally aimed at women and men. As we have seen throughout the book, sometimes it makes sense to have separate spaces for women and for men. It also makes sense to have separate strategies aimed at family violence and community violence, although there is no reason why they should not be linked under a single initiative at all scales of governance. Gender mainstreaming does not mean that family violence prevention should be privileged over community violence prevention; in fact, the good practice examples described in Chapters 4 to 6 represent an equal distribution of the two emphases.

Promoting equitable relationships is at the core of violence prevention (Michau and Naker, 2004, p71). Gender mainstreaming is one mechanism by which equitable relationships – between individuals, within families and throughout communities and societies – can take place. It means, in short, a new approach to community safety and violence prevention.

The majority of community safety efforts are still informed by public and political stereotypes. These include the notion that offenders are uncommon and substantially different from 'us'; that prevention is a matter of stopping a one-time act; that increasing the number of police will decrease the number of crimes; that making punishment more severe will decrease crime; that there was less crime in 'the good old days'; and that moral decline, somehow associated with urbanization, is responsible for crime (Tilley and Laycock, 2000, p214). Chapters 2 and 3 provided considerable evidence that suggests the opposite: violence is endemic; we all have the potential for violence, and a large number of us engage in violence either sometimes or regularly, thereby making violence 'our' problem; many forms of violence are iterative and generational in their impact; increasing the number of police or people in prison is a remarkably ineffective mechanism for reducing violence; there has always been considerable hidden violence, which is only now becoming more visible in public discourse; and cities represent opportunities as well as challenges for participatory democracy and 'moral betterment'.

Chapters 4 to 6 provided examples of what works well to prevent violence and insecurity around the world. There are huge differences in terms of culture, economics and politics around the globe. But it is important to build on what has worked elsewhere, adapting these ideas to local needs and resources and developing a menu of creative interventions as part of a comprehensive community safety plan (Shaw, 2002, piv). This is true whatever the scale of governance (neighbourhood, city, nation, region or globe) or scale of intervention (individual, family, community or society). Each scale has its opportunities and strengths. None operates in isolation, and jumping scales is a common practice. Individuals are shaped by their families, communities and societies, and, in turn, have the opportunity to influence others. Decisions made at the international scale can influence neighbourhoods. More optimistically, perhaps, examples have been provided of the opposite: where neighbourhood initiatives have inspired not only other neighbourhoods in other parts of the world, but national, regional and global action.

There are significant gaps in the material covered in this book. The prevention of self-directed violence such as suicide has not played a major role: it is a major source of disease and premature death, but very few community safety initiatives explicitly include it. Other issues, such as elder abuse, violence against people with physical or intellectual abilities, sexual trafficking and hate crimes, were largely neglected for the same reason. In general, there is more focus on high-income countries (HICs) than low-income countries (LICs), partly because there are more resources in HICs, including more researchers funded to provide evaluations and write up case studies. Several large countries, such as China and Indonesia, are generally absent from this book, partly because their governments have not hitherto been particularly involved in the international movement to prevent violence.

In 2008, the glass is either half full or half empty. There are global challenges affecting violence prevention at all scales. The growth of terrorism and transnational organized crime destroys lives on a daily basis, and dominates discussions of violence to the extent that resources could be shifted away from preventing violence in homes and streets to violence halfway across the world. Increased cultural and religious tensions have been exacerbated by a global migration to urban areas. Youth violence appears to be increasing in prevalence and severity, particularly in LICs, and is associated with international traffic of drugs, guns and people. There is growing anxiety about risk, with media and politicians telling people that they need to take precautions and be fearful, that their neighbours could be child molesters or terrorists. There are continuing threats to accessing public spaces and the 'right to the city', from the growth of gated communities and enclosed shopping malls, to the increasing privatization (or 'voluntarization') of security, to increasingly repressive laws and by-laws. There are growing inequalities, not only of income, employment and education, but of the basic necessity of security. The rich are voluntarily shutting themselves off from the poor, and the poor are spending much of their limited resources on individualized responses to violence and insecurity. Violence against women continues to be put in a box; responding to crime still gobbles up ten times the resources spent preventing it; and policy-makers continue to look out for the quick fix, the high-tech solution, the magic bullet or the 'one size fits all' nostrum (Shaw, 2006, p3–5).

At the same time, there are promising trends, which have been the focus of this generally optimistic book. There is a greater stress on grassroots ownership, participatory processes and leadership skills capacity-building, not only in community safety, but more generally in health promotion, urban planning and governance, and poverty reduction campaigns. Policy-makers are moving away from an emphasis on deficit models to resource-based models. There is greater attention being paid to the specificity of local contexts and the nuances of partnership building. A menu or tool kit of ideas is being developed and disseminated globally, and the 'one size fits all' model is being rejected. Increasingly, community safety initiatives are emphasizing a culture of violence prevention, from the home to the schoolyard, the workplace, sites of local and national decision-making, and global governance. These approaches are all complementary, not only to one another but to the greater aims of environmental sustainability, social equity, health and well-being, and economic and cultural resilience (Shaw, 2006, p4–6).

There are preconditions to this optimistic outlook. All of the initiatives described in this book rely on participatory democracy, which in general appears to be growing across the globe, but is hardly a 'done deal' in large swathes of Asia and Africa. Violence will continue to thrive until economic and social inequalities lessen. The diffusion of community safety efforts requires a common language of violence prevention in a field dominated by disciplinary jargon and obfuscating terms not generally understood by the general public. The growing community safety movement requires empathy, creativity and courage, and sometimes these resources are in short supply, whether in HICs or LICs.

This book seeks to describe and support a growing movement, linked by the technological wonders of the modern world, to prevent violence and make communities safer. Being involved in making communities safer requires an element of risk because you have to work against stereotypes and unlearn things that you have taken for granted. It also requires trust and respect for others, and the determination to succeed. In return, involvement in community safety and violence prevention offers the possibility of a better world for everyone. It is a risk worth taking in this world of horrific injustice and tremendous possibility.

References

Acero, H. (2006) 'Bogotá's success story', Comunidad Secura: Network of Ideas and Practices in Citizen Security, www.comunidadesegura.org/?q=en/node/31203, accessed 14 April 2007

Andersson, C. and Stavrou, A. (2000) *Youth Delinquency and the Criminal Justice System in Dar es Salaam, Tanzania*, UN-Habitat Safer Cities Programme, Nairobi

Andrew, C. (2000) 'Resisting boundaries? Using safety audits for women', in K. Miranne and A. Young (eds) *Gendering the City: Women, Boundaries, and Visions of Urban Life*, Rowman and Littlefield, Lanham, Maryland, pp157–168

Anti-Slavery International (2007) 'Child labour', www.antislavery.org/homepage/antislavery/childlabour.htm, accessed 30 January 2007

Association of London Government (2001) *One in Four: The London Domestic Violence Strategy*, Greater London Authority, London

Audit Commission UK (2004) *Youth Justice 2004: A Review of the Reformed Youth Justice System*, Audit Commission, London

Australian Bureau of Statistics (1996) *Women's Safety Australia*, Australian Bureau of Statistics, Canberra

Australian Bureau of Statistics (2006) *Personal Safety Survey (Reissue)*, Australian Bureau of Statistics, Canberra

Bart, P. and O'Brien, P. (1985) *Stopping Rape: Successful Survival Strategies*, Oxford University Press, Oxford

Bartlett, S. (2006) *Review of Child Friendly Cities Database*, Save the Children, Sweden

Baxi, P. (2003) 'Rape and Delhi's urban environment', *India Together*, November 2003, www.indiatogether.org/2003/nov/wom-delhienv.htm, accessed 13 March 2007

Benard, B. and Marshall, K. (2001) *Resilience Research for Protective Programs*, National Resilience Resource Center, Minneapolis

Blakely, E. and Snyder, M. G. (1997) *Fortress America: Gated Communities in the United States*, Brookings Institution Press, Washington, DC

Bloeman, S. (2006) 'Tackling gender violence in Papua New Guinea', UNICEF Real Lives series, www.unicef.org/infobycountry/papuang_30991.html, accessed 28 May 2007

Blomberg, S. B. and Mody, A. (2005) *How Severely Does Violence Deter International Investment?*, Claremont McKenna College, Claremont, California

Body Shop International (2006) 'Stop violence in the home campaign 2006', www.thebodyshopinternational.com/Whats+New/Stop+Violence+In+The+Home++Campaign+2006/, accessed 25 January 2008

Boraine, A. (2000) *A Country Unmasked*, Oxford University Press, Oxford

Brownlow, A. (2005) 'A geography of men's fear', *Geoforum*, vol 36, pp581–592

Burgess, J. (1998) '"But is it worth taking the risk?" How women negotiate access to urban woodland: a case study', in R. Ainley (ed) *New Frontiers of Space, Bodies and Gender*, Routledge, London and New York, pp115–128

Butchart, A., Phinney, A., Check, P. and Villaveces, A. (2004) *Preventing Violence: A Guide to Implementing the Recommendations of the World Report on Violence and Health*, World Health Organization Department of Injuries and Violence Prevention, Geneva

Caballero, M. C. (2004) 'Academic turns city into a social experiment', *Harvard University Gazette*, 11 March 2004

CAFSU (Women's Action Committee on Urban Safety) (2002) *Women's Safety: From Autonomy to Dependence*, CAFSU, Montreal

Capobianco, L. (2006) *Public–Private–Community Action towards Safety: A Focus on Housing in Disadvantaged Neighbourhoods*, International Centre for the Prevention of Crime, Montreal

Catallo, R. (1994) *Lessons from Success Stories: Making Communities Safer*, City of Toronto, Toronto

Cavanaugh, S. (1998) *Making Safer Places: A Resource Book for Neighbourhood Safety Audits*, Women's Design Service, London

Chalom, M., Leonard, L., Vanderschueren, F. and Vezina, C. (2001) *Urban Safety and Good Governance: The Role of the Police*, International Centre for the Prevention of Crime/ UN-Habitat Safer Cities Programme, Montreal

Cherney, A. (2006) *Problem-solving for Crime Prevention*, Australian Institute of Criminology, Canberra

City of Toronto (1999) *Toronto, My City, a Safe City: A Community Safety Strategy for the City of Toronto*, City of Toronto Taskforce on Community Safety, Toronto

Coalition for Gun Control (2007) 'Coalition for Gun Control – about us', Coalition for Gun Control, www.guncontrol.ca/English/About/About.htm, accessed 7 May 2007

Commonwealth Human Rights Initiative (2004) *Policing: A Human Rights Perspective*, Commonwealth Human Rights Initiative, Delhi

Commonwealth Secretariat (2003) *Integrated Approaches to Eliminating Gender-based Violence*, Commonwealth Secretariat, London

Community Safety Advisory Service (2007) 'Community Safety Advisory Service', www.csas.org.uk/index.html, accessed 27 January 2007

Connell, R. W. (2005) *Masculinities*, Allen and Unwin, Crow's Nest, New South Wales

Council of Europe (2003) *Urban Crime Prevention: A Guide for Local Authorities*, Council of Europe, Strasbourg

Council of Europe (2004) *Confronting Everyday Violence in Europe: An Integrated Approach*, Council of Europe, Strasbourg

Cowichan Safer Futures Program (2003) *The Next Stage: A Discussion Paper on Community Planning and Women's Security in Small, Rural, and Isolated Communities*, Cowichan Violence against Women Society, Duncan, British Columbia

Cowichan Safer Futures Program (2007) 'Safer futures', Cowichan Valley Safer Futures, www.saferfutures.org/, accessed 10 March 2007

Crawford, A. (1999) 'Questioning appeals to community within crime prevention and control', *European Journal on Criminal Policy and Research*, vol 7, pp509–530

Crime Reduction UK (2004) *Crime Reduction Toolkits: Fear of Crime*, Crime Reduction UK, London

Crime Reduction UK (2007) *Tools and Powers to Tackle Anti-Social Behaviour*, Crime Reduction UK, London

Daly, K. (2001) 'Conferencing in Australia and New Zealand: Variations, research findings, and prospects', in A. Morris and G. Maxwell (eds) *Restorative Justice for Juveniles: Conferencing, Mediation, and Circles*, Hart Publishing, Oxford, pp59–83

Dame, T. and Grant, A. (2002) *Women and Community Safety: A Resource Book on Planning for Safer Communities*, Cowichan Valley Safer Futures Program, Duncan, British Columbia

Davies, J., Lyon, E. and Monti-Catania, D. (1998) *Safety Planning with Battered Women: Complex Lives, Difficult Choices*, Sage, Thousand Oaks, California

Dean, S. (2000) *Hearts and Minds: A Public School Miracle*, Penguin Books, Toronto

Dobson, R. (2006) 'Urban renewal and prevention: The iTRUMP Warwick Junction (South Africa) experience', in R. Hastings (ed) *Sharing Across Borders/Learning from Experience: The ICPC's Annual Crime Prevention Training Institute Papers*, International Centre for the Prevention of Crime, Montreal, pp57–64

Dobson, R. (2007) 'Urban regeneration as a crime prevention strategy: The experience of Warwick Junction Thekwini (Durban), South Africa', in M. Shaw and K. Travers (eds) *Strategies and Best Practices in Crime Prevention in Particular in Relation to Urban Areas and Youth at Risk*, International Centre for the Prevention of Crime, Montreal, pp99–104

Donovan, R. and Vlais, R. (2005) *VicHealth Review of Communications Components of Social Marketing/Public Education Campaigns Focusing on Violence Against Women*, VicHealth (Victorian Health Promotion Foundation), Melbourne

du Mont, J. and Parnis, D. (1999) 'Judging women: The pernicious effects of rape mythology', *Canadian Woman Studies*, vol 19, no 1–2, pp102–109

du Plessis, A. and Louw, A. (2005) 'Crime and crime prevention in South Africa: 10 years after', *Canadian Journal of Criminology and Criminal Justice*, vol 47, no 2, pp427–446

EFUS (European Forum for Urban Security) (2007) 'European forum for urban security', European Forum for Urban Security, www.fesu.org, accessed 25 January 2008

Egger, S. (1997) 'Women and crime prevention', in P. O'Malley and A. Sutton (eds) *Crime Prevention in Australia: Issues in Policy and Research*, Federation Press, Sydney, pp84–104

Eisler, R. (1997) 'Human rights and violence: Integrating the public and private spheres', in J. Turpin and L. Kurtz (eds) *The Web of Violence*, University of Illinois Press, Urbana, pp161–186

Ellison, C. and Bartkowski, J. (1997) 'Religion and the legitimation of violence: Conservative Protestantism and corporal punishment', in J. Turpin and L. Kurtz (eds) *The Web of Violence*, University of Illinois Press, Urbana, pp45–68

Farrington, D. and Welsh, B. (2002) 'Family-based crime prevention', in L. Sherman, D. Farrington, B. Welsh and D. Mackenzie (eds) *Evidence-based Crime Prevention*, Routledge, London, pp22–55

Fenster, T. (1999) 'Gender and human rights: Implications for planning and development', in T. Fenster (ed) *Gender, Planning, and Human Rights*, Routledge, London, pp3–21

Fenster, T. (2005) 'The right to the gendered city: Different formations of belonging in everyday life', *Journal of Gender Studies*, vol 14, no 3, pp217–231

Fifth World Conference on Injury Prevention and Control (2000) *Delhi Declaration on People's Right to Safety*, http://web.iitd.ac.in/~tripp/righttosafety/deldeclaration.pdf, accessed 17 February 2007

First International Seminar on Women's Safety (2002) *The Montreal Declaration on Women's Safety*, www.femmesetvilles.org/english/sets_en/set_declaration_en.htm, accessed 19 February 2007

Focus Consultants (1998a) *Assessing Your Program: Tools for Measuring, Gathering Information, and Evaluating*, Aboriginal Justice Directorate, Department of Justice Canada, Victoria

Focus Consultants (1998b) *Developing Goals, Objectives, and Evaluation Plans: Tools for Charting Directions*, Aboriginal Justice Directorate, Department of Justice Canada, Victoria

Focus Consultants (1998c) *Doing Your Own Evaluation: Tools and Visions*, Aboriginal Justice Directorate, Department of Justice Canada, Victoria

Focus Consultants (1998d) *Laying the Groundwork for the Program: Tools for Assessing Community Needs, Strengths and Priorities*, Aboriginal Justice Directorate, Department of Justice, Victoria

Focus Consultants (1998e) *Reporting Results: Tools for Analyzing, Reporting, and Communicating*, Aboriginal Justice Directorate, Department of Justice Canada, Victoria

Friends of Dufferin Grove Park (2007) 'Friends of Dufferin Grove Park', www.dufferinpark.ca/home/wiki/wiki.php, accessed 3 June 2007

Garcia-Moreno, C., Jansen, H., Ellsberg, M., Heise, L. and Watts, C. (2004) *WHO Multi-country Study on Women's Health and Domestic Violence against Women*, World Health Organization, Geneva

Garrett, J. and Ahmed, A. (2004) 'Incorporating crime in household surveys: A research note', *Environment and Urbanization*, vol 16, no 1, pp139–152

Gauthier, L.-A., Hicks, D., Sansfacon, D. and Salel, L. (1999) *100 Crime Prevention Programs to Inspire Action throughout the World*, International Centre for the Prevention of Crime, Montreal

Gehl, J. (1987) *Life between Buildings: Using Public Space*, Van Nostrand Reinhold, New York

Gender Based Violence Prevention Network (2007) 'Activists and practitioners committed to preventing gender based violence in the Horn, East, and South Africa', Raising Voices, www.preventgbvafrica.org/, accessed 2 May 2007

Gold, M., Stevenson, D. and Fryback, D. (2002) 'HALYs and QALYs and DALYs, oh my: Similarities and differences in summary measures of population health', *Annual Review of Public Health*, vol 23, pp115–134

Gordon, M. and Riger, S. (1989) *The Female Fear*, Free Press, New York

Gottfredson, D., Wilson, D. and Najaka, S. (2002) 'School-based crime prevention', in L. Sherman, D. Farrington, B. Welsh and D. Mackenzie (eds) *Evidence-based Crime Prevention*, Routledge, London, pp56–164

Government of New Zealand Ministry of Social Development (2002) *Te Rito: New Zealand Family Violence Prevention Strategy*, Government of New Zealand, Wellington

Grabosky, P. (1995) *Fear of Crime and Fear Reduction Strategies*, Australian Institute of Criminology, Canberra

Graham, J. (2006) 'Preventing Youth Crime', in R. Hastings (ed) *Sharing Across Borders – Learning from Experience: ICPC's Annual Crime Prevention Training Institute Papers*, International Centre for the Prevention of Crime, Montreal, pp20–40

Gray, S. (2006) *Community Safety Workers: An Exploratory Study of Some Emerging Crime Prevention Occupations*, International Centre for the Prevention of Crime, Montreal

Greater London Authority (2005) *Second London Domestic Violence Strategy*, Greater London Authority, London

Greater London Authority (2006) *Annual Report of the London Domestic Violence Forum*, Greater London Authority, London

Healey, P. (1997) *Collaborative Planning: Shaping Places in Fragmented Societies*, Palgrave, Houndmills, Basingstoke, Hampshire

Heilig, L. (2002) 'An Empowering Approach to Women's Self-Defence', Presentation at First International Seminar on Women's Safety, Montreal, 9 May 2002

Hemson, D. (2003) *CBD Durban with Special Emphasis on Warwick Junction*, SARPN (Southern Africa Regional Poverty Network), Hatfield

Henderson and Associates (2002) *Good Practice Features of Community Crime Prevention Models*, Queensland Department of the Premier and Cabinet, Brisbane

Hester, M. and Westmarland, N. (2005) *Tackling Domestic Violence: Effective Interventions and Approaches*, Home Office, London

Heyzer, N. (1998) 'Working towards a world free of violence against women: UNIFEM's contribution', *Gender and Development*, vol 6, no 3, pp17–26

Hierlihy, D., Whitzman, C., Hwang, S. and Hamilton, A. (2003) *Models and Practices of Service Integration and Coordination for Women Who Are Homeless or at Risk of Homelessness*, Ontario Women's Health Council, Toronto

Hillman, M., Adams, J. and Whitelegg, J. (1990) *One False Move*, Policy Studies Institute, London

Holland, J. and Moser, C. (1997) *Urban Poverty and Violence in Jamaica*, World Bank, Washington, DC

Holtmann, B. (2006) 'Local crime prevention: The central Karoo experience', Presentation to the McCaughey Centre, University of Melbourne, Melbourne, 18 September 2006

Homel, P. (2004) *The Whole of Government Approach to Crime Prevention*, Australian Institute of Criminology, Canberra

Homel, P. (2005) 'A short history of crime prevention in Australia', *Canadian Journal of Criminology and Criminal Justice*, vol 47, no 2, pp355–368

Homel, R., Freiberg, K., Lamb, C., Leech, M., Batchelor, S., Carr, A., Hay, I., Teague, R. and Elias, G. (2006) *The Pathways to Prevention Project: Doing Developmental Prevention in a Disadvantaged Community*, Australian Institute of Criminology, Canberra

Homel, P., Nutley, S., Webb, B. and Tilley, N. (2004) *Investing to Deliver: Reviewing the Implementation of the UK Crime Reduction Programme*, Home Office, London

Hooks, B. (1984) *Feminist Theory from Margin to Center*, South End Press, Boston

Hume, M. (2004) 'It's as if you don't know, because you don't do anything about it: Gender and violence in El Salvador', *Environment and Urbanization*, vol 16, no 2, pp63–72

ICPC (International Centre for the Prevention of Crime) (2007) 'History', www.crime-prevention-intl.org/menu_item.php?code=history, accessed 22 May 2007

Immigrant Services Society of British Columbia (2007) 'Family and youth services', www.issbc.org/services/family_youth/default.htm, accessed 22 May 2007

International Centre for Assault Prevention (2007) 'CAP history', www.internationalcap.org/home/history.html, accessed 14 August 2007

International Centre for Municipal Development, Federation of Canadian Municipalities (2002) *A Community-based Approach is Reducing Violence against Women in the City of Bacolod, Philippines*, Federation of Canadian Municipalities, Ottawa

IULA (International Union of Local Authorities) (2001) *Local Governments Working for Gender Equity: A Collection of Cases*, IULA, The Hague

Jackson, S., Feder, L., Forde, D., Davis, R., Maxwell, C. and Taylor, B. (2003) *Batterer Intervention Programs: Where Do We Go From Here?*, National Institute of Justice, Washington, DC

Jacobs, J. (1961) *The Death and Life of Great American Cities*, Random House, New York

Jagori (2007) 'Safe Delhi: Make your city safe for women', http://safedelhi.jagori.org/, accessed 3 June 2007

Johnson, H. (2007) 'Preventing violence against women: Progress and challenges', *International Prevention of Crime Review*, vol 1, no 1, pp69–88

Johnson, H. and Sacco, V. (1995) 'Researching violence against women: Statistics from Canada's national survey', *Canadian Journal of Criminology*, vol 37, no 3, pp281–304

Kelling, G. and Coles, C. (1996) *Fixing Broken Windows: Restoring Order and Reducing Crime in our Communities*, Martin Kessler Books, New York

Kitchen, T. and Schneider, R. (2002) 'Crime and the design of the built environment: Anglo–American comparisons of policy and practice', in J. Hillier and E. Rooksby (eds) *Habitus: A Sense of Place*, Ashgate, Aldershot, pp239–265

Kretzmann, J. and McKnight, J. (1993) *Building Communities from the Bottom Up: A Path towards Finding and Mobilizing a Community's Resources*, ACTA Publications, Chicago

Krug, E. G., Dahlberg, L. L., Mercy, J. A., Zwi, A. B. and Lozano, R. (eds) (2002) *World Report on Violence and Health*, World Health Organization, Geneva

Kurtz, L. and Turpin, J. (1997) 'Conclusion', in J. Turpin and L. Kurtz (eds) *The Web of Violence*, University of Illinois Press, Urbana, pp207–232

Landry, C. (2000) *The Creative City: A Toolkit for Urban Innovators*, Earthscan London

Landry, C. (2006) *The Art of City Making*, Earthscan, London

Laprairie, C. (1998) 'The 'new' justice: Some implications for aboriginal communities', *Canadian Journal of Criminology*, vol 40, no 1, pp61–79

Lee, M. and Herborn, P. (2003) 'The role of place management in crime prevention: Some reflections on governmentality and government strategies', *Current Issues in Criminal Justice*, vol 15, no 1, pp26–39

Leeder, S., Ward, M. and Wilmouth, D. (2006) *Broadening the Scope of Inquiry: Including an Urban and Habitat Planning Perspective in Strategies for Better Health*, Oxford Health Alliance, Sydney

Lefebvre, H. (1996) *Writings on The City*, Blackwell, Oxford

Lemanski, C. (2004) 'A new apartheid? The spatial implications of fear of crime in Cape Town, South Africa', *Environments and Urbanization*, vol 16, no 2, pp101–112

Leonard, L., Rosario, G., Scott, C. and Bressan, J. (2005) 'Building safer communities: Lessons learned from Canada's National Strategy', *Canadian Journal of Criminology and Criminal Justice*, vol 47, no 2, pp233–250

Listerborn, C. (2002a) 'Understanding the geography of women's fear: Toward a reconceptualization of fear and space', in L. Bondi (ed) *Subjectivities, Knowledges, and Feminist Geographies: The Subjects and Ethics of Social Research*, Rowman and Littlefield, Lanham, pp34–43

Listerborn, C. (2002b) *Safer Cities: Is It Possible to Change the Places Which Generate Fear?*, City Planning Authority, Göteborg

Liverpool Safe Women Project (1998) *Plan It Safe: A Guide for Making Public Places Safer for Women*, New South Wales Attorney General's Department, Sydney

Local Partnerships and Government Unit (2003) *Future Directions of the Safer Community Council Network: Discussion Paper*, University of Auckland, Auckland

Lupton, D. (1999) 'Dangerous places and the unpredictable stranger: Constructions of fear of crime', *Australian and New Zealand Journal of Criminology*, vol 32, no 1, pp1–15

Lupton, D. (2000) 'Part of living in the late 20th century: Notions of risk and fear in relation to crime', *Australian and New Zealand Journal of Criminology*, vol 33, no 1, pp21–36

Mackenzie, D. (2002) 'Reducing the criminal activities of known offenders and delinquents: Crime prevention in the courts and corrections', in L. Sherman, D. Farrington, B. Welsh and D. Mackenzie (eds) *Evidence-based Crime Prevention*, Routledge, London, pp330–404

Maguire, M. and Nettleton, H. (2003) *Reducing Alcohol-related Violence and Disorder: An Evaluation of the TASC Project*, Home Office, London

Maslow, A. (1987) *Motivation and Personality*, Harper and Row, New York

McCauley, L. and Opie, A. (2007) *Research about the Use of Crime Prevention Through Environmental Design (CPTED) by Local Authorities in New Zealand*, Ministry of Justice/ Local Authorities New Zealand, Wellington

Meth, P. (2004) 'Using diaries to understand women's experiences of crime and violence', *Environment and Urbanization*, vol 16, no 2, pp153–164

METRAC (Metropolitan Action Committee on Violence against Women and Children) (2007) 'METRAC: About us', www.metrac.org/about/about.htm, accessed 7 May 2007

Michau, L. and Naker, D. (2003) *Mobilizing Communities to Prevent Domestic Violence: A Resource Guide for Organizations in East and Southern Africa*, Raising Voices, Kampala

Michau, L. and Naker, D. (2004) *Preventing Gender-based Violence in the Horn, East, and Southern Africa: A Regional Dialogue*, Raising Voices, Kampala

MINE (Mothers International Network for Empowerment) (2006) *International Mothers Centre Policy Paper and Platform of Action*, www.mine.cc/files/PlatformforActionSlovakConference. pdf, accessed 20 May 2007

Minnesota Program Development Inc (2007) 'The Duluth model and mending the Sacred Hoop project', www.duluth-model.org/, accessed 7 May 2007

Mitchell, D. (2003) *The Right to the City: Social Justice and the Fight for Public Space*, Guilford Press, New York

Modern Ghana (2003) 'Kadjebi district assembly wins gender sensitive award', *Modern Ghana*, 16 October 2003

Moe, A. and Bell, M. (2004) 'Abject economics: Effects of battering and violence on women's employability', *Violence against Women*, vol 10, no 1, pp29–55

Mohan, D. (2000) 'Injury control and safety promotion: Ethics, science and practice', in D. Mohan and G. Tiwari (eds) *Injury Prevention and Control*, Taylor and Francis, London and New York, pp1–12

Moser, C. (2004) 'Urban violence and insecurity: An introductory roadmap', *Environment and Urbanization*, vol 16, no 2, pp3–16

Moser, C. and McIlwaine, C. (2006) 'Latin American urban violence as a development concern: Towards a framework for violence reduction', *World Development*, vol 34, no 1, pp89–112

Mtani, A. (2002) 'Safety planning and design, "the women's perspective": The case of Manzese, Dar es Salaam, Tanzania', Presentation to the First International Seminar on Women's Safety, Montreal, Canada, 9 May 2002

Mtani, A. (2007) 'Local innovations for crime prevention: The case of safer cities Dar es Salaam', in M. Shaw and K. Travers (eds) *Strategies and Best Practices in Crime Prevention in Particular in Relation to Urban Areas and Youth at Risk*, International Centre for the Prevention of Crime, Montreal, pp69–79

Murray, C. J. L. and Lopez, A. D. (eds) (1996) *The Global Burden of Disease*, Harvard University Press on behalf of the World Health Organization and the World Bank, Boston

National Community Crime Prevention Programme Australia (1998) *Fear of Crime: Summary Volume*, Australian Government Attorney-General's Office, Canberra

National Community Crime Prevention Programme Australia (1999) *Pathways to Prevention: Developmental and Early Intervention Approaches to Crime in Australia*, Attorney General's Department, Canberra

National Crime Prevention Council Canada (1997) *The Dollars and Sense of a Comprehensive Crime Prevention Strategy for Canada*, Department of Justice, Ottawa

National Crime Prevention Council US (2001) *Are We Safe? The 2000 National Crime Prevention Survey*, National Crime Prevention Council, Washington, DC

National Development Plan (Ireland) Gender Equality Unit (2002) *Gender Equality and Crime Prevention Policies*, Department of Justice, Equality, and Law Reform, Government of Ireland, Dublin

New Zealand Ministry of Justice Crime Prevention Unit (2007a) 'Crime Prevention Unit', www.justice.govt.nz/cpu/, accessed 8 May 2007

New Zealand Ministry of Justice Crime Prevention Unit (2007b) 'Restorative justice', www.justice.govt.nz/cpu/restorative-justice/restorative.html, accessed 2 March 2007

Newman, O. (1972) *Defensible Space: Crime Prevention through Environmental Design*, Macmillan, New York

NIZW (Netherlands Institute for Care and Welfare) (2003) *Community Schools in the Netherlands: Fact Sheet*, Netherlands Institute for Care and Welfare, Utrecht

Northern Territory Office of Crime Prevention (2003) *Guide for Community Crime Prevention Partnerships*, Northern Territory Department of Justice, Darwin

OECD (Organisation for Economic Co-operation and Development) (1994) *Women in the City: Housing, Services, and the Urban Environment*, OECD, Paris

O'Malley, K. (2000) *Creating Consensus for Safer Rural Communities*, New Rural Partnerships Project, Christina Lake

Pain, R. (1997) 'Social geographies of women's fear of crime', *Transactions of the Institute of British Geographers*, vol 22, no 2, pp231–244

Pain, R. (2000) 'Place, social relations, and the fear of crime: A review', *Progress in Human Geography*, vol 24, no 3, pp365–387

Pain, R. (2001) 'Gender, race, age and fear in the city', *Urban Studies*, vol 38, no 5–6, pp899–913

Pain, R. and Townshend, T. (2002) 'A safer city centre for all? Senses of "community safety" in Newcastle upon Tyne', *Geoforum*, vol 33, no 1, pp105–119

Pain, R., Francis, P., Fuller, I., O'Brien, K. and Williams, S. (2002) *'Hard to Reach' Young People and Community Safety: A Model for Participatory Research and Consultancy*, Home Office, London

Panelli, R., Kraack, A. and Little, J. (2004) 'Claiming space and community: Rural women's strategies for living with, and beyond, fear', *Geoforum*, vol 36, pp495–508

Phadke, S. (2005) 'Take back the night', *Humanscape*, July 2005, p16

Phillips, R. (2006) 'Undoing an activist response: Feminism and the Australian Government's domestic violence policy', *Critical Social Policy*, vol 26, pp192–219

Pickup, F. (2001) *Ending Violence against Women: A Challenge for Development and Humanitarian Work*, Oxfam Publishing, London

Pitts, J. (1998) 'Young people, crime and citizenship', in A. Marlow and J. Pitts (eds) *Planning Safer Communities*, Russell House, Lyme Regis, pp84–100

Pitts, M., Smith, A., Mitchell, A. and Patel, S. (2007) *Private Lives: A Report on the Health and Wellbeing of LGBTI Victorians*, Gay and Lesbian Health Victoria, Melbourne

Poyner, B. (1983) *Design against Crime: Beyond Defensible Space*, Butterworths, London

Press, M. (2004) 'Communities for everyone: Redesigning contested spaces', in W. Weeks, L. Hoatson and J. Dixon (eds) *Community Practices in Australia*, Pearson Education Australia, Melbourne

Project for Public Spaces (1998) 'The big backyard: Neighbourhood park becomes centre of community activity', *Making Places Newsletter*, summer 1998, www.pps.org/info/design/success_toronto, accessed 17 March 2007

Project Respect (2007) 'Project respect', www.yesmeansyes.com/, accessed 8 March 2007

Quinn, J. (1999) 'Where need meets opportunity: Youth development programs for early teens', *The Future of Children*, vol 9, no 2, pp96–116

Rainero, L., Rodigou, M. and Perez, S. (2006) (English version) *Tools for the Promotion of Safe Cities from a Gender Perspective*, CISCSA (Centro de Intercambio y Servicios Cono Sur Argentina), Cordoba

Raising Voices (2007) 'Raising voices', www.raisingvoices.org/, accessed 6 June 2007

Ranade, S. (2007) 'The way she moves: Mapping the everyday production of gender-space', *Economic and Political Weekly*, 28 April, pp1519–1529

Randall, B. (2005) *Safe as Houses: EU Social Housing Organizations Dealing with Anti-social Behaviour*, CECODHAS (European Liaison Committee for Social Housing), Brussels

Red Mujer y Habitat de America Latina (2007) 'Red Mujer y Habitat de America Latina', www.redmujer.org.ar/, accessed 13 June 2007

RESOLVE Alberta (2005) *School-based Violence Prevention Programs: A Resource Manual*, RESOLVE Alberta, Calgary

Rogerson, R. (1999) 'Quality of life and city competitiveness', *Urban Studies*, vol 36, no 5–6, pp969–987

Rojas, C. (2002) *Forging Civic Culture in Bogotá City*, Asian Development Bank, Manila

Rosenbaum, D. (2002) 'Evaluating multi-agency crime partnerships: Theory, design and measurement issues', *Crime Prevention Studies*, vol 14, pp171–225

Roy, A., Jockin, A. and Javed, A. (2004) 'Community police stations in Mumbai's slums', *Environment and Urbanization*, vol 16, no 2, pp135–138

Safe Neighbourhoods Unit (1985) *After Entryphones*, Safe Neighbourhoods Unit, London

Safer Cities Tanzania Programme (2006) *Institutionalization of Safer Cities in Tanzania*, Government of Tanzania Regional Administration and Local Government Department, Dodoma

Schusterman, R., Almansi, F., Hardoy, A. and Urquiza, G. (2002) *Poverty Reduction in Action: Participatory Planning in San Fernando, Buenos Aires, Argentina*, International Institute of Environment and Development (Latin America), Buenos Aires

Schusterman, R. and Hardoy, A. (1997) 'Reconstructing social capital in a poor urban settlement: The integral improvement programme in Barrio San Jorge', *Environment and Urbanization*, vol 9, no 1, pp91–120

Scraton, S. and Watson B. (1998) 'Gendered cities: Women and public leisure space in the "postmodern city"', *Leisure Studies*, vol 17, no 2, pp123–137

Second International Conference on Safer Cities for Women and Girls (2004) *Bogotá Declaration on Safer Cities for Women and Girls*, http://ww2.unhabitat.org/programmes/safercities/documents/Declaration_of_Bogota.pdf, accessed 21 December 2007

Sen, A. (2005) *The Argumentative Indian: Writings on Indian History, Culture and Identity*, Penguin, New York

Shaw, M. (2001a) *The Role of Local Government in Community Safety*, International Centre for the Prevention of Crime, Montreal

Shaw, M. (2001b) *Promoting Safety in Schools: International Experience and Action*, International Centre for the Prevention of Crime, Montreal

Shaw, M. (2002) *Gender and Crime Prevention*, International Centre for the Prevention of Crime, Montreal

Shaw, M. (2006) *Communities in Action for Crime Prevention*, International Centre for the Prevention of Crime, Montreal

Shaw, M. (2007a) 'Introduction: Setting standards for progress in crime prevention', in M. Shaw and K. Travers (eds) *Strategies and Best Practices in Crime Prevention in Particular in Relation to Urban Areas and Youth at Risk*, International Centre for Crime Prevention, Montreal, pp9–17

Shaw, M (2007b) 'Strategies and best practices for crime prevention, in particular in relation to urban areas and youth at risk', in M. Shaw and K. Travers (eds) *Strategies and Best Practices in Crime Prevention in Particular in Relation to Urban Areas and Youth at Risk*, International Centre for the Prevention of Crime, Montreal, pp18–34

Shaw, M. and Andrew, C. (2005) 'Engendering crime prevention: International developments and the Canadian experience', *Canadian Journal of Criminology and Criminal Justice*, vol 47, no 2, pp293–316

Shaw, M. and Barchelat, O. (2001) *Preventing Hate Crimes: International Strategies and Practices*, International Centre for the Prevention of Crime, Montreal

Shaw, M. and Capobianco, L. (2004) *Developing Trust: International Approaches to Women's Safety*, International Centre for the Prevention of Crime, Montreal

Sheppard, M., Elliot, B., Falk, D. and Regal, R. (1999) 'Public health nurses' responses to domestic violence: A report from the enhanced domestic abuse intervention project', *Public Health Nursing*, vol 16, no 5, pp359–366

Sheppard, M. and Pence, E. (eds) (1999) *Coordinating Community Responses to Domestic Violence: Lessons from Duluth and Beyond*, Sage, Thousand Oaks

Sherman, L. and Eck, J. (2002) 'Policing for crime prevention', in L. Sherman, D. Farrington, B. Welsh and D. Mackenzie (eds) *Evidence-based Crime Prevention*, Routledge, London, pp295–329

Sherman, L., Farrington, D., Welsh, B. and MacKenzie, D. (eds) (2002) *Evidence-based Crime Prevention*, Routledge, London

Sherman, L., Gottfredson, D., Mackenzie, D., Eck, J., Reuter, P. and Bushway, S. (1997) *Preventing Crime: What Works, What Doesn't, What is Promising*, National Institute of Justice, Washington, DC

Sixth World Conference on Injury Prevention and Control (2002) *Montreal Declaration on People's Right to Safety*, http://web.iitd.ac.in/~tripp/righttosafety/Montreal%20declaration%2015-05-02.htm, accessed 27 January 2007

Smaoun, S. (2000) *Violence against Women in Urban Areas: An Analysis of the Problem from a Gender Perspective*, UN-Habitat Urban Management Programme Working Paper 17, Nairobi

Society for International Development (2002) *Latin American and the Caribbean Regional Dialogue: Reproductive Rights, Violence against Women: Men's Roles and Responsibilities*, Society for International Development, Rio de Janeiro

Solimano, A. (2004) *Political Violence and Economic Development in Latin America: Issues and Evidence*, Economic Commission for Latin America and the Caribbean, Santiago, Chile

Speak, S. (2004) 'Homelessness and safety in the city: A developing countries perspective', in R. del Caz, M. Rodriguez and M. Saravia (eds) *Report of Valladolid 2004: The Right to Safety in the City*, University of Valladolid School of Architecture, Valladolid, pp108–110

Stanko, E. (2000) 'Victims R Us: The life history of "fear of crime" and the politicisation of violence', in T. Hope and R. Sparks (eds) *Crime, Risk, and Insecurity: Law and Order in Everyday Life and Political Discourse*, Routledge, London, pp13–30

State Government of Victoria (Australia) Department of Human Services (2001) *Environments for Health: Promoting Health and Wellbeing through Built, Social, Economic and Natural Environments*, State Government of Victoria, Melbourne

Stepping Stones (2007) 'Stepping stones', www.steppingstonesfeedback.org/, accessed 3 June 2007

Sudjic, D. (1992) *The 100 Mile City*, André Deutsch, London

SWOVA (Saltspring Women Opposed to Violence and Abuse) (2007) 'Respectful relationships program', http://respectfulrelationships.swova.org/index.php, accessed 29 May 2007

Tilley, N. and Laycock, G. (2000) 'Joining up research, policy, and practice about crime', *Policy Studies*, vol 21, no 3, pp213–227

Turpin, J. and Kurtz, L. (1997) 'Violence: The macro/micro link', in J. Turpin and L. Kurtz (eds) *The Web of Violence*, University of Illinois Press, Urbana, pp1–28

Ullman, S. (2007) 'A 10-year update of *Review and Critique of Empirical Studies of Rape Avoidance*', *Criminal Justice and Behaviour*, vol 34, no 3, pp411–426

UN (United Nations) (2006) 'Some facts about persons with disabilities', UN, www.un.org/disabilities/convention/pdfs/factsheet.pdf, accessed 28 January 2007

UN (2007) *UN Millennium Development Goals*, UN, www.un.org/millenniumgoals/, accessed 14 August 2007

UN Economic and Social Council (2002) *Effective Community-based Crime Prevention*, UN Economic and Social Council, Vienna

UN-Habitat (2005a) *The Safer Cities Programme: Making Cities Safer from Crime*, UN-Habitat, Nairobi

UN-Habitat (2005b) *Diagnosis of Insecurity Report: Port Moresby, Papua New Guinea*, UN-Habitat, Nairobi

UN-Habitat (2006a) *UN-Habitat: The Agency for Cities and Shelter*, UN-Habitat, Nairobi

UN-Habitat (2006b) *Urban Planning: The Key to Better Cities*, UN-Habitat, Nairobi

UN-Habitat (2006c) *From Ideas to Action: 70 Actionable Ideas for the World Urban Forum 3*, UN-Habitat, Nairobi

UN-Habitat (2007) *Policy Makers Guide to Women's Land, Property, and Housing Rights around the World*, UN-Habitat, Nairobi

UNICEF (United Nations Children's Fund) (2006) *The State of the World's Children 2007*, UNICEF, New York

UNICJRI (United Nations Interregional Crime and Justice Research Institute) (2007) 'International Crime Victimization Survey Statistics', www.unicri.it/wwd/analysis/icvs/statistics.php, accessed 30 April 2007

UNIFEM (United Nations Development Fund for Women) (2007) 'Violence against women', www.unifem.org/gender_issues/violence_against_women/, accessed 22 May 2007

University College London Department for International Development (2007) 'Safer Cities Programme in Dar es Salaam', in *Drivers of Urban Change: A Collection of Resources*, www.ucl.ac.uk/dpu-projects/drivers_urb_change/urb_society/pdf_violence_rights/DFID_DPU_Tanzania_Safer_Cities_Dar_Es_Salaam.pdf, accessed 8 May 2007

UNODC (United Nations Office on Drugs and Crime) (2003) *Promoting the Prevention of Crime: Guidelines and Selected Projects*, UNODC, Vienna

UNODC (2005) *Crime and Development in Africa*, UNODC, Vienna

UNODC (2007) *Previous Congresses on the Prevention of Crime and the Treatment of Offenders*, www.unodc.org/unodc/en/crime_cicp_previous_congresses.html, accessed 22 May 2007

Vanderschueren, F. (2006) *Prevention of Urban Crime: Safer Cities Concept Note*, UN-Habitat Safer Cities Programme, Nairobi

VicHealth (Victorian Health Promotion Foundation) (2003) *Promoting the Mental Health and Wellbeing of New Arrival Communities: Learnings and Promising Practices*, VicHealth, Melbourne

VicHealth (2004) *The Health Costs of Violence: Measuring the Burden of Disease Caused by Intimate Partner Violence*, VicHealth, Melbourne

VicHealth (2005) 'Public health model for the prevention of violence', www.vichealth.vic.gov. au/assets/contentFiles/publichealthmodel%20VAW%20for%20campaign%20review_updated%20.pdf, accessed 6 June 2007

VicHealth (2006) *Two Steps Forward, One Step Back: Community Attitudes to Violence against Women*, VicHealth, Melbourne

Victorian Community Council against Violence (1995) *Safety Audits: Past Experiences and Future Strategies*, Victorian Community Council against Violence, Melbourne

Victorian Community Council against Violence (2003) *Family Violence is a Workplace Issue*, Victorian Community Council against Violence, Melbourne

Violence is Preventable Project (2007) 'Violence is preventable', www.violenceispreventable.org.uk/, accessed 30 May 2007

Walklate, S. (1995) *Gender and Crime: An Introduction*, Prentice Hall, London

Waller, I. and Sansfacon, D. (2000) *Investing Wisely in Crime Prevention: International Experiences*, US Department of Justice, Washington, DC

Waters, H., Hyder, A., Rajkotia, Y., Basu, S., Rehwinkel, J. A. and Butchart, A. (2004) *The Economic Dimensions of Interpersonal Violence*, World Health Organization Department of Injuries and Violence Prevention, Geneva

Watson, S. and Austerberry, H. (1986) *Housing and Homelessness: A Feminist Perspective*, Routledge and Kegan Paul, London

Wekerle, G. and Whitzman, C. (1995) *Safe Cities: Guidelines for Planning, Design and Management*, Van Nostrand Reinhold, New York

White, R. and Coventry, G. (2000) *Evaluating Community Safety: A Guide*, Government of Victoria (Australia) Department of Justice, Melbourne

White Ribbon Campaign (2007) 'The White Ribbon Campaign: The campaign', www.whiteribbon.ca/about_us/#2, accessed 7 May 2007

Whitzman, C. (1992) 'Taking back planning: Promoting women's safety in public places – the Toronto experience', *Journal of Architectural and Planning Research*, vol 9, no 2, pp169–179

Whitzman, C. (2002a) 'The voice of women in Canadian local government', in C. Andrew, K. Graham and S. Rankin (eds) *Urban Affairs: Back on the Policy Agenda*, Queens University Press, Montreal, pp93–118

Whitzman, C. (2002b) 'Feminist activism for safer social space in High Park Toronto: How women got lost in the woods', *Canadian Journal of Urban Research*, vol 11, no 2, pp47–67

Whitzman, C. (2004) 'Safer cities, gender and human rights', in R. del Caz, M. Rodriguez and M. Saravia (eds) *Report of Valladolid 2004: The Right to the City*, University of Valladolid School of Architecture, Valladolid, Spain, pp22–26

Whitzman, C. (2007) 'Stuck at the front door: Gender, fear of crime and the challenge of creating safer space', *Environment and Planning A*, vol 39, no 11, pp2715–2732

Whitzman, C. (forthcoming) 'Community safety indicators: Are we measuring what counts?' *Urban Policy and Research*

Whitzman, C., Canuto, M. and Binder, S. (2004) *Women's Safety Awards 2004: A Compendium of Good Practices*, Women In Cities International, Montreal

WHO (World Health Organization) (2005) *Milestones of a Global Campaign for Violence Prevention 2005: Changing the Face of Violence Prevention*, World Health Organization, Geneva

WHO (2007a) 'Injuries and violence prevention', WHO, www.who.int/violence_injury_ prevention/violence/global_campaign/en/, accessed 20 May 2007

WHO (2007b) 'World Health Organization regions', www.who.int/about/regions/en/, accessed 26 April 2007

WHO Collaborating Centre on Community Safety Promotion (2007) 'Introduction', www.phs.ki.se/csp/who introduction en.htm, accessed 25 August 2007

Whyte, W. (1980) *Social Life of Small Urban Spaces*, Conservation Foundation, Washington, DC

WICI (Women in Cities International) (2007a) 'Networking events of Women in Cities International at the World Urban Forum 3, Vancouver, 19 to 23 June 2006', www.womenincities.org/english/index_en.htm, accessed 18 May 2007

WICI (2007b) *Building Community-based Partnerships for Local Action on Women's Safety*, Women in Cities International, Montreal

Wilson, E. (1983) *What is to be Done about Violence against Women?*, Penguin Books, Harmondsworth, England

Wilson, E. (1991) *The Sphinx in the City: Urban Life, the Control of Disorder, and Women*, Virago Press, London

Woman Abuse Council of Toronto (2007) 'Projects: Diversity, alternative approaches, and best practices', Woman Abuse Council of Toronto, www.womanabuse.ca/projects/diversity.cfm, accessed 14 August 2007

Women's Action Centre against Violence (1995) *Safety Audit Tools and Housing: The State of the Art and Implications for the CMHC*, Canadian Mortgage and Housing Corporation, Ottawa

Women's Circus (2007) 'Women's circus: About us', www.womenscircus.org.au/briefinfo.html, accessed 7 June 2007

Women and Peace Network/Red de Mujeres por la Paz (2002) *Special Issue on Peace, Urban Governance, Land and Property Rights of Women*, Women and Peace Network/Red de Mujeres por la Paz, San José, Costa Rica

Womenkind Worldwide (2007) 'India: Helping women build their future', Womenkind Worldwide, www.womankind.org.uk/our-programme-india.html, accessed 22 May 2007

World Bank (2006) *Crime, Violence, and Economic Development in Brazil: Elements for Effective Public Policy*, Poverty Reduction and Economic Management Sector Unit, Latin American and Caribbean Region, World Bank, Buenos Aires

World Bank (2007a) 'Data: Country classification', http://cyberschoolbus.un.org/, accessed 13 February 2007

World Bank (2007b) 'Crime and violence prevention', http://wbln0018.worldbank.org/ LAC/LAC.nsf/ECADocByUnid/65A4BF3B8D10247D85256CFD007A5D62? Opendocument, accessed 22 May 2007

Worpole, K. (1992) *Towns for People: Transforming Urban Life*, Open University Press, Buckingham

Yeoh, B. and Huang, S. (1998) 'Renegotiating public space: Strategies and styles of migrant female domestic workers in Singapore', *Urban Studies*, vol 35, no 3, pp583–603

Young, I. M. (1990) *Justice and the Politics of Difference*, Princeton University Press, Princeton, New Jersey

Young, J. (1998) 'Zero tolerance: Back to the Future', in A. Marlow and J. Pitts (eds) *Planning Safer Communities*, Russell House, Lyme Regis, pp60–83

Index